# The Incas

## New Perspectives

## GORDON F. McEWAN

W. W. Norton & Company

New York · London

Reprinted by permission of ABC-CLIO

For information about permission to reproduce
selections from this book, write to Permissions,
W. W. Norton & Company, Inc.,
500 Fifth Avenue, New York, NY 10110

For information about special discounts for bulk purchases,
please contact W. W. Norton Special Sales at
specialsales@wwnorton.com or 800-233-4830

Manufacturing by Courier Westford
Production manager: Devon Zahn

Library of Congress Cataloging-in-Publication Data

McEwan, Gordon Francis.
The Incas : new perspectives / Gordon F. McEwan.
p. cm. — (ABC-CLIO's understanding ancient civilizations)
Includes bibliographical references and index.
ISBN 1-85109-574-8 (hardback : alk. paper) — ISBN 1-85109-579-9 (ebook)
1. Incas—History. 2. Incas—Social life and customs.
I. Title. II. Series: Understanding ancient civilizations.
F3429.M42    2005
305.898 323—dc22
2005031715

ISBN 978-0-393-33301-5 pbk.

W. W. Norton & Company, Inc.
500 Fifth Avenue, New York, N.Y. 10110
www.wwnorton.com

W. W. Norton & Company Ltd.
Castle House, 75/76 Wells Street, London W1T 3QT

1 2 3 4 5 6 7 8 9 0

This volume is dedicated to

FROILAN ITURRIAGA GUZMAN

in appreciaton of his valued contributions
to the author's archaeological projects in Cuzco.

# Contents

# Series Editor's Preface

In recent years there has been a significant and steady increase of academic and popular interest in the study of past civilizations. This is due in part to the dramatic coverage, real or imagined, of the archaeological profession in popular film and television and to extensive journalistic reporting of spectacular new finds from all parts of the world. Because archaeologists and other scholars, however, have tended to approach their study of ancient peoples and civilizations exclusively from their own disciplinary perspectives and for their professional colleagues, there has long been a lack of general factual and other research resources available for the nonspecialist. The Understanding Ancient Civilizations series is intended to fill that need.

Volumes in the series are principally designed to introduce the general reader, student, and nonspecialist to the study of specific ancient civilizations. Each volume is devoted to a particular archaeological culture (e.g., the ancient Maya of southern Mexico and adjacent Guatemala) or cultural region (e.g., Israel and Canaan) and seeks to achieve, with careful selectivity and astute critical assessment of the literature, an expression of a particular civilization and an appreciation of its achievements.

The keynote of the Understanding Ancient Civilizations series is to provide, in a uniform format, an interpretation of each civilization that will express its culture and place in the world as well as the qualities and background that make it unique.

Series titles include volumes on the archaeology and prehistory of the ancient civilizations of Egypt, Greece, Rome, and Mesopotamia, as well as the achievements of the Celts, Aztecs, and Incas, among others. Still others are in the planning stage.

I was particularly fortunate in having Kevin Downing from ABC-CLIO contact me in search of an editor for a series about archaeology. It is a simple statement of truth that there would be no series without him. I was also lucky to have Simon Mason, Kevin's successor from ABC-CLIO, continuing to push the production of the series. Given the scale of the project and the schedule for production, he deserves more than a sincere thank you.

*John Weeks*

# Preface

The empire of the Incas was the greatest native state ever to appear in the Americas. Overcoming the seemingly impossible obstacles of their environment and limitations of technology, the Incas created one of the world's most unusual civilizations. Their achievements have fascinated the world for close to five centuries, since the culture's discovery by the Spanish. I first encountered the realm of the Incas in 1964 on a visit to Peru and have been studying and learning about them ever since. I am one of the very few foreign archaeologists who have been privileged to work on the Inca legacy in Cuzco, and my studies have primarily focused on discovering who the Incas were and where they came from. I have spent my career examining this question in terms of their intellectual and cultural inheritance as well as their physical and geographic origins.

In this volume I have tried to present a fairly concise overview of the Incas that will be readily accessible to the average reader. There are few introductory textbooks on the Incas, and I hope that this effort will serve to fill that gap. I have drawn on many of the traditional ethnohistorical sources and tried to integrate archaeological knowledge wherever possible to provide a readily accessible synthesis. While this volume is not and should not be taken as the last word on the Incas, I hope that it will provide an introduction to the topic and guidance on where to look for detailed and comprehensive studies on individual aspects of Inca society and history.

One of the most difficult and confusing aspects of reading about the Incas is that there is no standardized orthography of their language that is generally accepted by the field of Andean studies. The Incas spoke a dialect of the language that we now call Quechua, but they never developed an alphabetic writing system. Since their language was unwritten, it left everyone free to try to render Quechua in the Latin alphabet as they saw fit. This has resulted in wildly varying spellings—such as Ynga, Inga, Inka, and Inca, or *bamba* and *pampa*—and very little consistency of usage. In writing this volume, I made a decision to try not to add to this confusion and have therefore tried to adhere to the spellings that are most commonly found in the literature. Thus I have retained the spelling of Inca with the letter "c," although some colleagues have changed to spelling it Inka with the letter "k." Most people first encounter the word with the traditional "c" spelling, and it is spelled that way in most dictionaries. For other words that are more recent in the literature, I have chosen to use the spelling that is easiest for an English speaker to pronounce. Thus I have used Wari instead of Guari or Huari, and Tiwanaku instead of Tiahuanaco.

Basic guidelines for pronouncing written Quechua words can be found in John Rowe's (1946: 186) classic article "Inca Culture at the Time of the Spanish Conquest" and in more widely available phrase books (Wright 1989). For the most part, Quechuan words are accented on the penultimate syllable as in MANco CApac (Manco Capac). The accented syllable changes (i.e., moves down the word) as suffixes are added to modify the meaning of a word. Most letters are pronounced as they are in English. There are basically three vowel sounds, since there is almost no difference in pronunciation between *i* and *e* and between *u* and *o*. The vowel *a* sounds like "uh"; the vowels *e* and *i* sound like their English counterparts in the words "get" or "hit"; and *o* and *u* have a sound midway between the pronunciations of these two letters in Spanish.

There are certain letter combinations that frequently occur and have distinct sounds. The combinations of *aw* and *au* sound like the end of the English word "how." *Hua* and *gua* sound like the English "w"; for example, the word Sacsayhuaman is pronounced Sacsaywaman. *Ay* sounds like the English "aye." *Ey* rhymes with the English "day." *Iy* sounds like the double "e" in the English word "seem." *Oy* sounds like the same letters in the English word "boy." *Uy* and *ui* sound like the English word "we."

Other sounds that Quechua uses are hard to describe with English equivalents. These are glottal stops, plosives, and aspirations that are generally marked with an apostrophe. Two sounds indicated by the Spanish letters *ll* and *ñ* are pronounced as they would be in Spanish.

Finally, I would remind the reader that although the Inca Empire fell to the Spanish conquerors in 1532, the descendants of the Incas and of their subject peoples continue to inhabit the Andes to this day. The Inca language is still spoken by millions of people, and their religion and many other customs survive in the rich and vital cultures of western South America.

## REFERENCES

Rowe, John H. 1946. "Inca Culture at the Time of the Spanish Conquest." In *Handbook of South American Indians*, Bureau of American Ethnology, bulletin 143, vol. 2, edited by Julian Steward, 183–330. Washington, DC: Smithsonian Institution.
Wright, Ronald. 1989. *Quechua Phrasebook.* Berkeley, CA: Lonely Planet.

# The Incas

New Perspectives

# PART I
## Introduction

# CHAPTER I

# Introduction

## OVERVIEW

At the time of the Spanish Conquest in A.D. 1532, the majority of the vast territory of Andean South America had been united into a single political entity now commonly called the Inca Empire. Known to its rulers as Tawantinsuyu, meaning roughly "The Land of Four Quarters" in the Inca language, this empire included parts of the modern countries of Colombia, Ecuador, Peru, Bolivia, Argentina, and Chile. This huge domain was the property of a small kin group called the Incas. From their capital city of Cuzco, located in the southern highlands of Peru, the rulers of this realm controlled a vast territory encompassing approximately 906,000 square kilometers. Measuring some 4,000 kilometers north to south along the west coast of South America, this territory comprised an extreme diversity of environments, ranging from the world's driest deserts on the Pacific coast, through the world's second highest mountain range, the Andean Cordillera, to the lush tropical lowlands of the upper Amazon Basin. Within the borders of this empire dwelled a population of perhaps 10 million people divided into a multitude of tribal groups, each with its own customs and language.

*[handwritten margin note: not just mtns]*

The Spanish conquerors were astonished at the size of the Inca Empire but even more so by its sophisticated political and economic structure and its monumental public works. Soon after the Conquest, the Spaniards made inquiries into the origins of the Inca state and learned that the empire had been in existence for only a little less than 100 years. They were told that the empire had been founded by the Inca Pachacuti circa A.D. 1438 and had endured until the Spanish Conquest in 1532. In the short span of three or four generations, the Incas had built the greatest of the Native American empires. Everywhere they went in the Inca Empire, the Spanish conquerors were amazed by the wealth, power, and organization of the Inca civilization. Never had they seen so much gold, silver, and other luxury goods, such quantities and varieties of foodstuffs, such huge flocks of domesticated animals, or such clean and orderly towns and settlements. The entire empire was interconnected by a highway system some 38,600 kilometers in extent that, as an engineering feat, rivaled or surpassed anything known in Europe.

An Inca hollow gold llama figurine. (Gordon F. McEwan)

Colombia

Ecuador

Brazil

Peru

Bolivia

Chile

Argentina

1000 km

N

Map of the Inca Empire

What most amazed the Spanish conquerors and continues to intrigue scholars to the present day is that the Incas were able to forge their society without many western European customs and practices. The Incas lacked the use of wheeled vehicles. They lacked animals to ride and draft animals that could pull wagons or plows. They were expert metallurgists but lacked the knowledge of iron and steel, making do with bronze for their tools and implements. Above all, they lacked a system of writing, which was essential to the administration of the European kingdoms and empires and for the transmission of knowledge and civilization. Despite these supposed handicaps, the Incas were still able to construct one of the greatest imperial states in human history.

Because of their isolation from the other great civilizations of the world, the Incas and their Andean ancestors were forced to come up with their own, often novel solutions to the common problems of human survival. They followed an alternate path to success from which the rest of humanity can learn a great deal. Among the most important contributions of the ancient Andean peoples to life in the modern world are foodstuffs and medicines. Our diet today is

Guinea pigs, or *cuy*, on a grill in Equador. A traditional food, the *cuy* has been an important source of protein for Andean peoples since before the arrival of the Spanish. (David L. Amsler)

tremendously influenced by this ancient society that developed such staples as potatoes, tomatoes, corn, beans, peanuts, and hot peppers, to name just a few of their agricultural products. Even our English term *beef jerky* comes from the Inca word *charqui,* a dried meat product carried by their soldiers on campaign.

Equally fascinating is the Inca view of reality. The Incas drew the boundary between the living and the dead in a different way from the rest of humanity. Deceased ancestors and former kings were viewed as being in a different stage of the life cycle but not departed from the human sphere of events. Mummified corpses were fed and clothed, maintained their households and wealth, and were consulted on all matters of importance. They traveled to visit each other and their living relatives, attended ceremonies and celebrations, and were thought to carry on with their lives as they had before death. This worldview was radically different yet very successful.

Ultimately, the Incas and their history are most valuable to us in the modern world for what they can teach us about how mankind arrived at the social and political conditions in which we find ourselves today. We live in a world of state-level governments, yet scholars are only just beginning to understand why. The worldwide processes that led to the development of complex state-level societies are so complicated that untangling the sequence of events and understanding the origins of the state are monumental tasks. We know that somebody somewhere invented the techniques and systems of statecraft, but because ancient civilizations had frequent contact with each other, it is exceedingly difficult to know who first created a particular idea or invention. Because they presumably developed their society in complete isolation from the rest of the world's complex civilizations, the Incas and their ancestors must have generated the necessary ideas and inventions independently. By studying the Incas, we can obtain a much clearer picture of the evolution of state-level society and perhaps understand the rules and principles governing the life cycle of complex states. All of the world's ancient societies eventually collapsed and disappeared. By learning why and how they functioned and failed, we can perhaps prevent our own civilization from experiencing the same fate.

## SOURCES OF INFORMATION ABOUT THE INCAS

Since the Incas did not develop a written language, there are no written sources of information about them from before the Spanish Conquest. Thus we have no Inca history books, novels, letters, or diaries to tell us how the Incas viewed themselves and their accomplishments. In order to learn about the Incas, scholars have had to rely on a variety of sources. These include Spanish documents and chronicles from the time of the Conquest and the colonial period, as well as ethnohistoric studies of the information contained in these documents, ethnographies of the Incas' modern descendants, and archaeological studies of the remains of the Inca culture.

### Documentary Evidence

The best scholarly source regarding the early Spanish colonial documents and their authors remains the classic article by John Rowe (1946) published in the

Frozen mummy of an Inca boy sacrificed on the mountain peak of El Plomo in northern Chile. (Charles & Josette Lenars/Corbis)

*Handbook of South American Indians.* Rowe's article should be consulted for a comprehensive discussion of the Spanish sources. I will present here a brief list of the most important sources.

The earliest written records of the Incas were made by the invading Europeans. These sources comprise Spanish chronicles and early colonial-period documents. The chronicles are works written at the time of the European invasion or shortly afterward. These sources can be generally divided into three types of documents: eyewitness primary accounts, post-Conquest secondary accounts, and accounts of Spanish-trained native authors.

Spanish legal and ecclesiastical documents of the colonial period also provide a great deal of information on the Incas. The Catholic Church, in its attempt to control and exterminate the Inca religion, kept voluminous records concerning Inca religious beliefs and practices. The Spanish colonial legal system, which heard lawsuits by natives attempting to regain their rights, and the colonial government, which conducted periodic inspections and censuses of the population, were both sources of a wealth of documentation regarding the Incas and other native peoples with whom the Incas interacted. Many of these documents are preserved in the archives of the cities of Cuzco and Lima, as well as in the royal archives in Spain.

It is important for the reader to be aware of a variety of biases that distort the accuracy of the Spanish accounts. The foremost influence in these narratives is the sixteenth-century worldview. These authors did not have our modern knowledge of the world's history and geography. They had to contend with reconciling what they saw with a worldview based on biblical history. There was a tendency, therefore, to try to connect and interpret the events of Inca history with those of the Old Testament of the Christian Bible. There were also biases introduced by the position of the authors in the Spanish hierarchy and their attitudes toward the controversies of their day. At various times the Incas were vilified as cruel tyrants and usurpers or glorified as enlightened and benevolent god-kings. The descriptions were tailored to suit the audience, depending on whether one wanted to justify or condemn Spain's destruction of the Incas.

Distortions and biases also resulted from attempts by Incas and their descendants to improve their reputation with the Spanish and their standing in colonial society by glorifying their ancestors. As a result, a variety of versions of the most important events of Inca history were recorded. Inca factions vied with each other in recounting their history to improve their status with the Spanish.

Finally, there is the problem of the drastic cultural differences between the European and Andean peoples. The Inca concept of history and its purposes were very different from those of the Europeans. The Spanish were attempting to understand a linear, sequential history of the Inca past, whereas the Incas recorded history in a ruler-centric manner. Each king had his own history composed with himself in the central role. Therefore, each royal lineage kept a different version of history that was focused on the king to whom they were related. Some Inca rulers were known to have rewritten and edited history to remove inconvenient predecessors, to claim the successes and glory of others, and to improve their legitimacy. In addition to these factors, there was a language barrier. Few Spaniards had command of the Inca language, and few Incas spoke Spanish. Much was lost in the translations through misunderstandings.

**Eyewitness Accounts of the Incas.** There are only six known eyewitness accounts of the Incas at the moment of Spanish contact. These are records of what was seen, experienced, and understood by members of Pizarro's invading Spanish force. Four of these were written immediately after the Conquest by Francisco de Xérez (1917), Miguel de Estete (1918), Pedro Sancho de la Hoz (1917), and an unknown author referred to by scholars as the Anonymous Conqueror, published in an English translation by Joseph H. Sinclair in 1929. These accounts, although invaluable, are colored by the writers' sixteenth-century worldview, the fact that they were not trained observers, and the fact that they were describing something totally new and strange to them. The accounts also lack comprehensiveness, since each author was relating what he individually saw and experienced. The two other eyewitness accounts were written well after the conquest. Pedro Pizarro (1986), who was a cousin of expedition leader Francisco Pizarro, wrote his account in 1570. An English translation of this work by Philip Ainsworth Means was published in 1921. Cristóbal de Molina de Santiago (1916) wrote his account in 1556. Because some time had passed between the events themselves and their recording, these last two documents are considered somewhat less reliable.

Portrait of Francisco Pizarro (1470–1541), the Spanish conqueror of Peru. (Mansell/Time-Life Pictures/Getty Images)

**Secondary Accounts.** There are a large number of secondary accounts, some written soon after the Conquest, although their authors were not eyewitnesses. As Rowe (1946: 193–197) points out, these documents are so numerous and vary so much in reliability that consulting them can be an arduous task. Many authors borrowed from others without crediting the original so that it becomes difficult to know the true source of some information. Many of the original manuscripts were not published until modern times. In general, the further away in time from the Conquest, the less reliable the account. Among the most useful and reliable of the secondary accounts are those of Cieza de León, Betanzos, Polo de Ondegardo, Sarmiento de Gamboa, and Cobo. A more obscure and problematic but still important source is the account of Montesinos.

Pedro Cieza de León wrote a work titled *Crónica del Perú* in 1551. He traveled throughout the Andes and fought as a soldier in the post-Conquest civil wars among the Spaniards. He is regarded as an honest and careful observer who distinguished between fact and opinion. An English translation titled *The Incas of Pedro Cieza de León* was published in 1959 by the University of Oklahoma (Cieza de León 1959).

Juan de Betanzos was a Spaniard who was considered in his day to be the finest interpreter into Spanish of the Inca language called Quechua. He married an Inca princess who was the former wife of both the last independent Inca ruler, Atahuallpa, and the Spanish conquistador Francisco Pizarro. Because of his wife, Betanzos had remarkable access to the Inca viewpoint of both the pre-Conquest history and the European occupation. Nevertheless, his account is biased by the fact that his informants were of the kin group of the emperor Pachacuti and so related Inca history with Pachacuti and his descendants in the leading roles. In 1557, Betanzos finished a manuscript titled *Suma y narración de los Yngas*. An English translation titled *Narrative of the Incas* was published by the University of Texas in 1996 (Betanzos 1996).

During the 1550s, Juan Polo de Ondegardo was an official of the Spanish government in Cuzco. Trained as a lawyer, he made a number of careful investigations of Inca governmental and religious practices. His reports on rites and laws of the Incas (e.g., Polo de Ondegardo 1873) are considered very reliable and were used extensively by authors of other early accounts, most often without attribution.

The Viceroy Toledo, who ruled Peru for the Spanish crown from 1569 to 1581, ordered that a history of the Incas be prepared by Pedro Sarmiento de Gamboa. This work was completed in 1572. In order to gather information for his history, Sarmiento interviewed Inca survivors and descendants in Cuzco. His work is considered to be quite accurate by scholars, but its interpretations of Inca history are biased by the desire of the Viceroy Toledo to depict the Incas as illegitimate usurpers. This work was translated into English by Clements Markham and published by the Hakluyt Society in Cambridge, England, in 1907. It has recently been reprinted by Dover Press (Sarmiento de Gamboa 1999).

One of the most respected sources used by scholars is the work of the Jesuit priest Father Bernabé Cobo titled *Historia del Nuevo Mundo*, which was completed in 1653. He conducted research in Peru in the early 1600s and also drew on the works of some of the earlier authors previously mentioned, especially Polo de Ondegardo. He produced four books that provide one of the most complete descriptions of Inca culture. English translations of his works have been published in two volumes by the University of Texas (Cobo 1979 and 1990).

A controversial but very important work was written by another Catholic priest, Fernando de Montesinos, around 1642. His book *Ophir de España. Memorias Antiguas Historiales y Politicas del Perú* presents a remarkably different dynastic history for the Incas and their ancestors. Montesinos presents a long list of kings extending back in time before the Incas that possibly includes rulers of the earlier Wari and Tiwanaku empires. Because it departs so dramatically from the histories recorded by the other chronicles, this work was, until recently, ignored by most scholars. A comprehensive new study of Montesinos and his work by the Finnish scholar Juha Hiltunen (1999) has caused a revival of scholarly interest. Recent archaeological discoveries in Cuzco have also supported some of the events in the history related by Montesinos (Hiltunen and McEwan 2004; McEwan, Chatfield and Gibaja 2002).

**Native Accounts.** A small number of secondary accounts of the Incas and aspects of Andean culture were written by native Andean authors. The most famous and influential of these is by Garcilaso de la Vega, the son of a Spanish conquistador and an Inca princess. Garcilaso left Peru for Spain at the age of twenty-one and never returned. His work *The Royal Commentaries of the Incas* was composed at the end of the sixteenth century, near the end of his long life, and was based on the memories of his childhood. Garcilaso presented the Incas in a favorable light, and because he had access to information through relatives who were Inca nobility, he was for many years considered the authority on Inca history. In modern times, his authority has been questioned and his reputation has declined to the extent that he is no longer considered a prime source by scholars. An English translation of his book was published in 1966 by the University of Texas.

In the early seventeenth century, Felipe Huaman Poma de Ayala, the mestizo son of a Spaniard and an Indian, wrote a massive 1,400-page letter to King Phillip III of Spain. This work, titled *Nueva Corónica y Buen Gobierno*, gives a history of the Incas before and during Spanish rule and complains of colonial abuses of the natives by the Spaniards. It is written in a mixture of Spanish and Quechua and is of dubious value as a history. What is important about this work are the numerous detailed pen-and-ink drawings illustrating the text that are considered to be a very reliable visual record of Inca culture. This letter was sent to Spain but never seen by the king. It eventually made its way to Denmark, where it lay unread in the Royal Library in Copenhagen until 1908. It was finally published in 1936 in Paris and more recently has been translated into English and published by Dutton Press in New York in 1978.

Also writing in the early part of the seventeenth century was Joan de Santacruz Pachacuti Yamqui Salcamaygua (1879). His work titled *Relación de antigüedades deste Reyno del Perú* is described by Rowe (1946: 196) as "confused and difficult to use," although it contains "valuable material on Inca history and religion."

## Ethnohistoric Studies

William Prescott's (1847) classic *History of the Conquest of Peru* is perhaps the most widely known synthesis of the Spanish sources. Since its publication, however, some new major sources have come to light, including such works as Felipe Huaman Poma de Ayala's manuscript and the complete Palma de Mallorca manuscript of the work of Juan de Betanzos. The second half of the twentieth century saw an explosion of interest in the original Spanish sources on the Incas, with scholarship dominated by John H. Rowe of the University of California at Berkeley, R. Tom Zuidema at the University of Illinois, John V. Murra of Cornell University, Richard Schaedel of the University of Texas, and their many students. Outside the United States, major contributions to Inca studies were made by Maria Rostworowski de Diez Canseco, Franklin Pease, Waldemar Espinosa, and Pierre Duviols. The field of ethnohistory remains very active moving into the twenty-first century, and new works appear yearly.

## Ethnographic Studies

Ethnographic studies of modern groups descended from the Incas and other Andean peoples, which are too numerous to list here, have provided a great deal of information on a variety of topics. These studies shed light on religious beliefs, the structure of family and kinship, craft production, and many aspects of social organization. Although separated from the Incas by almost five centuries, modern Andean society is very conservative in its basic structure, and many social practices are still observed. These can be very illuminating in explaining and understanding Inca society.

## Archaeology of the Incas

Given that the Inca civilization was the greatest of the Native American empires, it is surprising that relatively few archaeological studies of the Incas have been done. This is due to a variety of factors. Scientific archaeology in Peru in general is a relatively new phenomenon dating from the turn of the twentieth century. Until the advent of aviation and rapid travel, Cuzco and much of the highlands were remote and difficult to access. The number of trained archaeologists was very small and research funding difficult to come by. Most scholars in the early part of the century, with the notable exceptions of Julio C. Tello, Luis Valcárcel, and Hiram Bingham, confined their work to the coastal regions of Peru. With plenty of sites to investigate and amazingly good preservation of artifacts in the coastal deserts, there was little incentive to venture to inland sites. Since the Incas and their history had already been described in Spanish documents, there seemed less urgency to research them. By the middle of the twentieth century, John H. Rowe began his pioneering efforts in Cuzco and was followed by his students and other scholars throughout the second half of the century. The Peruvians also began training archaeologists through their university system and taking a great interest in studying their heritage. Archaeological understanding of the Incas continues to develop each year as more fieldwork is accomplished by an increasing number of scholars in an exciting and dynamic field of study. It is only very recently, however, that it has been possible to begin comparing the archaeological record to histories recorded by the Spaniards. This process will, over time, permit clarification of the contradictory and confusing accounts of Inca history recorded in the chronicles.

## Publication of Inca Research

There are many sources of published scholarship regarding the Incas. Major works are normally published as monographs or edited volumes by publishing houses such as Thames and Hudson, Crown, Kluwer, and Blackwell.

University presses also publish major scholarly works. Those that concentrate on the Incas and Inca-related themes include the following:

- The University of Iowa Press
- The University of Texas Press
- The University of Oklahoma Press
- The Institute of Archaeology at the University of California, Los Angeles
- Cambridge University Press
- Oxford University Press

Several major museums also publish volumes on Inca archaeology. These include the following:

- The Field Museum of Natural History in Chicago
- The Smithsonian Institution and Dumbarton Oaks in Washington, D.C.
- The American Museum of Natural History in New York

Scholarly articles about Inca research are generally published in specialized professional journals. The leading journal in the Americas is *Latin American Antiquity,* published by the Society for American Archaeology (prior to 1990 *American Antiquity* published Inca-related articles for the society). Articles also occasionally appear in *American Anthropologist,* the journal of the American Anthropological Association. Other important journals include the following:

- *Journal of Field Archaeology,* published at Boston University
- *Andean Past,* published at Cornell University
- *Ñawpa Pacha,* published by the Institute of Andean Studies at Berkeley, California
- *Tawantinsuyu: International Journal of Inka Studies,* published by Brolga Press in Australia

In Peru the following journals, among others, carry articles about Inca archaeology:

- *Boletin de Arqueologia,* published by Pontificia Universidad Católica Peru, Lima

- *Revista del Museo Nacional*, Lima
- *Gaceta Arqueologica Andina*, Lima
- *Boletin de Lima*
- *Revista Andina*, Cuzco
- *Revista del Museo e Instituto de Arqueologia*, Cuzco

Additional sources for published studies include the following:

- Instituto Nacional de la Cultura, Peru
- Instituto Nacional de Arqueologia, Bolivia
- Academia Nacional de Ciencias, Bolivia
- United Nations Educational, Scientific and Cultural Organization (UNESCO)

Outlets publishing popular, nontechnical articles on the Incas include *National Geographic* magazine, *Archaeology* magazine, books published by Time-Life Books, and Newsweek Books.

## Libraries

Most major university libraries in the United States contain works on the Incas. The following are among the most important and comprehensive library collections for studying the Incas:

- The Library of Congress, Washington, D.C.
- Dumbarton Oaks Research Library and Collection, Washington, D.C.
- The Benson Latin American Library Collection, the University of Texas, Austin
- The New York City Public Library
- Biblioteca del Museo Inka, Cuzco, Peru
- Biblioteca Bartolomé de las Casas, Cuzco, Peru

## Museum Collections

There are not many collections of Inca material culture found outside Peru. Many major museums have only one or two pieces, and others erroneously exhibit material from other Peruvian cultures as being Inca. The most important museum collections are in Peru, and a few are in the United States. These include the following:

- Museo Inka, Cuzco, Peru
- Museo Histórico Regional, Casa Garcilaso, Cuzco, Peru
- El Museo de la Nación, Lima, Peru
- El Museo Nacional de Antropología, Arqueología e Historia, Lima, Peru
- Museo del Oro, Lima, Peru
- Museo Larco Hoyle, Lima, Peru
- The American Museum of Natural History, New York
- The National Museum of the American Indian, New York
- The Peabody Museum of Archaeology and Ethnology, Harvard University

- The Peabody Museum of Natural History, Yale University
- The Phoebe A. Hearst Museum of Anthropology, University of California, Berkeley
- Dumbarton Oaks Research Library and Collection, Washington, D.C.
- The Textile Museum, Washington, D.C.
- The Smithsonian Institution, Washington, D.C.

## Research Symposia

A number of conferences are held annually in which current Andean and Inca research is presented and discussed. These include:

- The annual meeting of the Society for American Archaeology
- The annual meeting of the Institute for Andean Studies, Berkeley, California
- The Northeast Conference on Andean Archaeology and Ethnohistory
- The Midwest Conference on Andean and Amazonian Archaeology and Ethnohistory

## REFERENCES

Anonymous Conqueror. 1929. *The Conquest of Peru as Related by a Member of the Pizarro Expedition.* Edited and translated by Joseph H. Sinclair. New York: New York Public Library.

Betanzos, Juan de. 1996. *Narrative of the Incas.* Translated and edited by Roland Hamilton and Dana Buchanan. Austin: University of Texas Press.

Cieza de León, Pedro de. 1959. *The Incas of Pedro de Cieza de León.* Translated by Harriet de Onis and edited by Victor W. von Hagen. Norman: University of Oklahoma Press.

Cobo, Bernabé. 1979. *History of the Inca Empire: An Account of the Indians' Customs and their Origin Together with a Treatise on Inca Legends, History, and Social Institutions.* Translated and edited by Roland Hamilton. Austin: University of Texas Press.

———. 1990. *Inca Religion and Customs.* Translated and edited by Roland Hamilton. Austin: University of Texas Press.

Estete, Miguel de. 1918. "Noticia del Perú, o El descubriemiento y conquista del Perú." Published with introduction and notes by Carlos Larrea. *Boletín de la Sociedad Ecuatoriana de Estudios Históricos* 1(3): 300–350.

———. 1967. *La Relación del viaje que hizo el señor Capitán Hernando Pizarro por mandado del señor Gobernador, su hermano, desde el pueblo de Caxamalca a Pachacamac y de allí a Jauja.* Edited by Concepción Bravo. Madrid: Historia 16.

Garcilaso de la Vega, El Inca. 1966. *Royal Commentaries of the Incas and General History of Peru, Parts One and Two.* Translated by Harold Livermore. Austin: University of Texas Press.

Guaman Poma de Ayala, Felipe. 1936. *Nueva corónica y buen gobierno.* Paris: Travaux et Mémoires de L'Institut d'Ethnologie 22.

Hiltunen, Juha J. 1999. *Ancient Kings of Peru: The Reliability of the Chronicle of Fernando de Montesinos; Correlating the Dynasty Lists with Current Prehistoric Periodization in the Andes.* Helsinki: Suomen Historiallinen Seura.

Hiltunen, Juha J., and Gordon F. McEwan. 2004. "Knowing the Inca Past." In *Andean Archaeology,* edited by Helaine Silverman, 237–254. Oxford: Blackwell.

Huamán Poma de Ayala, Don Felipe. 1978. *Letter to a King: A Peruvian Chief's Account of Life under the Incas and under Spanish Rule.* Translated by Christopher Dilke. New York: E. P. Dutton.

McEwan, Gordon F., Melissa Chatfield, and Arminda Gibaja O. 2002. "The Archaeology of Inca Origins: Excavations at Chokepukio, Cuzco, Peru." In *Andean Archaeology,* edited by W. Isbell and H. Silverman, 287–301. New York: Kluwer Academic.

Molina de Santiago, Cristóbal. 1916. "Relación de muchas cosas acaescidas en el Perú, en suma, para entender a la letra la manera que se tuvo en la conquista y poblazon destos reinos." In *Colección de libros y documentos referentes a la historia del Perú,* edited by C. A. Romero and H. H. Urteaga, 1(1): 105–190.

Pachacuti Yamqui Salcamaygua, Joan de. 1968. *Relación de antigüedades deste Reyno del Perú.* Biblioteca de Autores Españoles, 209: 279–319. Madrid: Ediciones Atlas.

Pizarro, Pedro. 1921. *Relation of the Discovery and Conquest of the Kingdoms of Peru.* Translated and edited by Philip Ainsworth Means. Boston: Milford House.

———.1986. *Relación del descubrimiento y conquista de los reinos del Perú.* Edited by Gjillermo Lohmann Villena. Lima: Pontificia Universidad Católica, Fondo Editorial.

Polo de Ondegardo, Juan. 1873. *The Rites and Laws of the Incas.* Edited and translated by C. R. Markham. London: Hakluyt Society.

Prescott, William H. 1847. *History of the Conquest of Peru.* New York: Harper and Brothers Publishers.

Rowe, John H. 1946. "Inca Culture at the Time of the Spanish Conquest." In *Handbook of South American Indians,* edited by Julian Steward, bulletin 143, vol. 2, 183–330. Washington, DC: Bureau of American Ethnology.

Sancho de la Hoz, Pedro. 1917. *An Account of the Conquest of Peru.* Translated and edited by P. A. Means. New York: Cortés Society.

Sarmiento de Gamboa, Pedro. 1960. *Historia de los Incas.* Biblioteca de Autores Españoles, vol. 135, 193–297. Madrid: Ediciones Atlas.

———. 1999. *History of the Incas.* Translated and edited by Sir Clements Markham. Mineola, NY: Dover. English translation originally published 1907. Cambridge: Hakluyt Society.

Xérez, Francisco de. 1872. *Reports on the discovery of Peru.* Translated and edited by C. R. Markham. London: Hakluyt Society.

———. 1985. *Verdadera Relación de la Conquista del Perú y Provincia del Cuzco llamada la Nueva Castilla.* Edited by Concepción Bravo. Madrid: Historia 16.

# PART 2

## Inca Civilization

CHAPTER 2

# Location of the Inca Civilization and Environmental Setting

## LOCATION

The Inca Empire was located in the Andes mountain range and coastal deserts that run the length of the west coast of South America. At its height, the empire extended from near the modern Colombia-Ecuador border south through highland and coastal Peru, most of modern Bolivia, to the extreme northwest of Argentina and to the Maule River in northern Chile. The Incas confined themselves to the highlands and coast and did not significantly penetrate the lowland Amazonian areas to the east of the Andes.

## THE ANDEAN ENVIRONMENT

The west coast of South America is dominated by the Andes mountain range, home of some of the world's highest mountains. The central Andes comprise two parallel ranges known as the Cordillera Negra or Occidental in the west and the Cordillera Blanca or Oriental in the east. The Andean environment, although rich and varied, is an exceptionally difficult one for human survival. The elevation changes drastically over short distances, water is often scarce, and climatic fluctuations cause frequent droughts. Andean society was profoundly affected by this challenging environment and was in many ways uniquely adapted to it. Despite the fact that only about 2 percent of the land area is suitable for agriculture, this region became one of the world's great centers of civilization (Burger 1992: 12).

The Andean region is essentially composed of three different major environmental zones running north-south longitudinally and parallel to each other. To the west is the coastal desert zone bordered by the Pacific Ocean. A short distance inland from the coast, the Andes rise steeply to form the highland zone. To the east of the Andean range lies the tropical forest of the Amazon Basin.

### The Coastal Zone

The desert coastal zone comprises a narrow, gently sloping plain that varies in width from 20 to 100 kilometers. It is narrow in the south and widest in the extreme north of Peru. Here the Humboldt Current turns west into the Pacific Ocean; the climate of the coastal plain in Ecuador is thus different, and the area

Aerial view of the dry desert coast showing the Paracas Peninsula. (Yann Arthus-Bertrand/ Corbis)

is covered with tropical forest. However, most of this land along the Pacific coast forms one of the world's driest deserts.

This desert results from the cold waters of the Humboldt Current sweeping north from Antarctica along the west coast of South America. Upwelling of this current, caused by the prevailing winds, keeps the air temperature cool over the sea. The capacity of the air to hold moisture is therefore diminished and not much evaporation takes place. As the air moves inland, it slowly warms. This warming increases the capacity of the air to hold what little moisture it has, and thus no precipitation can occur. As the warmed air rises in altitude, it gradually cools and forms clouds. During the South American winter, from June to November, these clouds are trapped beneath a layer of warmer high-altitude air, resulting in a constantly overcast sky. Some mist and light sprinkling occur during this time, but no significant rain falls. When the South American summer comes, during the months of December through May, the upper air layers become cooler, allowing the clouds to rise over the Andes. As the clouds gradually cool in response to the increase in elevation, their moisture precipitates and falls as rain in the mountains.

On some parts of the coast, the interval between rainfalls can be as much as fifty years or more. These infrequent rains are often the result of temporary shifts in the ocean currents, a climatological phenomenon called El Niño (after

*why there are deserts on Pac. Coast*

the Christ Child) that usually occurs in December. At intervals varying from sixteen to fifty years, the equatorial countercurrent is deflected to the south and unites with the eastern equatorial current. This causes a warming of the normally cold waters off the coast and results in conditions that permit precipitation. The rains, when they do come, are usually so heavy that they are catastrophic.

Crossing this dry desert coast are about forty relatively short rivers flowing out of the highlands. The bulk of the Andean watershed flows into the Amazon River to the east and then to the Atlantic Ocean, but a small portion flows to the Pacific Ocean. Although these rivers are small and some flow only seasonally, they provide enough water to turn the desert river valleys into oases capable of supporting life. Once the inhabitants began to expand the extent of the rivers through networks of irrigation canals, they made an otherwise inhospitable environment capable of supporting large populations. Many common plants were domesticated and farmed in these valleys. Such foods as avocados, peanuts, beans, squash, gourds, maize, peppers, manioc, sweet potatoes, and a variety of fruits, including pineapples, guavas, cherimoyas, and *lúcumas*, among others, were produced.

Some of the coastal valleys have climatic variation resulting from elevation changes between the coast and the mountains. Midvalley zones between 500 and 2,500 meters in elevation, called *yungas*, are sometimes especially productive since they are warmer and more sheltered than the coast (Burger 1992, 16).

The same cold waters that cause the desert conditions on the coast by precluding rainfall paradoxically produce an exceptionally rich environment for marine fauna. The upwelling waters of the cold current bring nutrients to the surface that support plankton species, which in turn provide the food source for numerous species of small fish and shellfish. The food chain extending from these species includes larger fish species, many types of waterfowl, and even sea lions. These waters are among the richest fishing grounds in the world and are a vital source of animal protein for the human coastal population. Like the coastal deserts, the ocean biomass is also subject to severe disturbance by the El Niño phenomenon. The resulting warming of the offshore waters can result in catastrophic death rates among the wildlife, depleting the food source of human populations.

## The Highland Zone

As little as 50 kilometers inland from the desert coast, the Andes mountains rise steeply, and thus the environment changes markedly. These mountains are among the world's tallest, with the highest peaks near 6,700 meters in altitude. The rapid change in elevation over very short distances in the sierra provides a large number and variety of microclimates. Crossing over the Andes from the desert coast in the west to the Amazon lowlands to the east, one can encounter twenty of the world's thirty-four life zones in the course of only a few hundred kilometers (Burger 1992: 12). Despite this huge ecological variety, the steep slopes of the Andes mountains hold very little fertile soil that can be farmed. Through the centuries, Andean farmers learned to make maximum use of

View of the high Andes. (Yann Arthus-Bertrand/Corbis)

what little farming land they had. They fully exploited all of the best land in the highland river basins and created additional fields by constructing agricultural terraces on mountain slopes. Because not all zones would be affected at once, diverse crops were grown in different ecological zones to ensure against famines caused by climatic fluctuations or plant diseases. Farmers would sometimes plant as many as two hundred varieties of potatoes in a single field (National Research Council 1989). As on the coast, a great variety of crops were domesticated and grown, including more than 1,000 kinds of potatoes and other tubers such as *achira, ocas, mashua, ulluco,* at least 150 varieties of maize, grains called *kaniwa, kiwicha,* and quinoa, as well as amaranth, squash, and chili peppers.

The high, rugged Andes are geologically young mountains with considerable volcanic and seismic activity. Most river canyons and valleys are very steep; only a few have narrow strips of bottomland suitable for farming. Although the central Andes are within the tropics, their climate is temperate because of the high elevations. The cold increases with altitude, and mountains with elevations of 4,800 meters or higher are capped with snow and ice year-round.

In the highlands there are several distinct geographic zones where particular crops are cultivated. The lowest of these in terms of elevation is called the *quechua* (the same word is also used for the name of the predominant modern native ethnic group in Peru and for the language that they speak) zone and is found between 2,300 meters and 3,200 meters above sea level. These warm, frost-free lower valleys are excellent for the production of maize and other crops. Above the *quechua* zone is the *suni* zone at 3,200 meters to 4,000 meters above sea level. This is an area of steep slopes suitable for growing potatoes and other tubers as well as native grains.

Higher still is the *puna* zone, from 4,000 meters to 4,800 meters above sea level. Although agriculture is impossible at these altitudes, this zone provides abundant grasslands. Llamas and alpacas were herded in great numbers on the high, cold plateaus of the southern Andes, which provided ideal pasturage for camelids. Llamas provided meat and were used as pack animals. In the absence of wheeled vehicles and large animals to pull them, llama caravans provided the means of moving trade goods over long distances, connecting the coast with the highlands and the cloud forests of the eastern Andean slopes. Alpacas were prized for their fine wool used to make cloth, which became the most valued commodity in Andean culture. Two other camelids, the vicuña and guanaco, are also native to this zone. Although prized for their wool, these animals could not be domesticated like their larger relatives.

Additional food sources were to be found in the abundant highland lakes and rivers. Many species of fish were available as well as aquatic birds. Many human populations supplemented their diet hunting animals such as deer. One of the most important protein sources for Andean peoples is the *cuy*, or

Bushels of corn and beans in an Ecuador farmers' market, products that were introduced to Europeans by the Incas. (Tom Schumacher)

guinea pig. These creatures have the advantage of being cheap to raise and maintain, and they reproduce very rapidly. They are an excellent inexpensive source of protein even today.

Over the millennia, humans adapted the land through irrigation and terracing. Selective breeding adapted plants to the many ecological niches, and the most productive species were developed for each area. Humans also adapted physically to the severe mountain environment. Highlanders developed a much greater lung capacity and a more efficient circulatory system that allowed them to thrive in the thin air and cold temperatures of the high altitudes.

## The Tropical Lowlands

To the east, the highlands drop into the Amazon Basin. This transition zone is known as the *montaña*. Here there are dense jungles covering extremely rugged mountainous terrain. This area is the home of jaguars, caimans, large snakes, and tropical birds frequently represented in Andean art. The higher elevations are quite cool, but as the altitude decreases, the temperature and humidity rise. This environmental zone does not appear to have been as heavily populated in antiquity as the highland and coastal zones and was economically less productive. The Incas exploited the upper elevations, called the Ceja de Selva, or eyebrow of the jungle. Here there are magnificent cloud forest environments with exotic plants, spectacular views, and a very agreeable climate. Some of the more spectacular Inca monuments, including Machu Picchu, are found in this environment. The most valued products of this region were brightly colored feathers, tobacco, and the all-important leaves of the coca plant. When chewed together with chemical lime, coca leaves have a mildly narcotic effect. Coca was much prized in the ancient Andes and is still widely used today. It was so valued that in Inca times, and perhaps earlier, colonies were established in this zone to produce coca for consumption in the highlands and on the coast.

Further to the east, the highlands give way to the Amazon Basin. Here there are dense tropical rainforests and high rainfalls but poor soils for intensive agriculture. Although the Incas traded for some products of this zone, such as brightly colored macaw feathers, they seem to have seldom penetrated this area. What little information we have of the Incas' expeditions indicates that their attempts at conquest ended in disaster.

## ANDEAN CULTURE AND ITS ENVIRONMENT

More than most historical locales, the Andean environment dictated that humans could survive in relatively few places in this immense landscape. A very large part of this territory was uninhabitable because of high altitude, desert conditions, and limited water resources. On the coast, formidable deserts had to be crossed in order to travel between river valley oases. Although obstacles to movement were not insurmountable, the choice of places to live was severely limited by the availability of water. Yet the larger of the coastal river valleys were ultimately able to support large human populations and permitted the development of advanced civilizations.

Coca leaves for sale. The highly prized leaves of the coca plant provide a mild narcotic effect when chewed. Andean peoples use it not only as a stimulant but also for religious purposes and for cooking and healing. (Corel)

The Amazon Basin rainforest was never occupied by the Incas. Nevertheless they prized many of the products of the zone, especially colored feathers. (Danny Lehman/Corbis)

In the highlands, movement throughout the terrain was largely determined by the path of least resistance. One could practically pass from one river drainage to another only through a limited number of mountain passes. Crossing the narrow gorges of the fast-flowing highland rivers was possible only at certain places where bridges could be built. These natural obstacles resulted in restricted options for movement and in the development of a number of diverse population centers distributed in a chainlike fashion from north to south. These include the Cajamarca or Middle Marañón river basin, the Callejon de Huaylas, the Mantaro river basin, the Upper Urubamba and Vilcanota basin, and the northern and southern basins of Lake Titicaca. Each of these major highland basins became a population center and developed its own distinctive cultural features. Throughout time, these population centers gave rise to a series of complex civilizations that culminated in the Inca Empire.

Since ancient times, the population of the Andes has comprised many different ethnic groups. These peoples originally spoke their own languages and had their own distinct cultural practices. The Spanish Conquest had a homogenizing effect in that much of the linguistic diversity disappeared. Most of the population of the Andes now speaks one or more of only three languages: Quechua, Aymara, and Spanish. Despite the ethnic diversity, certain commonalities bind these people into an Andean culture. Much of this culture is shaped by the universal subsistence activities of farming, fishing, and herding. The difficulty of farming the steep Andean slopes and desert river valleys made cooperative ef-

Boats made of totora reeds were used by fishermen on highland lakes and also on the coast. (Corel)

forts essential. With no draft animals, plowing had to be done by hand. A group of farmers, each digging one furrow, could plow a field much more efficiently than a single farmer. In areas where irrigation was required, construction and maintenance of canals could only be carried out by large groups coordinating their labor. The reciprocal obligation to help neighbors or kinsmen with their labors in return for their help became a key feature of Andean society.

Communal holding of land and its surplus is also an important feature of many Andean societies. In Inca times, surplus food was stored in warehouses by the state for insurance against times of want. In times of famine, this food would be redistributed to those in need. On a community level, widows, orphans, the sick, and people too old for work were taken care of by the surpluses of their kin groups or had their lands worked for them. The storage and redistribution of surpluses, together with farming strategies involving the use of multiple and varied eco-niches, were the main means by which the Andean population could cope with the unpredictability of their environment.

## REFERENCES

Burger, Richard L. 1992. *Chavin and the Origins of Andean Civilization.* London: Thames and Hudson.

National Research Council. 1989. *Lost Crops of the Incas: Little Known Plants of the Andes with Promise for Worldwide Cultivation.* Washington, D.C.: National Academy Press.

CHAPTER 3

# Historical and Chronological Setting

Because the Incas had no writing, our knowledge of their empire begins with the accounts of those who brought about its end. Some of the Spanish conquerors wrote down their impressions of what they saw and the events in which they participated, and reports were written to the Spanish authorities. There are thus a very limited number of eyewitness accounts of the Incas from the very short period between the first contact with the Spaniards and the Conquest. Ironically, history in the European sense as a written record of events of the Incas begins at the end of their empire.

## EUROPEAN DISCOVERY OF THE INCAS

Following Columbus's voyage of discovery, the Spanish explored and settled first in the islands of the West Indies, working their way slowly westward. In 1513 an expedition led by Vasco Núñez de Balboa crossed the Isthmus of Panama and discovered the Pacific Ocean. Among Balboa's lieutenants was Francisco Pizarro, who would continue explorations to the south in subsequent years.

Just twenty-seven years after Columbus's first voyage to the "New World," the potential wealth of the Americas was deeply impressed upon the Spaniards with the discovery of the Aztec Empire by Hernán Cortés in 1519. Eager Spanish adventurers inspired by the success of the expedition to conquer the Aztecs set out to explore the Americas in hopes of finding additional empires rich with gold. The success of Cortés made it possible for other would-be conquerors to receive royal license from Spain to mount expeditions.

By 1522 the explorer Pascual de Andagoya had pushed down the Pacific coast to the south and reported finding the province of "Birú." Tales of this fabulously wealthy land spurred Francisco Pizarro to begin organizing an expedition of conquest. He launched this first expedition in late 1524 and throughout 1525 explored the coast south to the San Juan River in what is now Colombia. This venture ended disastrously, with many men dying of disease and hunger and very little gold to show for their efforts upon their return to Panama.

Undeterred, Pizarro found two backers for a second expedition and entered into an agreement with Father Hernando de Luque, a Catholic priest, and Diego de Almagro, another Spanish explorer. This second voyage was em-

Balboa discovers the Pacific Ocean. Among his lieutenants on his expedition was Francisco Pizarro, who went on to conquer the Inca Empire. (Library of Congress)

barked on in 1526 and lasted through 1527. Moving further down the coast of Colombia, the expedition came to rest on the island of Gallo after being blocked by hostile natives in northern Ecuador. Here, upon receiving news that the governor in Panama had recalled the expedition, considering it a failure, Pizarro issued his famous challenge to his companions. Drawing a line in the sand with his sword, he summoned his men to follow him on to Peru. Only thirteen chose to do so, and the rest returned to Panama. After a delay of nearly five months awaiting a ship, Pizarro and his small band pushed on to the south. During this second voyage, the Spaniards obtained their first glimpse of the wealth to be found in the Inca Empire. Just south of the equator, the Spanish ships encountered a large ocean-going raft engaged in a trading expedition to Ecuador. The raft held twenty natives as well as silver, gold, jewels, and fine cloth. Three of the native crew were captured and were taught to speak Spanish in order to serve as translators.

The Spanish expedition landed at a place called Tumbes in northern Peru and received gifts from the local ruler. Eventually, the explorers followed the coast as far south as modern Chimbote before turning back. When they returned to Panama, the governor was not impressed with their account, even though they brought evidence of gold as well as plants and animals from Peru. He refused to sanction another expedition, and Pizarro was forced to go home to Spain to seek backing from the royal court.

Pizarro's third voyage was undertaken on December 27, 1530, after the trip back to Spain, where he secured for himself from the king the titles of governor and captain general of Peru. During 1531 and part of 1532, the Spaniards advanced cautiously down the coast as far as Piura in northern Peru. Much of this time was spent waiting for reinforcements to arrive from Panama. By September 1532, Pizarro and his men had lost patience with waiting, and a decision was made to head into the interior of the Inca realm, leaving only a small party of men at the newly founded Spanish town of San Miguel de Piura. On September 24, Pizarro set out for the highland town of Cajamarca with 62 horsemen and 106 foot soldiers, hoping to encounter the Incas (Hemming 1970).

Near Cajamarca, the Spaniards found a huge Inca army and the Inca Atahuallpa. Having defeated his brother Huascar in a civil war over succession to the throne, Atahuallpa and his army were on their way from Quito in the north to the Inca imperial capital of Cuzco. Unknown to the Spaniards, the Inca Empire had just suffered two prolonged traumatic events. Between 1525 and 1527, an epidemic disease that was probably smallpox, introduced into the native populations by the Europeans, had ravaged the populace of the empire. Among the thousands of victims were the reigning emperor Huayna Capac and his heir apparent, Ninan Cuyochi. The sudden death of Huayna Capac and his heir left a power vacuum that precipitated a civil war between two of the surviving claimants to the throne. Atahuallpa had been with his father in Ecuador at the time of the emperor's death. He enjoyed the loyalty of the large armies that had been engaged in expanding the empire to the north. His rival was his brother Huascar, who had actually ascended to the throne in the capital at Cuzco upon learning of the death of Huayna Capac. The Incas divided into factions, supporting one or the other of these brothers, and a bitter struggle ensued that lasted nearly five years. Atahuallpa had just defeated Huascar and was marching to Cuzco to claim the throne and be crowned emperor at the moment of his fateful encounter with the Spaniards. Francisco Pizarro had the phenomenal luck of having arrived in Peru at just the right moment, when the Inca Empire was between rulers, its most vulnerable condition (Hemming 1970).

At Cajamarca, the tiny force of 168 Spaniards attacked the Incas and captured Atahuallpa, effectively decapitating the Inca state. In an attempt to free himself from captivity, Atahuallpa agreed to pay a ransom by filling a room once with golden objects and twice with silver objects. The Spaniards readily agreed to this arrangement and settled in to wait for the treasure to accumulate and for reinforcements to arrive from Panama. During this period, Pizarro sent parties out to scout the highlands and coast and allowed Atahuallpa to continue to conduct the business of his empire despite his captivity. Atahuallpa ordered that the treasure be brought but also plotted his own escape and had his defeated brother Huascar executed to prevent him from presenting himself to the Spanish invaders as a legitimate alternative ruler. Ultimately 13,420 lb. of gold and 26,000 lb. of silver were collected as Atahuallpa's ransom, but it was not enough to save him. On July 26, 1533, the last independent ruler of the Incas was killed by the Spaniards, who feared a rescue attempt by the Inca army (Hemming 1970).

Following the death of Atahuallpa, the Spaniards attempted to rule the Inca Empire through a series of puppet emperors. Some of these were assassinated by their own people when they seemed too cooperative with the foreign invaders, while others escaped into the *montaña* and led resistance to the Spanish from their last stronghold at Vilcabamba. The last Inca ruler, Tupac Amaru, was finally captured and executed by the Spanish in 1572. With his death, the Inca dynasty ended (Hemming 1970).

Soon after the conquest was consolidated, the Spaniards made inquiries into the origins of the Incas. Survivors of the upper classes of Inca society were interviewed as well as some of the oldest and best educated people of Cuzco. They were questioned about their history, and the Spanish chroniclers duly recorded what they were told. They learned that the empire had been in existence for only a little less than a hundred years. It had been founded by the Emperor Pachacuti in approximately 1438 and was brought to an end by the Spanish Conquest in 1532. Although the Inca dynasty comprised twelve rulers—this number did not include Atahuallpa, who was never formally crowned—it was not until the reign of the ninth Inca, known as Pachacuti, that the Inca Empire began its conquests. Before the rule of the first Inca, Manco Capac, the Spaniards were told, the world had been inhabited by barbarians who lived like animals. The Incas said that they had been especially created by the sun god to bring civilization to the world. Thus everything that the Spanish saw and admired in the realm of Peru was credited to the enlightened rule of the Incas. At least one Spanish chronicler, Pedro Cieza de León, observed that the Incas could not have been responsible for all of the impressive ruins found in Peru. He visited the ruined sites of Wari near Ayacucho in the Peruvian highlands and Tiwanaku near Lake Titicaca in modern Bolivia and noted that the ruins at these sites and those at Inca sites were of different styles. The ruins he visited also appeared to be much older than any of the Inca buildings (Cieza de León 1959). Despite these observations, the civilization of Peru was credited entirely to the Incas until the nineteenth century. Only then did the true antiquity of ancient Peruvian civilization begin to be revealed, along with the proper place of the Incas in ancient Andean culture history.

Map showing some of the archaeological sites mentioned in the text.

## ANDEAN HISTORY BEFORE THE INCAS

Prior to the rise of the Incas, a multitude of cultures flourished and died out in ancient Peru, each one adding its unique contributions to the Andean cultural legacy inherited by the Incas. Only a few of these are well known and have been studied by archaeologists. The earliest widespread cultural influence is manifested in the style associated with the religious cult of Chavín.

By 1400 B.C., this new religious movement had begun to spread across northern Peru. It incorporated elements from older Peruvian coastal religions and combined them with religious elements such as the caiman and jaguar from the tropical forests of the *montaña* and Amazon Basin. Although named for the site of Chavín de Huantar, a ceremonial center and temple complex on the eastern watershed of the north-central highlands, the cult seems to have originated throughout a broad area of northern Peru and represents a synthesis of a variety of traditional religious beliefs. By 1300–1200 B.C., temples and artworks associated with this cult had been built in the northern highlands and on the northern coast of Peru. By 1000 B.C., the influence of Chavín had appeared as far south as the area near where the modern city of Lima now stands. The cult continued to expand, and by 500 B.C., Chavín influence had extended from the

Relief sculpture in the ruins of Chavín de Huantar depicting a caiman or crocodile figure. (Charles & Josette Lenars/Corbis)

modern cities of Cajamarca in the north to Ayacucho in the south. The local culture in the Inca heartland at this time is called Marcavalle by archaeologists, named for the site where its remains were first discovered near the city of Cuzco. Very little is known about these people. They seem to have been farmers who probably occupied a number of villages and lived under a relatively simple political system. In terms of material culture, the Marcavalle peoples seem to be related to those of the Lake Titicaca basin to the south.

Although direct Chavín influence does not appear to have reached the Cuzco region, it appears to have profoundly influenced the peoples of the Ayacucho region to the north of Cuzco, who would later invade and occupy the Valley of Cuzco during the Wari imperial expansion of the Middle Horizon (A.D. 540–900). Chavín influence is also seen in some of the principal deities of the Tiwanaku Empire, which developed to the south of Cuzco at the same time as the Wari expansion. The nature of the religion represented by the Chavín cult remains obscure in its details. The actual names of the gods and their interaction with the population cannot be recovered, but it is possible to make some general observations about this powerful cult. The artistic canons strongly suggest an overriding concern with duality. The perfect balance of Chavín compositions in their bilateral symmetry and reversibility suggests the importance of maintaining balance between the natural and supernatural worlds. Interaction and reconciliation of opposites was a central theme, perhaps most forcibly expressed in the extraordinary black and white portal built in the final stages of occupation of the temple at Chavín de Huantar.

This portal was a major artistic statement of the fully developed Chavín tradition. Its approach steps were divided in the center; the southern half were made of white granite and the northern half of black limestone. Flanking the portal were a black and a white stone column supporting a carved lintel. The columns were decorated with incised winged figures. Here in this portal are seen most clearly the merging of opposites, day and night, light and dark, north and south, right and left. It seems likely that the purpose of the Chavín cult was to maintain the balance of the forces of nature. In an agricultural society living in the harsh and extremely unpredictable environment of the Andes, natural phenomena such as floods, droughts, hailstorms, and earthquakes were always of paramount concern. A cult that was perceived as influencing the supernatural powers to cooperate with agricultural food production would have had profound influence over society.

Enduring for centuries, the Chavín cult was enormously successful, but by about 400 B.C., the cult seems to have disappeared, as a number of new regional traditions asserted themselves. The influence of the Chavín artistic tradition continued to be felt, however. In succeeding generations and in the later art styles, the representations of the main Andean deities continued to reflect the attributes of the Chavín gods (Burger 1992).

Following the heyday of the Chavín cult, which roughly corresponds to the Early Horizon time period (circa 1500–370 B.C.), archaeologists believe that there was a florescence of many strong regional cultures. The best known of these are the Moche of the Peruvian north coast and the Nazca, who lived on

Hummingbird image, part of the famous Nazca lines on the southern coast of Peru. (Corel)

the south coast. During the Early Intermediate Period (370 B.C.–A.D. 540), the Moche and Nazca cultures achieved a high degree of civilization. Building on the Chavín religious tradition, these societies became increasingly complexly organized and, in the case of the Moche, may have developed into centrally governed states.

In the Cuzco region at this time, there was a culture called Chanapata by archaeologists. The Chanapata peoples are little known and in many respects seem to be a continuation of the preceding Marcavalle culture. Recent excavations have shown that they lived in villages of small rectangular houses and made their living as farmers. They seem to have had a well-developed ceramic art style similar to the styles of the peoples living farther south toward Lake Titicaca. The principal outside cultural influence continued to be the peoples of the Titicaca basin.

During the time that the Nazca and Moche cultures were at their height on the Peruvian coast, other cultures were beginning to rise in the highlands of Peru and Bolivia. These highland cultures would expand their influence until it encompassed most of the Andean world. After dominating the Andes for centuries, their cultural legacy greatly influenced succeeding cultures and the course of Andean prehistory until the Spanish Conquest.

In the southern Andes, in what is today Bolivia, a large ceremonial center developed on the shores of Lake Titicaca. This magnificent city, called

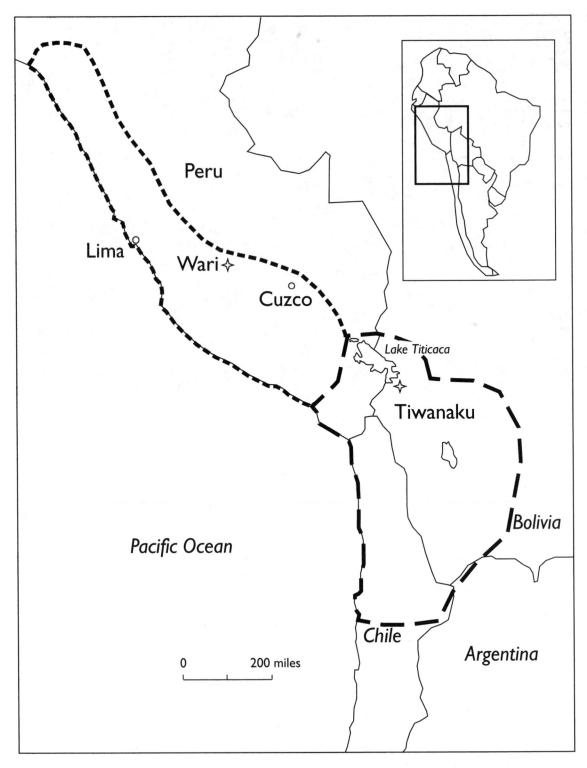

Map showing the extent of the Wari and Tiwanaku empires.

Tiwanaku, was built at an elevation of 3,850 meters above sea level on the cold, treeless plateau called the altiplano. The exact dimensions of the city are not yet known, but preliminary studies indicate an urban center of nearly 4 square kilometers. Although Tiwanaku is above the tree line, the altiplano produces abundant grass, making it prime grazing land for alpacas and llamas. Some high-altitude crops such as potatoes, *ocas* (a sweet potato–like tuber), and quinoa (a grain high in protein) could also be grown. The cold waters of Lake Titicaca, the world's highest navigable freshwater lake, also provided resources such as fish and waterfowl. Although this severe environment seems hostile, in prehistoric times this area supported one of the densest population concentrations in the ancient New World. Population estimates for the city of Tiwanaku and its sustaining area range between 570,000 and 1,111,500 people (Kolata 1993: 201).

First settled around 1000 B.C., the site of Tiwanaku was occupied for nearly 2,000 years. It began as a small farming village, but around A.D. 100 the people began to construct monumental architecture, and the site grew to be the capital city of an empire that dominated the southern Andes between A.D. 500 and 1000. It is believed that the Tiwanaku Empire established administrative centers and economic colonies throughout the altiplano of Bolivia and Peru and along the coasts of southern Peru and northern Chile.

The city of Tiwanaku was dominated by its platform mounds and temples. The largest is the platform mound called the Akapana, which measures about 200 by 200 meters at its base and was more than 15 meters high. A second large platform mound, called the Pumapunku (lion gate), measures 150 meters long at its base and was more than 5 meters high. Each of these platform mounds has a sunken rectangular court in the center of its top platform. In addition to platform mounds, other monumental structures at Tiwanaku include large rectangular walled enclosures and semisubterranean temples. All of these structures were built of finely cut stone.

Entrance to these elaborate buildings and ceremonial precincts was made through monumental gateways, the most famous being the so-called Gate of the Sun. The gateways were often monolithic, with the uprights and lintels all carved from a single piece of stone. The lintels were frequently decorated with complex relief carvings that are believed to depict deities of the Tiwanaku pantheon. The most important of these is thought to be the figure on the Gate of the Sun. This is the Tiwanaku interpretation of the old Chavín staff god.

The expansion and consolidation of Tiwanaku power appear to have been accomplished principally through three economic strategies. The first was a state policy of intensive land reclamation around the shores of Lake Titicaca. This was accomplished through the construction of raised and ridged fields by subject populations paying their tribute or taxes in labor. These fields can still be seen and have been dated to the Tiwanaku period. Associated with these large land reclamation projects are large administrative centers; the two best known are Luqurmata and Pajchiri, located to the north of Tiwanaku. These secondary centers dominated the tertiary centers, where local administrations were formed. Like the capital, the secondary centers contain several massive

An alpaca in the Peruvian highlands. (Corel)

platforms and architecture of finely cut stones, including monumental gateways and rectangular sunken courts. Elite artifacts suggesting considerable wealth, such as fine pottery, fragments of precious metal, semiprecious stone pendants, and fragments of statues, have been recovered from these sites.

The second strategy was the establishment of economic colonies located at a considerable distance from the capital. Tiwanaku populations were moved into regions along the coasts of northern Chile and southern Peru and into the edge of the jungle to the east of the altiplano. These colonies provided the capital with a secure and steady supply of large quantities of highly desired products from a variety of ecological zones. Among these products were maize, coca, medicinal plants, seashells, and feathers from tropical birds.

A third strategy was based on llama caravans. Llamas, a member of the camel family, can carry up to about 40 kilograms of cargo as beasts of burden. Large caravans traveled throughout the altiplano and down into the coastal valleys, bringing large quantities of goods to be exchanged and redistributed. Vast herds of llamas and alpacas were raised on the altiplano, their native habitat; animals were therefore readily available for the assembly of large pack trains or caravans.

These activities, in addition to conquest and tribute, contributed to the vast wealth that permitted the construction of the great ceremonial monuments of Tiwanaku and the other major administrative centers. However, sometime between A.D. 1000 and 1200, the Tiwanaku Empire disintegrated, and the great city and its satellite centers were abandoned. The causes of the collapse are not well understood, but it seems likely that a climatic fluctuation contributed substantially to the demise of Tiwanaku. Kolata (1993: 284) argues persuasively that the climatic shift was massive and that it undermined the agroeconomic base of the state. Ice cores taken from the Quelccaya glacier located in southern Peru approximately midway between Cuzco and Lake Titicaca and sediment cores taken from Lake Titicaca indicate that a great drought ensued after A.D. 1000 (Kolata 1993: 285).

The legacy of Tiwanaku was tremendous. Even in Inca times, the site was revered as a holy place. The Incas invented an official history that claimed their place of origin as an island in Lake Titicaca and themselves as the true inheritors of the prestigious Tiwanaku tradition.

The other great culture of the Middle Horizon is that of the Wari. About 965 kilometers to the north of Tiwanaku, the Wari capital was located in the Ayacucho Valley of the central Peruvian Andes, at an elevation of 2,743 meters. The Wari Empire is represented archaeologically by large architectural complexes found throughout the Peruvian highlands. Wari and Tiwanaku shared some of the same religious iconography, but they seem to have been separate entities. There is no evidence that one ever dominated the other, although the exact nature of their relationship remains unknown. The only place where Wari and Tiwanaku archaeological remains are found together is on the site of Cerro Baúl in the Moquegua Valley on the south coast of Peru, where there is some evidence of a violent confrontation (Moseley, Feldman, Goldstein, and Watanabe 1991).

The site of Wari was first occupied around 200 B.C. Like Tiwanaku, it was only a small settlement until around A.D. 500. Between A.D. 500 and 900, however, the site grew very rapidly to become one of the largest urban centers in South America. Ultimately a city of 500 hectares (5 square kilometers), it was occupied by a population between 35,000 and 70,000 people. Unlike Tiwanaku, the city of Wari had little finely cut stonework. Most of its buildings were constructed of fieldstone set in mud mortar and were then covered with smooth coats of clay and gypsum plaster. The scale was monumental: walls were 2–3 meters thick, stood 9–12 meters high, and supported two and three stories. Many residential buildings, some as long as 36 meters, were rectangular enclosures with central courtyards. The portion of the building surrounding the central court was probably roofed with thatch. Underground conduits supplied water and drainage to these structures. In addition to these residential buildings, there were elaborate temples and tombs, as well as specialized craft production areas for the manufacture of such items as pottery and obsidian implements. Some of the more elaborate tombs exhibit finely cut stone reminiscent of the Tiwanaku style, but these are the only examples of cut stone at the site (Isbell, Brewster-Wray, and Spickard 1991).

A new religion is presumed to have been introduced to the Wari through contact with Tiwanaku, but little is understood about this religion. As with most agricultural societies, the Wari religion was undoubtedly concerned with ensuring fertility and a water supply and protecting against natural disasters such as drought or flood. Religious iconography suggests that there were several deities in a ranked hierarchy, some with several aspects. Most prominent and presumably most important was the staff god or front face deity derived from the Chavín staff god. This deity is often shown grasping staffs that take the form of serpents, which are associated in Andean cosmology with lightning and rain. It is also sometimes depicted as either male or female, grasping various plants in place of the staff, perhaps indicating a connection with fertility and agriculture. Another motif is a figure shown with a knife and severed human heads who is interpreted as the "sacrificer." Human sacrifice seems to have been practiced. Offering caches have been discovered containing the bodies of sacrificed young women and ritually broken, elaborately painted pottery. Other caches contain high-status goods including objects of gold, bronze, and shell as well as human skulls. Two temples have been excavated at Wari, but the rituals that took place within them are not yet understood to any great extent (Bragayrac 1991; Cook 2001).

Following the introduction of the new religion, Wari soon emerged as the center of an expansionist movement, and its inhabitants embarked on a series of conquests. Although the motive for this expansion is unclear, an environmental deterioration may have caused the Wari to conquer their neighbors in an attempt to gain more arable land in a greater variety of ecological zones to ensure against universal crop failure. Whatever the cause, the Wari appear to have organized one of the first, if not *the* first, conquest empires in the Andes. Between A.D. 540 and 650, the Wari conquered the central and southern highlands (including Cuzco) and the central and south coast of Peru. Around A.D. 650, the empire appears to have suffered a severe crisis, possibly a revolt or epidemic that is reflected in the archaeological record by changes in settlement distribution and burial patterns. This crisis was successfully overcome, and the empire expanded very rapidly a second time to encompass most of what is today highland and coastal Peru.

The Wari imperial economy was based on agriculture and herding. A great variety of foodstuffs were produced. Numerous ecological zones at varying altitudes throughout the empire were exploited to raise such diverse products as potatoes, maize, coca, peanuts, chili peppers, *ocas,* lima beans, squash, and many fruits. In drier environments, the state built canals and irrigated fields. Terracing opened new lands, which also increased production. Llamas and guinea pigs were raised as sources of meat, supplemented by some hunting of deer and fowl. Like the Incas, the Wari may well have built state-sponsored storage facilities that were used to preserve agricultural surplus as insurance against drought and other natural disasters.

Long-distance exchange also supplied scarce luxury goods such as *Spondylus* shells from Ecuador and feathers from the Amazon jungles. To what extent trading affected the economy is unknown. It may have been an upper-class monopoly designed solely to provide the ruling elite with luxury goods.

The empire seems to have been divided into regions governed by subcapitals and administrative centers. The largest provincial capitals are the sites of

Pikillacta and the Huaro complex, near the city of Cuzco in the southern high-lands, and Viracocha Pampa near Huamachuco in the north highlands. Smaller Wari administrative complexes exist at Jincamocco in the southwest highlands, at Azangaro and Wari Wilka in the central highlands, and at Honco Pampa in the north highlands. On the coast, the Wari occupied the huge shrine and oracle at Pachacamac just south of the modern city of Lima. Many elaborate high-status burials were interred in the sacred ground around the temple at Pachacamac. Other coastal valleys were also home to Wari administrative centers, such as Cerro Baúl in the Moquegua Valley, and Maymi in the Pisco Valley. On the north coast, the Wari seem to have been responsible for the collapse of the Moche culture. It is unclear whether this was by outright conquest or by taking advantage of an internal collapse caused by severe environmental disruptions.

Most Wari administrative complexes seem to have been built to a standard plan and were linked to the capital at Wari by a state-constructed highway network that allowed for rapid communication and movement of goods and people. Those studied in detail have a standardized administrative unit surrounded by satellite sites that form a segmented town in which each section had a specific function (e.g., defense, lower-class housing, and craft production). The administrative architectural units are remarkably uniform throughout the empire. Indeed, they are so uniform that they appear to have been planned by the same individual or group of individuals. This evidence of centralized planning suggests that the Wari Empire was tightly controlled from the center. These architectural units seem to have functioned both as provincial administrative palaces, with residences for the governing elite, and as religious centers. The architecture is similar to that of the capital at Wari but is often laid out in perfectly rectangular ground plans, regardless of the terrain, whereas the architecture of the capital conforms to the topography.

The largest and best preserved of these provincial administrative centers is the site of Pikillacta, located in the Valley of Cuzco. Pikillacta and the nearby Wari site at Huaro, along with their numerous satellite sites, indicate that the Wari directly ruled the Inca heartland during the Middle Horizon from A.D. 600 to 1000. During this time, the settlement system of the Valley of Cuzco was reorganized, and a number of large-scale and monumental works were undertaken. Pikillacta itself required more than 5 million man-days to construct. It was linked to the rest of the Wari Empire by a well-engineered road system. Large hydraulic works were also undertaken, with canals and aqueducts built to bring water to the site of Pikillacta and other Wari establishments. The local Cuzco people at this time were a culture that archaeologists called Qotakalli. Not much is known about these people except that their cultural artifacts occur in small numbers at local Wari sites and in larger numbers at what seem to be their own residence sites. These people seem to be descendants of the Marcavalle and Chanapata cultures, but their surviving art shows Wari influence and it is likely that they were completely dominated by the Wari culture.

Wari imperial power lasted for more than 400 years, until sometime between A.D. 1000 and 1100, when it rapidly disintegrated. The exact reasons are unknown, but the Wari state seems to have suffered from severe overcentraliza-tion. As the empire grew, it became increasingly difficult to administer over the vast distances when all communication was carried on foot. This was fur-ther complicated by the fact that there was no system of written communica-tion. Further, the empire had to cope with a huge diversity of ethnic groups and languages. These problems were no doubt aggravated by highly variable and unpredictable weather patterns that could severely affect agricultural pro-ductivity and state wealth. Like the Tiwanaku, the Wari were very vulnerable to major climatic fluctuations.

The capital at Wari continued to grow throughout the life of the empire and eventually became the largest city in pre-Columbian South America. The rulers were thus faced with the twin problems of administering the empire and trying to cope with managing a gigantic urban center that no doubt con-sumed more and more of the agricultural production. This meant that more and more food had to be brought in from farther and farther away, making it increasingly expensive to maintain the city. Whatever the cause, by A.D. 1100 all of the major Wari centers were abandoned and never reoccupied. The em-pire had collapsed.

Although the Wari Empire had dissolved, like the Tiwanaku, they left an en-during legacy. Throughout much of the Peruvian Andes, they introduced the concept of the imperial state. Many peoples had undoubtedly increased their cultural complexity under the Wari and were now ready to try their own ex-periments in statecraft. The Wari, then, set the stage for the formation of nu-merous predatory states that would compete with one another to fill the power vacuum left by the imperial collapse. Out of this ferment would eventu-ally rise the empire of the Incas. In the culture of the Incas, we can see many legacies of the Wari inheritance. The famous Inca highway system was founded on the Wari road network. The woven tunics of the Inca nobility are descended from the Wari tapestry tunics. The imperial architecture of Cuzco was influenced in its design by the old provincial capital of Pikillacta nearby. Polychrome ceramics and certain vessel forms, such as the *kero* drinking cup, were introduced to the Valley of Cuzco through the Wari at Pikillacta. And most important, a body of statecraft—invaluable information on state admin-istration and organization—was the legacy of the Wari that enabled the forma-tion of the Late Intermediate Period states and ultimately the rise of the Incas.

Following the collapse of both the Wari and Tiwanaku empires, there was a period of great political fragmentation throughout Peru. The two great impe-rial states dissolved into numerous competing kingdoms and chiefdoms. On the north coast of Peru, the great empire of the Chimu developed, beginning around A.D. 900, in the territory that was formerly home to the Moche king-doms. It ultimately expanded along the coast as far south as modern Lima and would eventually become the principal rival to the Incas. In the highlands, the situation remained fragmented for a much longer period of time. In Cuzco, the Inca heartland, there were numerous small kingdoms contesting for su-premacy. By about A.D. 1438, the Incas emerged supreme among these warring kingdoms and were able to launch their empire making use of knowledge of statecraft and a physical infrastructure that they inherited from both the Wari and Tiwanaku empires.

The Inca version of their history begins with a small band of highlanders migrating into the Valley of Cuzco in the southern Peruvian sierra. This event does not have a fixed date, but scholars believe that if it actually occurred, it would have been around the year A.D. 1200. Over the next few centuries, the huge empire of the Incas sprang from this small group. According to Inca legends, their place of origin was called Pacariqtambo and was located about 30 kilometers from Cuzco. Here their ancestors had come forth into the world from three caves. Led by the first Inca (or ruler), Manco Capac, this ancestral family was made up of his three brothers and four sisters. Other stories claim that the place of origin was an island in Lake Titicaca, to the south of Cuzco, from which the Incas were led by Manco north to the Valley of Cuzco. Some accounts combined these two legends into one, having the Incas migrating underground from Lake Titicaca to Pacariqtambo, where they emerged from the caves of origin. After many adventures, Manco led his siblings into the Valley of Cuzco, where they were said to have established themselves by force of arms and brought order and civilization.

Following their arrival in Cuzco, the Incas slowly increased their influence through strategic alliances and marriages and by military raids against their neighbors. The city of Cuzco was founded by Manco, but through the reign of the eighth Inca in the traditional dynastic list, it was little more than an ordinary Andean highland town. The turning point in the history of the city and the Incas themselves was the great Chanca crisis near the end of the reign of the eighth ruler, Inca Viracocha (A.D. 1438). By this time, the Incas had increased their domain to include the whole of the Valley of Cuzco, including the Oropesa and Lucre basins, and a large part of the neighboring Urubamba Valley. The Chanca, a powerful warlike confederation located to the north of Cuzco, began to expand to the south, threatening Cuzco and nearly defeating the Incas. The emperor, Inca Viracocha, abandoned the city and fled to the neighboring Urubamba Valley, but at the last moment, one of his royal sons, Inca Yupanqui, rallied the Inca armies and heroically defeated the Chanca forces. Following this victory, he deposed his father, Inca Viracocha, whose failure to defend Cuzco was viewed as a disgrace. Inca Yupanqui took the name Pachacuti and assumed the throne, becoming the first of the great Inca emperors.

The name Pachacuti—or Pachacutec, as it is sometimes given in the chronicles—means "earth shaker" or "cataclysm" in Quechua, the language of the Incas. It also refers to the Inca belief that periodically the time-space continuum was overturned and a new world order put in place. It was an appropriate name for the man who literally reorganized the Inca world. His first acts as emperor included subduing the neighboring peoples in the Cuzco region. Whereas they had previously been loosely associated with the Incas, mostly by persuasion and family ties, they were now forcibly brought under control as vassals of the lords of Cuzco. Pachacuti launched a series of conquests that rapidly evolved the tiny Inca domain into an expanding empire. Large areas of the sierra, north into the central Peruvian highlands and south to the shores of

Idealized portrait of the ninth Inca ruler Pachacuti. (Louis Glanzman/National Geographic Collection)

Lake Titicaca, were rapidly conquered. He also turned his attention to reorganizing and rebuilding the city of Cuzco and designing the empire.

Pachacuti conceived of the city of Cuzco as the center of the empire where the four quarters into which it was divided came symbolically and physically together. Four highways coming from each of the four quarters, or *suyus,* converged in the great central plaza of the city. From this four-part division the empire took its name of Tawantinsuyu, meaning literally "four parts together" but usually glossed as "the land of four quarters."

In addition to rebuilding Cuzco into a suitable imperial capital, Pachacuti initiated building projects in the environs of Cuzco and on his royal estates in the Urubamba Valley. The most famous of these is the so-called lost city of Machu Picchu, but he also built royal estates at Pisac, Ollantaytambo, Patallacta, and many smaller sites in the Cuzco region.

Other building projects initiated by Pachacuti included the famous royal highway of the Incas that provided for communication within the expanding empire and a means of rapidly moving the army to wherever it was needed. Following and expanding the routes of the old highways of the earlier Wari Empire, this network linked the various regions of the growing empire to Cuzco. Storehouses called *qolqa* and rest stops called *tambos* were built to provision and serve the army as it marched. A system of relay runners called *chasqui* formed an effective postal system for the transmission of verbal messages and instructions. Towns and provincial administrative centers were also built by Pachacuti and his successors in the various conquered territories as the empire expanded.

Pachacuti's son Topa Inca succeeded him as emperor in A.D. 1471. Topa Inca continued to move the imperial frontier north into what is now Ecuador and south into modern Bolivia, northern Chile, and northwestern Argentina. By 1476 he had achieved the conquest of the Chimu Empire on the Peruvian north coast, the last serious rival for total control of the Andean area. Topa Inca reigned until 1493 and was succeeded in turn by his son Huayna Capac.

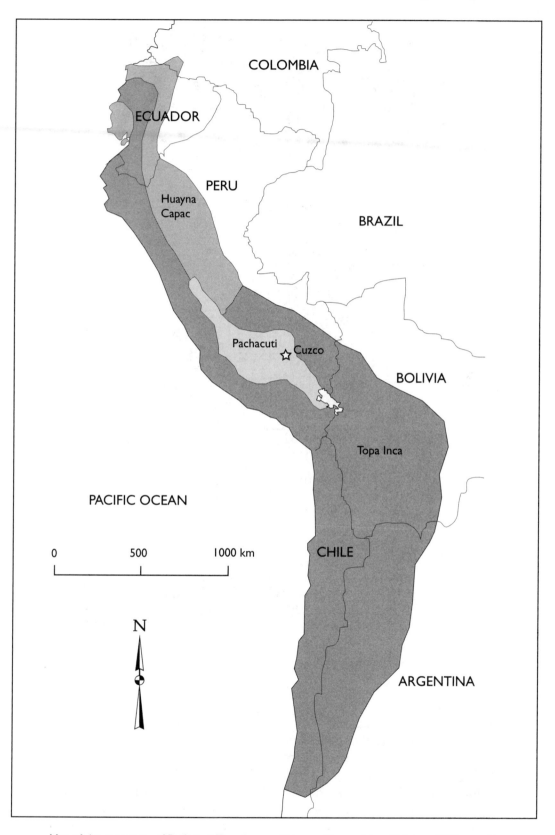

Map of the conquests of Pachacuti, Topa Inca, and Huayna Capac. After McIntyre 1975 page 19.

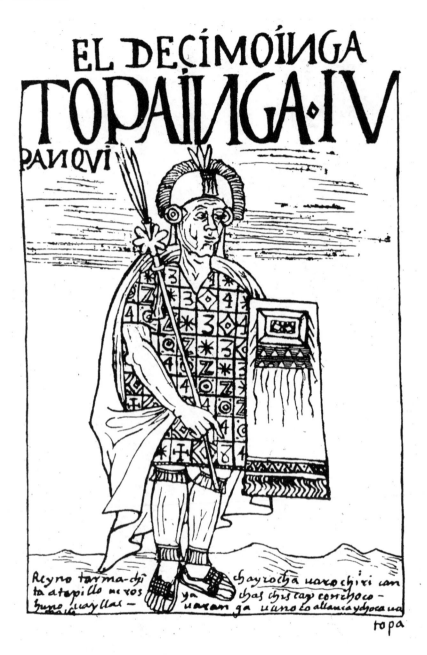

Topa Inca, the tenth ruler. (Felipe Huamán Poma de Ayala)

Huayna Capac continued to expand the boundaries of the empire to the north and east, incorporating much of modern Ecuador and the northeastern Peruvian Andes. He also made minor incursions into modern Colombia. Compared to his father, however, his conquests were difficult and more modest. Huayna Capac spent so much time on his northern campaign that severe strains began to grow in the social fabric of the Inca Empire. Because Huayna Capac was absent for many years at a time, surrogates had to stand in for him at important festivals and ceremonies, and the people of Cuzco began to feel

Huayna Capac, the eleventh ruler. (Felipe Huamán Poma de Ayala)

out of touch with their emperor. A new and potentially rival court even grew up around him at his northern headquarters at Tomebamba in Ecuador. Administratively, the empire was becoming increasingly difficult to govern. Decisions from the emperor took a long time to reach Cuzco and to be disseminated to the rest of the empire.

A severe crisis finally came when Huayna Capac suddenly died of what may have been smallpox in 1527. The disease, introduced by Europeans arriving in the New World, preceded the Spanish conquistadores as they journeyed across South America. Thousands died in a very short space of time, including Huayna Capac's appointed heir, who survived his father by only a few days. Confusion about the succession created even more strain on Inca society, and finally a civil war broke out between two brothers who were rival claimants for the throne. One of the brothers, Huascar, had succeeded to the throne in Cuzco in 1527. He was challenged by Atahuallpa, who had been with his father and the imperial army in Ecuador at the time of Huayna Capac's death. A large part of the army rallied behind Atahuallpa, and a bloody war ensued. Taking the city of Cuzco in 1532, the forces of Atahuallpa eventually prevailed. The emperor Huascar was captured and imprisoned, but soon afterward the European invasion took place, resulting in the end of the empire and the death of Atahuallpa in 1533.

## DEVELOPMENT OF ANDEAN CULTURAL CHRONOLOGY

Until the second half of the nineteenth century, historians, such as William Hickling Prescott (1847), exclusively used the various accounts of the Spanish chronicles as their primary source on the Incas. Because there is considerable variation among the Spanish accounts of Inca dynastic history, the historian's task became one of attempting to reconcile these accounts into a synthetic and coherent story.

By mid-century, a great deal of interest in the prehistoric Andes was aroused by the publication of several detailed travel accounts and archaeological works. In the 1840s the Swiss scientist J. J. von Tschudi collaborated with Mariano Rivero, director of the Peruvian national museum, in a study of ancient Peruvian civilization. Their work was published in 1855 and received wide attention in Europe and America. Perhaps the most influential volume was that published in 1877 by Ephraim George Squier recounting his travels in Peru during the 1860s. Squier was a serious avocational archaeologist who had the opportunity to travel throughout Peru as a U.S. government purchasing agent. He was a careful observer whose work was as much a volume on archaeology as a travelogue. Other travelers, including Charles Wiener, Thomas Hutchinson, and E. W. Middendorf, also published travelogues containing detailed descriptions of a number of archaeological sites, but the quality and accuracy of these accounts was variable. By the 1880s, however, truly scientific inquiries had begun and some of the earliest archaeological studies were being carried out. Two German geologists, Wilhelm Reiss and Alphonse Stübel, excavated at Ancon, on the central Peruvian coast. Stübel also visited the Tiwanaku site in Bolivia and recorded many of the sculptures and architectural monuments. The information gathered by Stübel was studied in Germany by Max Uhle, who was to become the father of scientific archaeology in Peru.

The contribution of Max Uhle to the field of Andean archaeology was of enormous importance. Working with Stübel's data from Tiwanaku, he demonstrated that the Tiwanaku art style was pre-Inca and also predated the peoples that the Incas had conquered in the region of Lake Titicaca. In 1896, Uhle began fieldwork in Peru at the huge archaeological site of Pachacamac, near the city of Lima, and later at many other archaeological sites throughout Peru. Uhle introduced rigorous scientific methodology into the study of cultural sequence and focused his work on establishing a chronology in Peruvian prehistory. Using stratigraphic analysis of the archaeological material that he excavated, Uhle was able to devise the first chronological framework for organizing Andean prehistory. His four-phase scheme included an early phase, a Tiwanaku-style phase, a late phase, and an Inca-style phase. This system provided a means of ordering archaeological material in relative chronology, based on stylistic similarity. Most important, Uhle recognized that there had been an earlier period of stylistic unity, before that of the Incas, which he characterized as the Tiwanaku-style phase. He realized that this period did not immediately precede the Inca style but was separated from it by a considerable amount of time, which he termed the late phase. He also observed that the Tiwanaku phase had been preceded by a phase of unrelated material. His conception of the Tiwanaku phase as a great dividing point between the early and late stylistic phases provided the basic framework for most subsequent interpretations of Andean prehistory (Uhle 1903).

## Chronological Schemes

The principal preoccupation of early Andean archaeologists was the establishment of a chronology for Andean prehistory. A large part of the history of Andean archaeological studies involves the development of a satisfactory chronological and classification scheme that could be applied throughout the region. In the first half of the twentieth century, as more archaeological work was done and more archaeologists became involved in interpreting the Andean past, a number of chronology models were proposed. Some of these also included or implied an evolutionary classification of cultural development. In the 1920s, Alfred L. Kroeber postulated a sequence built on the framework established by Uhle. Kroeber's scheme consisted of periods called Pre-Tiahuanaco, Tiahuanacoid, Post-Tiahuanaco and Pre-Inca, and Inca. He later modified the names as Early Period, Middle Period, Late Period, and Inca Period. Kroeber's periods were simply units of chronology, independent of style or evolutionary development (Kroeber 1926).

In the 1920s and 1930s Julio C. Tello, the great Peruvian archaeologist, concentrated his work in the highlands and is generally credited with discovering the Chavín culture and recognizing it as a widespread phenomenon. Because he worked in the highlands, his perspective differed from that of Uhle, who had worked mostly on the coast. Tello devised a chronological scheme of four major divisions (Tello 1942). He believed that civilization was earliest in the eastern Andes and *montaña,* and his temporal divisions, from earliest to latest, consisted of civilizations of the Eastern Andes, Western Andes, Pacific Coast, and Tawantinsuyu (Inca Empire). Tello's scheme was, however, never fully articulated in his writings and was never widely accepted.

In 1946 Wendell C. Bennett devised a chronological scheme that began with the Chavín Periods, followed in time by the Early Period, Middle Period, Late Period, Inca Period, and Spanish Conquest. This scheme had much in common with the chronological systems of Uhle and Kroeber. Like them, Bennett considered the Tiwanaku style to be the great dividing point in Peruvian prehistory and thus used the Tiwanaku styles to define his Middle Periods.

About the same time in the mid-1940s the landmark Virú Valley project was undertaken by a group of North American and Peruvian scholars. This project, sponsored by the Institute of Andean Research and the Viking Fund, represented the first attempt at a comprehensive multidisciplinary study of a single valley on the Peruvian coast. The archaeology of the Virú Valley was studied by Gordon Willey and Julian Steward of the Smithsonian Institution; Wendell C. Bennett of Yale University; William Duncan Strong, James Ford, and Clifford Evans of Columbia University; Donald Collier of the Chicago Natural History Museum; and Junius Bird of the American Museum of Natural History. The geography and ethnology of the Virú Valley was studied by F. Webster McBryde and Allan Holmberg of the Institute of Social Anthropology and by Jorge C. Muelle of the Peruvian Instituto de Estudios Etnológicos. Several of the participants in this project proposed additional ordering schemes for Peruvian prehistory based on their research.

A remarkable 1947 conference, "A Reappraisal of Peruvian Archaeology," sponsored by the Institute of Andean Research in New York, provided a forum for the proponents of several of these new ordering schemes (Bennett 1948a). By this time, Bennett had devised a new ordering scheme different from the one that he had proposed in 1946. His new scheme was based on cultural development and complemented his concept called the Peruvian co-tradition. Bennett's co-tradition combined the notion of culture area with time depth in history. This provided a meaningful way to conceptualize five geographically centered cultural traditions composed of multiple cultures that had interacted continuously throughout Andean prehistory. His scheme supposed that all of the cultures represented in the co-traditions changed essentially in the same ways about the same times. Thus, ancient society moved through a series of developmental stages that began with a Cultist Period, followed by the Experimenters, Master Craftsmen, Expansionists, City Builders, and Imperialists periods. In this scheme, the Chavín culture corresponded to the earliest period, the Tiwanaku culture to the Expansionists Period (more or less the middle), and the Inca culture to the Imperialists Period (Bennett 1948b).

At the same conference, William Duncan Strong proposed a different sequential scheme based on his stratigraphic studies in midden excavations in the Virú Valley. Strong's sequence included the following divisions: Pre-Agricultural, Developmental, Formative, Florescent, Fusion, Imperial, and Colonial (Strong 1948). Again, this system assumes a general and more or less uniform evolutionary movement of all cultures through the same set of stages.

Gordon Willey put forward yet another organizational scheme that employed both the horizon concept that had been implicit in Uhle's scheme and the later sequences modeled on it and a series of developmental stages. The horizons in Willey's scheme represented the geographically widespread occurrence of specific stylistic or technical traits. These were considered in the context of the developmental stages called Formative, Regional Classic, and Expansionistic. Thus the spread of an early horizon style such as Chavín must have been the result of a peaceful spread of religious concepts and the absence of organized warfare and military hierarchy at the Formative level of development. In contrast, the spread of the Tiwanaku horizon was likely due to military expansion since it occurred during the Expansionistic Period, a time of crisis and unrest when military power was paramount (Willey 1948).

Two additional organizational schemes were proposed in the 1960s. The Peruvian archaeologist Luis G. Lumbreras devised a system incorporating and combining many elements of the earlier systems discussed above. His scheme includes the following divisions from earliest to latest: Lithic Period, Archaic Period, Formative Period, Regional Developmental Period, Wari Empire, Regional States, and Inca Empire. The earlier divisions in this scheme were based on technological development, whereas the later divisions were based on level of political organization (Lumbreras 1974).

In the early 1960s John H. Rowe put forward a system that has become the most influential and widely used by present-day Andean scholars. Building on Kroeber's scheme, which employed periods that were independent of style or stage of cultural development, Rowe devised a system combining periods and horizons. This system began with an Initial Period followed by the Early Horizon (Chavín influence), Early Intermediate Period, Middle Horizon (Tiwanaku and Wari influence), Late Intermediate Period, and Late Horizon (Inca influence). In devising this scheme, Rowe sought deliberately to avoid the value-laden terminology and evolutionary assumptions of the stage systems, such as Bennett's, Strong's, and Willey's schemes. Instead he intended that his system be strictly a chronological organization. Rowe's scheme was particularly useful in that he took the novel step of tying the units of time to a master chronological sequence in the Ica Valley. Thus the beginning and ending of each unit was arbitrarily defined by events in the Ica Valley ceramic sequence. This meant that the periods and horizons had the same temporal span everywhere in the ancient Andes regardless of the local cultural development of any particular location (Rowe 1965).

The chronological framework that evolved through the work of the pioneers of Andean archaeology allows us to view and understand the vast body of new data that is now available with a degree of coherence that would otherwise have been impossible. It is possible to comprehend the developmental and evolutionary trends of nearly 5,000 years of Andean civilization through this chronological scheme and to appreciate the astonishing continuity in Andean cultural tradition.

In the twentieth century, the field of Inca studies came into being, and a great amount of new information continues to be brought to light. Max Uhle excavated and studied several important Inca sites, including Pachacamac on the coast near Lima and Tomebamba in the highlands of southern Ecuador. Hiram Bingham's visit to Machu Picchu in 1911 and subsequent publications in *National Geographic* magazine and several books he authored greatly popularized the Incas in the public imagination. Despite this popularization, it was not until the 1930s that true archaeological investigation of the Incas was undertaken in their heartland. Peruvian scholars Luis Valcárcel and Luis Pardo were among the pioneers in this effort (Valcárcel 1946; Pardo 1937). In the late 1930s and the early 1940s, John H. Rowe began work in Cuzco, and the publication in 1944 of his dissertation "An Introduction to the Archaeology of Cuzco" marked the first systematic scientific study of the Cuzco area. Two years later in 1946, he published his seminal work, "Inca Culture at the Time of the Spanish Conquest." Rowe's work has provided the foundation for most of the studies of the second half of the twentieth century. Today there are scholars from many countries in the Americas and Europe as well as Peru who are actively pursuing Inca studies.

## Advances and Developments in Andean Chronology

Until the development of the radiocarbon dating technique, there was no way to assign absolute dates to any but the very latest events in the Late Horizon (Inca period). Rates of cultural change were calculated rather arbitrarily and varied drastically at times. Arthur Posnansky, working at the site of Tiwanaku in Bolivia, argued in favor of 12,000 years of Andean civilization. Other scholars took a much more modest view. Tello dated his four divisions from 1000 B.C. to A.D. 1532. Bennett's scheme encompassed the years from 200 B.C. to A.D. 1532. Willey's scheme had the Chavín Horizon beginning at about the start of the Christian era, the Tiwanaku or Middle Horizon about A.D. 1000, and the Inca Horizon beginning a relatively short time before the Spanish invasion in 1532. Strong provided only vague "guess dates" for his culture sequence, which began considerably before the Christian era. He dated the Coastal Tiwanaku style to shortly after A.D. 1000 and ended the sequence with the historical date of the conquest in A.D. 1532.

With the advent of the radiocarbon dating process in 1947, it became possible for the first time to assign approximate absolute dates to archaeological materials. In 1965 John Rowe published a series of radiocarbon determinations that he synchronized with the master sequence that he had developed for the Ica Valley on Peru's south coast on which he had based his organizational scheme. The approximate beginning dates for each of his periods and horizons are as follows:

Late Horizon: A.D. 1476
Late Intermediate Period: A.D. 900
Middle Horizon: A.D. 540
Early Intermediate Period: 370–420 B.C.
Early Horizon: 1300–1500 B.C.
Initial Period: 2050–2120 B.C.

The results of the radiocarbon dating sequence indicated that there was much greater time depth to Andean civilization than had been previously suspected, although not as great as the extreme estimates of Posnansky (1945). Most recent research and additional radiocarbon dating have tended to corroborate these dates, lending additional reliability to Rowe's sequence, which is now the most widely used organizational framework in Andean studies.

## Problems in Dating the Inca Civilization

The most commonly accepted dates for the Inca civilization and empire are those suggested by John H. Rowe in his work, "An Introduction to the Archaeology of Cuzco" (Rowe 1944: 55–59). Rowe reasons that the reigns reported by the Spanish chronicler Cabello Balboa (1586) for the Inca Pachacuti (A.D. 1438–1471), his son Topa Inca (A.D. 1471–1493), and his grandson Huayna Capac (1493–1525) are probably quite close to the truth. The length of the reigns is reasonable and Spanish writers such as Cieza de León commented that in their day many people were still alive who had known Topa Inca and Huayna Capac, fought in their armies, and heard tales from their own fathers about participating in the wars of Pachacuti and witnessing his deeds. There were no living witnesses with direct knowledge of the times before Pachacuti's reign at the time of the Spanish Conquest, so specific dates earlier than the reign of the ninth Inca emperor are probably not reliable. Rowe points out that since the genealogical record of the Inca dynasty is complete, we at least know that there were twelve reigns before the time of the European invasion and the Incas said that Pachacuti was the ninth ruler. Assuming an average of between three and four generations to the century, Rowe calculates that the most reasonable date for the founding of the Inca dynasty is approximately A.D. 1200. This means that the dynasty began long before the empire. Between A.D. 1200 and 1438 eight Incas ruled without the Incas expanding much outside their heartland in Cuzco. The empire began sometime after Pachacuti ascended the throne around 1438 and lasted only until the arrival of the Spanish in A.D. 1532, which is the first absolute historical date that can be assigned to the Inca civilization.

Because of its short life span, dating the Inca civilization by scientific methods is difficult. The most commonly used technique in archaeological dating is the radiocarbon method. This method permits the dating of any organic material belonging to the Incas but cannot discriminate individual dates with sufficient accuracy to correctly place them within the life span of the civilization. Radiocarbon relies on statistical counts of particle emissions, and the results typically have a margin of error as great as several hundred years. Even the most accurate radiocarbon dates produced through accelerator mass spectrometry (AMS) will still have a margin of error as great as plus or minus thirty years. Considering that the life span of the Inca Empire was perhaps only eighty years, these large error ranges cause all Inca radiocarbon dates to overlap. It is impossible to define an object as being early Inca or late Inca using the radiocarbon method. Obsidian hydration as a dating methodology for Inca materials suffers from similar accuracy difficulties. Although abundantly used by pre-Inca cultures, obsidian is much less common in Inca archaeological contexts, and little of this material has been recovered scientifically that is suitable for dating purposes.

Seriation studies will eventually allow the determination of chronology in the Inca artifact sequence even if exact dates are unknown. A detailed seriational study of Inca artifacts has not yet been published, although a number of scholars are working with Inca ceramic materials. Likewise, stratigraphic studies will greatly aid in establishing the seriation of Inca materials. Until quite recently, however, few stratigraphic studies had been carried out. A great many of the archaeological deposits in the Valley of Cuzco have been seriously disturbed by a variety of activities, including urban sprawl, urban renewal, the construction of infrastructure, and looting during Inca, colonial, and modern times. This disturbance has resulted in mixed stratigraphic contexts of little or no value for archaeological purposes. A few undisturbed sites have been located, and recent excavations will surely shed light on the Cuzco series.

## REFERENCES

Bennett, Wendell C. 1946. "The Archaeology of the Central Andes." In *Handbook of South American Indians*, edited by Julian Steward, Bureau of American Ethnology, bulletin 143, vol. 2, 61–147. Washington, DC: Smithsonian Institution.

———, ed. 1948a. *A Reappraisal of Peruvian Archaeology.* Society for American Archaeology memoir, vol. 4.

———. 1948b. "The Peruvian Co-Tradition." In *A Reappraisal of Peruvian Archaeology*, edited by Wendell C. Bennett, Society for American Archaeology memoir, vol. 4, 1–7.

Bingham, Hiram. 1913. "In the Wonderland of Peru." *National Geographic* (April 23): 387–574.

Bragayrac, Enrique. 1991. "Archaeological Excavations in the Vegachayoq Moqo Sector of Huari." In *Huari Administrative Structure: Prehistoric Monumental Architecture and State Government*, edited by William Isbell and Gordon McEwan, 71–80. Washington, DC: Dumbarton Oaks.

Burger, Richard L. 1992. *Chavin and the Origins of Andean Civilization.* London: Thames and Hudson.

Cabello Valboa, Miguel. 1951. *Miscelánea antártica: una historia del Perú antiguo.* Lima: Universidad Mayor de San Marcos, Instituto de Etnología y Arqueología.

Cieza de León, Pedro de. 1959. *The Incas of Pedro de Cieza de León.* Translated by Harriet de Onis and edited by Victor W. von Hagen. Norman: University of Oklahoma Press.

Cook, Anita G. 2001. "Huari D-Shaped Structures, Sacrificial Offerings, and Divine Rulership." In *Ritual Sacrifice in Ancient Peru*, edited by Elizabeth P. Benson and Anita G. Cook, 137–164. Austin: University of Texas Press.

Hemming, John. 1970. *The Conquest of the Incas.* London: MacMillan.

Hutchinson, Thomas. 1873. *Two Years in Peru.* London: Sampson Low, Marston, Low & Searle.

Isbell, William, Christine Brewster-Wray, and Lynda Spickard. 1991. "Architecture and Spatial Organization at Huari." In *Huari Administrative Structure: Prehistoric Monumental Architecture and State Government*, edited by William Isbell and Gordon McEwan, 19–53. Washington, DC: Dumbarton Oaks.

Kolata, Alan L. 1993. *The Tiwanaku: Portrait of an Andean Civilization.* Oxford: Blackwell.

Kroeber, Alfred L. 1926. "Culture Stratification in Peru." *American Anthropologist* 28: 311–351.

Lumbreras, Luis G. 1974. *The Peoples and Cultures of Ancient Peru.* Washington, DC: Smithsonian Institution Press.

Middendorf, E. W. 1893–1895. *Peru.* 3 vols. Berlin: R. Oppenheim.

Moseley, M. E., Robert A. Feldman, Paul S. Goldstein, and Luis Watanabe. 1991. "Colonies and Conquest: Tiahuanaco and Huari in Moquegua." In *Huari Administrative Structure: Prehistoric Monumental Architecture and State Government*, edited by William Isbell and Gordon McEwan, 121–140. Washington, DC: Dumbarton Oaks.

Pardo, Luis A. 1937. *Ruinas precolombinas del Cuzco*. Cuzco

Posnansky, Arthur. 1945. *Tihuanacu: The Cradle of American Man*. 2 vols. New York: J. J. Augustin.

Prescott, William Hickling. 1847. *History of the Conquest of Peru*. 2 vols. New York: Harper and Brothers Publishers.

Reiss, W., and Alfons Stübel. 1880–1887. *The Necropolis of Ancon in Peru*. Translated by A. K. Keane. 3 vols. Berlin: A. Asher and Co.

Rivero, Mariano, and Johan von Tschudi. 1851. *Antiguedades Peruanas*. Vienna: Impr. Imperial de la Corte y del Estado.

Rowe, John H. 1944. "An Introduction to the Archaeology of Cuzco." *Papers of the Peabody Museum of American Archaeology and Ethnology* vol. 27, no. 2. Cambridge, MA: Harvard University Press.

———. 1946. "Inca Culture at the Time of the Spanish Conquest." In *Handbook of South American Indians,* edited by Julian Steward, Bureau of American Ethnology, bulletin 143, vol. 2., 183–330. Washington, DC: Smithsonian Institution.

———. 1965. "An Interpretation of Radiocarbon Measurements on Archaeological Samples from Peru." In *Proceedings of the Sixth International Conference, Radiocarbon and Tritium Dating, Held at Washington State University, Pullman, Washington, June 7–11, 1965*, 187–198.

Squier, E. George.1877. *Peru, Incidents of Travel and Exploration in the Land of the Incas*. New York: Harper and Brothers.

Strong, William Duncan. 1948. "Cultural Epochs and Refuse Stratigraphy in Peruvian Archaeology." In *A Reappraisal of Peruvian Archaeology*, edited by Wendell C. Bennett, Society for American Archaeology memoir, vol. 4, 93–102.

Tello, Julio C. 1942. "Origen y desarollo de las civilizaciones prehistóricas Andinas." In *Actas y Trabajos Científicos, 27th International Congress of Americanist*, Lima Session, 1939, vol. 1, 589–720.

Uhle, Max. 1903. *Pachacamac: Report to the William Pepper, M.D.L.L.D., Peruvian Expedition of 1896*. Philadelphia: Department of Archaeology, University of Pennsylvania.

Valcárcel, Luis E. 1946. "Cuzco Archaeology." In *Handbook of South American Indians,* edited by Julian Steward, Bureau of American Ethnology, bulletin 143, vol. 2. 177–182. Washington, DC: Smithsonian Institution.

Wiener, Charles. 1880. *Perou et Bolivie, Recit de Voyage suivi D'Etudes Arqueologiques et Ethnographiques et de Notes sur L'Ecriture et les Langues des Populations Indiennes*. Paris: Librairie Hachette.

Willey, Gordon R. 1948. "Functional Analysis of 'Horizon Styles' in Peruvian Archaeology." In *A Reappraisal of Peruvian Archaeology*, edited by Wendell C. Bennett, Society for American Archaeology memoir, vol. 4, 8–15.

CHAPTER 4

# Origins, Growth, and Decline
# of Inca Civilization

The Spanish were very impressed by the Inca Empire that they had so im-
probably overthrown. Inca cities were as large as those of Europe, but
more orderly and by all accounts much cleaner and more pleasant places in
which to live. Nothing comparable to the Inca highways and aqueducts had
been seen in Europe since Roman times. The efficiency of economic production
and distribution surpassed anything ever encountered by the Spaniards. It
was important for the Spanish to understand the history of the Inca Empire if
they were to govern it legitimately in the eyes of the rest of the world. The Europeans were thus interested in the origins of the Inca Empire for a variety of
reasons, ranging from simple curiosity to moral justification of the Spanish
Conquest.

To the Europeans, the peoples of the Western Hemisphere represented an
enormous chapter in human history that could not be explained by existing
knowledge. European understanding of man's descent was based on biblical
history and the historical records of times since. Despite great efforts to find a
historical basis for the peoples and civilizations of the New World in biblical
narratives, a satisfactory explanation of the existence of the Inca Empire was
difficult to achieve. The difficulty was compounded by the need felt after the
fact to justify the conquest of the Inca Empire and the judicial murder of its
emperor. Although the Spanish sovereign was very pleased to have acquired
new lands, subjects, and a vast hoard of gold, he was not at all happy about the
fact that regicide had been used to effect the conquest. The killing of another
monarch by common soldiers was not acceptable. As a result, there was a con-
certed effort made by the Spanish Viceroy Toledo to discredit the Inca dynasty.
The Inca history that he commissioned, written by Pedro Sarmiento de Gamboa, was designed to demonstrate that the Inca were illegitimate usurpers of
power who had ruled cruelly and despotically over unwilling subjects. The
Spanish invaders could then be cast as moral saviors who had delivered op-
pressed people from a cruel government and introduced them to Christianity.

Unfortunately, the Incas had no writing and had recorded their history only
orally. The purposes of the history that was recorded also varied from what the
Europeans expected. Rather than an accurate, unbiased account of a succession of chronological events, Inca oral histories were basically propaganda devices used by various rulers for their own ends. Each ruler kept an account of
his deeds and actions that portrayed him as the central and most important

figure in Inca history. Each took credit for as many major events as plausible. Therefore, it mattered very much which of the Inca oral historians the Spanish chroniclers listened to in compiling their written accounts. Spanish authors wrote down considerably different accounts. To further compound the problem, the events of the earliest part of Inca history occurred well beyond the limits of any living memory and could not be verified by either Spanish or Inca historians.

## WHAT THE INCAS TOLD THE SPANISH ABOUT THEIR ORIGINS

There were some forty different accounts of Inca origins recorded after the conquest by the Spanish. Most of these can be divided into two basic versions of Inca origins (see Rowe 1946, Urton 1990, and Hiltunen 1999 for a complete discussion of these myths). Most accounts locate the place of origin (*pacarina* in Quechua) at the town of Pacariqtambo. Some accounts give Lake Titicaca on the modern Peruvian-Bolivian border as the origin place. Other accounts combine elements of these two stories or refer to another possible origin place called Tambo.

### The Pacariqtambo Legend

The most frequently told legend of Inca beginnings is that the first Inca emperor, Manco Capac, was created by the creator Viracocha and the sun god Inti and emerged with his brothers and sisters from three caves in a hill called Tambo Tocco near a place called Pacariqtambo about seven leagues' distance (approximately 33 kilometers) from Cuzco. In which direction from Cuzco it lay is not indicated. The central cave at Tambo Tocco was named Capac Tocco, and it was flanked by two caves called Maras Tocco and Sutic Tocco. In Spanish colonial times, a small town about 30 kilometers south of Cuzco became identified as Pacariqtambo, the official origin place of the Inca dynasty. Recent scholarship has shown that this identification came about largely because of political maneuverings among surviving Incas in the colonial period (Urton 1990).

The founders of the Inca dynasty, comprising a group of eight brothers and sisters who were paired as married couples, came out of the middle cave, Capac Tocco. The men held the title Ayar (translated from Quechua as the wild form of the grain quinoa) and the women the title Mama (translated as mother or lady). The pairs were named: Ayar Manco and Mama Ocllo, Ayar Auca and Mama Huaco, Ayar Cachi and Mama Cora, and Ayar Ucho and Mama Rahua. Auca means "warrior," Cachi means "salt," Ucho means "chili pepper," Ocllo means "pure," and Cora means "weed." There is no known translation of the other names. Out of the other two caves, Maras Tocco and Sutic Tocco, emerged the rest of the nonroyal Inca kin groups.

Ayar Manco was selected as leader of the group and adopted the title Capac (roughly translated as King). As Manco Capac, he led the group toward a promised land where they were to settle. In his possession was a golden staff or rod that he was to use to test the soil of the places that they visited. At the place where it sank into the soil, they were to found their settlement. After a

*Similarities to Greek gods? origins*

The modern reenactment of the Inca Inti Raymi festival in Cuzco. (Corel)

prolonged series of adventures, Manco Capac led his followers into the Valley of Cuzco, conquered the local inhabitants, and set up the Inca state.

During the course of these events, three of the Ayar brothers were eliminated and a son was born to Manco Capac and Mama Ocllo. Ayar Cachi was deemed too disruptive because he was given to fits of ferocity in which he would hurl boulders with his sling, knocking down mountains and gouging out new valleys. His siblings tricked him into returning into the cave of origin, Tambo Tocco, on the pretext of needing to retrieve something left behind. Once inside, he was sealed in by the others, who closed off the entrance with stone slabs. Later in the journey, Ayar Ucho was transformed into a stone at the hill of Huanacauri, which became the central shrine involved in the coming-of-age rites for Inca males. Upon arrival in Cuzco, Ayar Auca transformed himself into a *huaca* (sacred object) that became the guardian of the Incan agricultural fields. At one of the stops along the way, a son named Sinchi Roca was born to Manco Capac. He was to succeed Manco as the second ruler of the Inca dynasty. At the end of the journey, only Manco and his sisters remained from the original group. Manco became the sole ancestor from whom all of the royal Incas traced their lineage.

### The Lake Titicaca Legend

A second common version of the origin story is that Manco Capac and Mama Ocllo were children of the sun, created by the sun god Inti on an island in Lake

# DE INGAS
## MANGO CAPAC INGA

est ynga reayno ſoleel cuz̃ a camama

Manco Capac, founder of the Inca dynasty. (Felipe Huamán Poma de Ayala)

Titicaca in modern Bolivia. The Incas were given the mission of civilizing the peoples of the world. Manco Capac and his followers migrated northward to Cuzco, using the golden staff along the way to test the soil. Upon their arrival in Cuzco, the staff sank into the ground, signifying that the Incas had arrived in their promised land. The royal residence and temple of the sun were built

on the spot where the staff had sunk. The local people recognized Manco Capac as divine and chose him as their ruler.

## Other Origin Myths

A few of the Spanish accounts refer to an Inca origin place called Tampu or the
Valley of Tambo. This was thought to be in the Urubamba Valley or Sacred Valley of the Incas near Cuzco (Hiltunen 1999: 130–133). The American explorer
Hiram Bingham located Tambo Tocco in the Urubamba Valley, arguing that the
ruins of the site of Machu Picchu that he made famous were actually those of
the Inca origin place (Bingham 1948: 245–252).

Bingham was attempting to reconcile his discoveries with the account of the
chronicle of Fernando de Montesinos written around 1642. While Montesinos's version basically follows the Pacariqtambo version of the origin myth,
it differs significantly in that it presents a much greater time depth. In four dynasties, 108 kings are listed, extending back in time from Huascar Inca, the last
independent ruler crowned. The dynastic lists of Montesinos, if they are accurate, extend back to the Middle Horizon (A.D. 540–900), when the empires of
Wari and Tiwanaku ruled the land.

The origin story related by Montesinos speaks of a great dynasty of powerful kings called the Amautas. They ruled for a very long time but were eventually defeated in battle south of Cuzco at the pass of Vilcanota. The survivors of
this disaster fled northward and settled at Tambo Tocco, near Cuzco. Over
time, they recovered and founded the dynasty of Tambo Toccans. The throne
of this dynasty was usurped during the fifteenth reign by a king from the
south named Tupac Cauri. Somewhat later, still another group from the south
caused the end of the Tambo Toccan dynasty. About this time, a legitimate heir
of the Tambo Toccans led his followers from Tambo Tocco to Cuzco and
founded the Inca dynasty, which begins with Inca Roca as the first ruler rather
than Manco Capac.

## The Historical Veracity of the Inca Version of History

The thrust of these stories is that the Incas were supermen chosen by the gods
to rule the earth. They essentially invented ancient Peruvian culture and civi-
lized the barbarian tribes that existed until then. All of the marvelous things
that the Spanish conquerors encountered were attributed to the Incas. In the
sixteenth century, the Spanish chroniclers had no way of verifying or judging
the accuracy of the Inca version of their origins. They tended to accept them at
face value or at least record them without comment.

Most modern scholars view the story of Manco Capac and his siblings as a
myth. Its function was, as Rowe (1946: 318) points out, to explain the Inca dynasty and justify its rule, to explain and justify the practice of royal incest or
marriage between siblings, and to explain the origins of some of the most important *huacas.* With these purposes in mind, the Incas were less interested in
recording the actual sequence of events that led to their rise. In historical
terms, modern scholarship has tended to look skeptically on all of the Inca emperors who preceded the ninth emperor, Pachacuti. Because there were reliable
witnesses available from his reign onward, relatively accurate approximate

ELSESTO INGA SVHIIA

IINGAROCA.CON

Reyno hasta
andesuyo -

ynga

Inca Roca. (Felipe Huamán Poma de Ayala)

dates can be determined for events during and after his reign. The Incas also said, however, that Pachacuti reorganized their entire culture and their history for his own purposes. It is therefore impossible to tell which parts of the origin story that he retained were original and which he may have created himself. It is likely that there is a kernel of truth buried in these legends, and archaeologists have begun to try to find it. The detailed history in Montesinos's chronicle is proving to be especially promising for archaeological analysis.

## WHAT SCHOLARS HAVE LEARNED ABOUT INCA ORIGINS

Despite the renown of the Inca Empire and the passage of nearly five centuries since its conquest, it is only very recently that scholars have undertaken detailed archaeological study of Inca origins. During the twentieth century, the outline of ancient Peruvian civilization began to be understood and dated. As discussed in Chapter 3 of this volume, it is now clear that the Incas were the last of a very long line of highly sophisticated civilizations that flourished in the South American Andes. Studies have shown that the Incas most likely inherited many aspects of infrastructure and statecraft from the earlier empires of Wari and Tiwanaku. Building on this base, they were able to construct the grandest empire of them all in only fifty to eighty years' time. The Incas possessed undoubted genius for empire building and military conquest, but they did not operate in a cultural vacuum. Instead, they were keen students of other cultures and adapted and borrowed whatever they themselves did not invent. This complex process is very difficult to understand and interpret in terms of the archaeological and ethnohistoric record. Several approaches are currently being used to address the question of Inca origins, and headway is gradually being made.

### The Ethnohistoric Approach to Inca Origins

Inca ethnohistory is the study of the Incas' own version of their history as recorded by the Spanish chroniclers. It has been studied by historians, art historians, anthropologists, and of course archaeologists. The limitations of these documents have been described in Chapter 1. Despite their shortcomings, these documents are all that we have of the Inca version of their history, so it is worthwhile to mine them for whatever truth they may contain.

Since the 1940s, the most prominent ethnohistorical scholars of the Incas have been John H. Rowe, R. Tom Zuidema, Maria Rostworowski de Diez Canseco, and their various students. These scholars represent two very different ways of looking at the Inca history preserved in the Spanish chronicles.

Rostworowski de Diez Canseco believes that the Spanish sources have a historical basis that was distorted by the Spaniards, who imposed a European model and forced the Inca material into descriptive and analytical categories that did not properly fit (Rostworowski de Diez Canseco 1999: ix–x). Her work has attempted to disentangle the European and Inca approaches to a real history.

While acknowledging the mythical character of the story of Manco Capac, John H. Rowe has approached the material on the later Inca rulers as true history (Rowe 1946). Recently, Catherine Julien, a former student of John Rowe's, has argued that there is a true history embedded in the material recorded by the Spanish. She has published a seminal work on how to approach the task of reading Inca history (Julien 2000). Her comparative approach to reading the multiple versions of Inca history makes it possible to attempt to separate history from myth. In the process, one can also learn a great deal indirectly about social and political relations by the manner in which the events are narrated. These scholars take an approach that can be characterized as historicist.

R. Tom Zuidema takes an opposing approach to the Inca stories in the Spanish chronicles that can be characterized as structuralist-functionalist. He denies their historical content and treats them purely as myths. Although mythical, these accounts encode important information regarding social organization and other knowledge (Zuidema 1995). Thus they can be mined for valuable information but cannot tell us what actually happened in Inca history.

For the past half century, these two very different approaches have dominated Inca scholarship. First the historicists and then the structuralists had great influence, yet neither approach could be strongly supported by the physical evidence because so little Inca archaeology had been done. This state of affairs began to change during the last two decades of the twentieth century.

## The Archaeological Approach to Inca Origins

Despite the intense interest and scholarly debates over the origin of the Incas, there was, surprisingly, no archaeological study of this subject undertaken until the 1990s. At that time, two projects with very different methodological approaches were begun. Gordon McEwan, Arminda Gibaja, and Melissa Chatfield initiated the study of Inca origins using the strategy of extensive excavation at a well-stratified archaeological site called Chokepukio in the eastern end of the Valley of Cuzco. About the same time, Brian Bauer and his students undertook a large-scale archaeological survey project that encompassed the western end of the Valley of Cuzco.

Both of these projects depended on the previous work of a number of scholars. Although the Valley of Cuzco had been previously explored for archaeological sites by John Rowe, Edward Dwyer, Luis Barreda, Manuel Chavez, and Gordon McEwan, among others, very little excavation had been done. The first systematic archaeological survey in the Cuzco Valley was carried out by McEwan in 1978, 1979, and 1981 (McEwan 1984). This work covered only the eastern third of the valley known as the Lucre Basin. Starting in 1980–1981, a much larger systematic survey encompassing the entire valley was conducted by Ruben Orellana and Fernando Astete of the Peruvian National Institute of Culture. They recorded and mapped all of the detectable archaeological sites in the valley in great detail.

**The Strategy of Archaeological Excavation.** The most accurate way of establishing the sequence of events in early Inca prehistory is to observe the remains of the activities of the early Incas as they sequentially occur in the stratigraphic deposits on archaeological sites. Unfortunately for the archaeologist, there were a number of elements in Inca culture that made it very difficult to find suitable locations in which to conduct stratigraphic excavations. The Incas are famous as engineers, having built some of the most impressive monuments in history. They were avid farmers and landscape designers. Each succeeding emperor from Pachacuti onward engaged in large construction projects. In building new structures and terraces throughout the Valley of Cuzco, the early

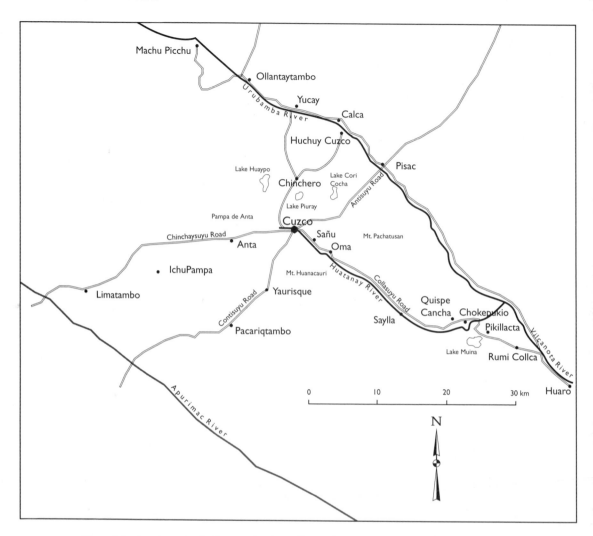

Map of the Inca heartland. (Source: Instituto Geografico Militar del Perú hojas Cuzco 28s, Calca 27s, Anta 27r)

stratified deposits left by the first Incas and their predecessors were very often destroyed, moved, rearranged, or otherwise disturbed, rendering them useless for archaeological dating and sequencing purposes. After the Spanish Conquest, there was additional disturbance caused by the construction of the Spanish city on top of Cuzco and numerous other towns and haciendas. After a long period of exploration, a complete undisturbed stratigraphic sequence was finally located at the Chokepukio archaeological site in 1993.

Between 1993 and 2005 extensive excavations have been carried out at Chokepukio, and although by no means have all questions about Inca origins been answered, we now have some idea of what occurred in the Valley of Cuzco in ancient times. As a result of this work, it is possible to outline the cultural sequence and chronology of the region with some degree of precision as well as focus on the culture history of Inca origins (McEwan, Gibaja, and Chatfield 1995, 2000; McEwan, Chatfield, and Gibaja 2002).

The ruins of the enormous Wari center of Pikillacta. Located in the valley of Cuzco, it covers an area of almost two square kilometers. (Gordon F. McEwan)

It is now known that the Cuzco region was on the periphery between two great early empires. During the Early Horizon and Early Intermediate Period (ca. 1500 B.C.–A.D. 600), Cuzco was originally in the orbit of the Lake Titicaca cultural sphere, seat of the later Middle Horizon Tiwanaku Empire. Around the year A.D. 600, the Wari Empire conquered the Cuzco area and built there the Pikillacta-Huaro complex, the largest Wari imperial settlement other than their capital in Ayacucho. The Wari occupied the Valley of Cuzco region for perhaps 400 years and had a tremendous cultural impact. After the collapse of Wari control around A.D. 1000–1100, the local center of power in Cuzco seems to have shifted to the site of Chokepukio, in the Valley of Cuzco. This site was a major power center until after A.D. 1400 and probably was overthrown with the founding of the Inca Empire in 1438. There was clearly a lot of complicated local history involving large-scale complex polities well before the appearance of the Incas. So the question then arises, who were the Incas? Were they locals who were influenced by these outside empires from whom they learned statecraft? Were they the remnants of the collapsed Wari Empire? Or were they a group that migrated northward from the seat of the Tiwanaku Empire in Bolivia when it collapsed around A.D. 1100?

The data from our excavation project at Chokepukio provides some potential answers. There is strong Wari cultural influence in the ceramics and architecture of the Late Intermediate Period at Chokepukio, suggesting a continuity of cultural elements after the collapse of the Wari Empire. However, there is also evidence of outside influence at Chokepukio during this period. The chronicle of Montesinos, mentioned earlier, suggests that there may have been a migration north to Cuzco from the area near Tiwanaku in Bolivia around A.D. 1100. A royal lineage possibly moved north and usurped power in the Valley of Cuzco after the fall of the Wari Empire. Archaeological evidence that can be radiocarbon dated suggests that there was an influx of new people at Chokepukio in 1100. These people brought with them their ancestors' remains and possibly interred whole lineages in the wall niches of a series of huge temples constructed on the Chokepukio site. These people also brought with them ceremonial ceramics very similar to the Mollo culture of northern Bolivia. This group flourished at Chokepukio until around 1440, at which time imperial Inca buildings and artifacts began to appear on the site. From archaeological analysis of the site and its artifacts, it seems that the group at Chokepukio eventually joined with their immediate neighbors to the northwest at the opposite end of the Valley of Cuzco to become part of the royal Inca line.

If this is true, then the Incas, or at least a large part of them, did in fact come from Lake Titicaca to the south, just as the legend suggests, and not from the traditional origin place of Pacariqtambo. It may also turn out that Tambo Tocco is Chokepukio. In the Quechua language of Cuzco, Tambo Tocco seems to refer to caves or windows, but in the Aymara language, spoken by the peoples around Lake Titicaca, it can refer to a place with niches. It is important to note that the name of the site, Chokepukio, means "Golden Spring" in the Aymara language. When the Incas said that they came out of Tambo Tocco, they may have referred to the fact that their ancestors were physically in the walls of the temples of Tambo Tocco (Chokepukio).

Because of its unique position on the periphery of two empires, the strategic Cuzco area is well situated for imperial regeneration. Peoples in Cuzco were significantly influenced over long periods of time by the two great empires of Wari and Tiwanaku. The Cuzqueños likely inherited not only imperial ideology but a great deal of practical statecraft information as well. Equally important was their inheritance of infrastructure. The hydraulic and highway systems of the earlier empires would have provided the basis for rapid expansion of the early Inca state. These systems likely had unused capacity left over from the former empires that could easily be used to supply the physical resources to begin the Inca expansion. A further advantage to the Incas was that their closest neighbors, those they conquered first, had also been heavily exposed to the prior imperial states. As in Cuzco, there were likely many other territorial fragments of the old empires that could be relatively easily grafted on to the new Inca state. With these advantages, the Incas rapidly expanded into the largest of the pre-Columbian Andean empires.

**The Strategy of Archaeological Survey.** The approach to understanding the origin of the Inca state through the strategy of archaeological survey is based on the idea that the changes over time observed in regional settlement patterns will reveal the development of political organization. This method relies on intense exploration for sites visible on the ground surface and is predicated on the notion that the artifacts discovered at these sites will indicate the ethnic groups occupying them and will also help date them. Using this strategy, Brian Bauer and his students resurveyed the western end of the Valley of Cuzco and combined their results with his earlier surveys south of Cuzco in the region around Pacariqtambo. The results of these surveys were interpreted by the investigator to reveal a pattern of centralization leading to the formation of the Inca state. He argues that a centralized Inca state was formed as early as A.D. 1000 that gradually incorporated its neighbors through a variety of strategies, ranging from marriage alliances to violence (Bauer 1992; Bauer and Covey 2002).

Most scholars feel that when used without being backed up by extensive excavation, this strategy is very problematic in the conditions prevailing in modern Cuzco. As previously mentioned, the Incas were great engineers and engaged in large-scale construction and massive terraforming projects. In the process they eliminated or obscured numerous sites, both Inca and pre-Inca, in the Cuzco area. The western end of the Valley of Cuzco was especially affected by this process, since it contains the city of Cuzco. According to the Incas, the Emperor Pachacuti completely reconstructed the city of Cuzco during his reign. The emperors who followed him likewise engaged in great building projects. Fill dirt for construction was excavated in and around Cuzco and carried, along with the artifacts that it contained, some distance to new locations. This process occurred again when the Spaniards rebuilt Cuzco. As years of excavation have shown, the remains visible on the surface or their absence may bear little or no relationship to what may be present underground and out of sight.

An additional problem compounding the disturbance of the settlement pattern data is the fact that Inca ceramics and their immediate precursors are not well known. It is not yet known with any certainty what the early Inca ceramic styles were. Pachacuti is said by the chroniclers to have standardized the style that we know today as imperial Inca, but what came before is still under study. There are at least two major ceramic styles that have been identified: the Lucre style and the K'illke style. Technological analysis suggests that elements of each of these styles were combined to form the classic imperial Inca style. What is not yet agreed upon is what these styles reflect in social terms. Are they ethnic markers, or did more than one group use similar ceramics? Dating these styles is also problematic. Stratigraphically, they can be dated to begin in the Late Intermediate Period before the creation of the imperial Inca style. However we cannot accurately date when they went out of use. People tend to use a functional pot until it breaks, and it may be handed down several generations.

**Summary of Knowledge of Inca Origins.** Given the limitations of the ethnohistoric record and the difficulties in interpreting the archaeological record, it is impossible to say precisely what transpired during the period of origins of the Incas. Nevertheless, it is possible to make some general observations that are likely to be quite accurate. Chief among these is the fact that the Incas were the last in a long line of complex civilizations that appeared in ancient Peru. As such, they inherited a tremendous body of knowledge from their forebears. Specifically, there is evidence that the Incas were influenced by both the Wari and Tiwanaku empires, which preceded them. It also seems that some peoples migrated into Cuzco from the Lake Titicaca Basin not long before the beginning of the Incas. This group may have combined with a local kingdom to form the imperial Incas. This in turn may account for there being two versions of the origin myth, in which case both may contain a kernel of truth. This state of affairs is possibly reflected in the social organization of the Incas into two distinct groups called moieties by anthropologists. Moiety division was typical of communities within the Inca Empire, resulting in a community being more or less equally divided into upper and lower parts. Those in the upper division took symbolic precedence in all ceremonial or ritual behavior, but in all other respects the two divisions were equals. The first five kings of the Inca dynasty came from the lower moiety called Hurinsaya, and the remainder belonged to the upper moiety called Hanansaya. In the final analysis, the Incas found themselves in the right place at the right time with the necessary knowledge of statecraft and a well-developed infrastructure that allowed them to launch and rapidly expand the greatest of the Native American empires.

## THE INCA DYNASTY

Andean peoples were fundamentally organized by descent groups or lineages that traced their origins to a founding ancestor. The royal Incas were related through the male line in a lineage descended from their founding ancestor Manco Capac. As such, members of this lineage held a status called Capac. As a status, the term refers to a class of people but it was also used as a title for hereditary rulers. There is no exact European equivalent for this term, but the Spanish used it to denote persons of exalted status of "very much more than king," according to the chronicler Betanzos (1996: 123). The term "Inca" was said to mean "ruler" or "king," but a whole class of people were called Inca, so to single out the ruler of the empire, the title "Sapa Inca" meaning "unique Inca" was applied to the emperor (Julien 2000: 27–25). The Spaniards referred to this whole class of people as "Orejones," meaning "big ears." This name was a reference to the fact that the Inca males wore large golden earplugs as insignia. The lineage of the Capac Incas that comprised the imperial dynasty is reported by most of the Spanish sources in Table 4.1.

This list of emperors that Hiltunen (1999: 366–367) describes as the official or canonic dynasty does not include all of the Inca rulers. Atahuallpa was never formally installed as Inca emperor, although he ruled de facto after the defeat of Huascar. The succession of Inca rulers was never as simple and clear-cut as the European model of crown prince following the king to the throne. The change of rulers often involved infighting, violence, and even civil war among numerous eligible contenders and their factions. A ruler named Tarco Huaman was apparently deposed in order to place Capac Yupanki on the throne, and his name was not included in the canonic line. Capac Yupanki was then poisoned to death, and his favored heir, Quispe Yupanki, was also killed (Rostworowski

Table 4.1  Reigns of the Inca Dynasty

| Name | Reign |
|------|-------|
| 1. Manco Capac | ? |
| 2. Sinchi Roca | ? |
| 3. Lloque Yupanqui | ? |
| 4. Mayta Capac | ? |
| 5. Capac Yupanki | ? |
| 6. Inca Roca | ? |
| 7. Yahuar Huacac | ? |
| 8. Viracocha Inca | ?–A.D. 1438 |
| 9. Pachacuti (Pachacutec) | 1438–1471 |
| 10. Topa Inca (Tupac Inca Yupanqui) | 1471–1493 |
| 11. Huayna Capac | 1493–1525 |
| 12. Huascar | 1525–1532 |

de Diez Canseco 1999: 102). There is also mention made in the works of the chroniclers Cieza de León and Sarmiento de Gamboa of an Inca called Urcon who was the successor to Viracocha Inca but was murdered and replaced by Inca Pachacuti. Afterward, Inca Pachacuti had Inca Urcon's name stricken from the official dynastic list and Inca histories. There also appears in Sarmiento de Gamboa's account a passage suggesting that the heir to Pachacuti was to have been his son Amaru Tupac Inca but that he was for some reason replaced by Topa Inca, who instead became the ruler. It is unknown whether Amaru Tupac Inca was ever formally made emperor (Sarmiento de Gamboa 1999: 124–140).

## The Hurin Cuzco Dynasty

The first five Incas who appear on the canonic or official king list were said to be members of the lower moiety called Hurinsaya. The lineages of these kings resided in lower or Hurin Cuzco. Both moiety divisions however traced their lineage back to the founder Manco Capac. In addition to the origin stories related earlier, which are basically stories of Manco Capac, each of the succeeding Inca rulers had a history attached to his reign. These histories are often contradictory and confusing, attributing an event or achievement to the reign of two different emperors. At this distance, it is not often possible to accurately sort out who actually did what. At best, we can only follow the weight of the testimony of the oral histories recorded in the chronicles.

**Sinchi Roca (Dates unknown).** Sinchi Roca was the son of Manco Capac and Mama Ocllo and was said to have been born during the epic journey of the Inca founders to Cuzco. Despite having an unwarlike reputation, this ruler held the title of Sinchi, which denotes a war chief or captain of a relatively small community and was often a temporary honor assumed during a military threat. This title suggests that at this time the Incas did not have a strong mili-

SEGVNDO INGA
CINCHEROCA GA

con quis to hasta
hatun colla aniquipa

feruente

The second Inca ruler Sinchi Roca, wearing a tunic decorated with *tocapu* designs that mark him as a royal personage. (Felipe Huamán Poma de Ayala)

tary. Sinchi Roca is said to have married Mama Coca, a lady of the town of Sañu (modern San Sebastián), which cemented an important political alliance. Curiously, their son whose name was remembered as Manco Sapaca did not succeed his father as ruler for reasons that are not clear in the stories (Brundage 1963: 24–41).

**Lloque Yupanqui (Dates unknown).** The next ruler was a younger brother of Manco Sapaca who was called Lloque Yupanqui, which seems to mean left-handed (*lloque* means "left" in Quechua and *yupay* is the verb meaning "to count"). Lloque Yupanqui was remembered as an ineffectual ruler and some said a coward. In any case, he was unable to advance the Inca cause by either conquest or alliance. He is said to have had no children until very late in life, when a new young wife bore him a son and heir (Brundage 1963: 24–41).

**Mayta Capac (Dates unknown).** Following Lloque Yupanqui's lackluster reign, the new ruler, Mayta Capac, became the first Inca to be considered a great military leader. He was legendarily tough and aggressive. He managed to militarily control all of the Incas' nearest neighbors and set up a strong rule. He is also credited with first promoting the cult of the sun god Inti (Brundage 1963: 24–41).

**Capac Yupanki (Dates unknown).** Succeeding Mayta Capac as ruler, this leader continued the warlike ways of the Incas. It is said that he led the first Inca military expedition outside of the Valley of Cuzco. He also moved out of the Inti Cancha sun temple, where all of the previous rulers from Manco Capac onward had resided, and established the first royal palace. Each of the succeeding Inca rulers followed his example and built their own palaces. Capac Yupanki's reign ended with his assassination by one of his concubines and with the death of his son and heir (Brundage 1963: 24–41).

## The Hanan Cuzco Dynasty

With the assumption of power by the sixth ruler there is a significant change to the dynasty. All previous kings have been from the lower Hurin moiety but the sixth and all subsequent rulers were members of the upper Hanan moiety. These rulers built their palaces and resided in upper or Hanan Cuzco. From this point onward, all of the rulers also adopted the title Inca. Why this change occurred is a mystery that shrouds some very important events in Inca history. One theory is that Inca Roca was not the son and heir of Capac Yupanki but instead a usurper. His legitimacy stemmed from being a descendant through his mother of the last ruler of the ancient Tambo Tocco dynasty. If this is true, then he represents an entirely new line of kings and thus explains both the assassination of the preceding ruler and the cultural changes that came about at this time (Hiltunen 1999: 329–330).

**Inca Roca (Dates unknown).** The events of this reign are primarily concerned with the consolidation of the Incas' power against their strongest rivals in the immediate Cuzco region. A conflict was ignited with the marriage of Inca Roca to a woman named Mama Micay of the Guayllacan ethnic group. She had been promised to Tocay Capac, the ruler of another powerful group in Cuzco called the Ayarmaca. While the Guayllacan and Ayarmaca went to war over this woman, she and Inca Roca produced a son and heir named Yahuar Huacac. The price of peace was to have been the kidnapping of the boy by the Guayllacan, who were to hand him over to Tocay Capac to be killed. Legend says that when presented before Tocay Capac, the boy wept tears of blood, which frightened Tocay Capac into releasing him. From that point on, the boy was known as Yahuar Huacac, which means "blood weeper" (Brundage 1963: 24–41). Perhaps the most significant indication of the rising power of the Incas was a marriage alliance Inca Roca was later able to form with Tocay Capac that brought peace on favorable terms. It is said that Inca Roca gave a daughter to Tocay Capac in marriage and in turn married a daughter of Tocay Capac. These events signified the emergence of Inca power, since those who gave wives for marriage were viewed in Inca society as symbolically superior to those who received wives. Since both parties in this exchange were "givers" of wives, they must have been viewed as equals (Julien 2000: 245–246).

**Yahuar Huacac (Dates unknown).** Aside from the story of how he received his name, there is little information that has come down to us about the reign of Yahuar Huacac. He apparently presided over turbulent times. There were numerous conspiracies and revolts and his heir Pahuac Gualpa was murdered (Rostworowski de Diez Canseco 1999: 102). Considered a weak ruler by the Incas, he was eventually assassinated at a feast by some of the captains of Contisuyu, one of the four quarters of the empire (Cieza de León 1959: 206).

**Viracocha Inca, ?–A.D. 1438.** With the assassination of Yahuar Huacac, the Incas found themselves without a ruler, and numerous sons of the former king wanted to ascend the throne. According to Cieza de León (1959: 207), the principal lords of the Incas met and elected the next ruler. Hatun Topa Inca was elevated to the office of Sapa Inca and reigned throughout the formative years of the Inca state as Viracocha Inca. Although the historical significance of his accomplishments was enormous, his son and successor, Pachacuti, rewrote official Inca history to the extent that it is difficult to determine which achievements should be credited to Viracocha Inca and which were those of Pachacuti. The sources indicate that after his election, this emperor embarked on a series of conquests, as opposed to the raids and withdrawals of his predecessors. Viracocha Inca first incorporated the town of Calca and the neighboring sections of the Urubamba Valley. Next he turned his attention to the eastern end of the Valley of Cuzco and subdued the Pinagua and the Muyna peoples, which opened the path to advance farther south. He is said to have conquered as far as the territory of the Canchas, some 120 kilometers to the southeast, and then peacefully incorporated the Canas. He finally emerged into the Titicaca Basin, but there encountered the armies of the Colla ethnic group, which were evenly matched to his own. Rather than engage this power, he negotiated a peace and withdrew. During this campaign, the Incas had taken the holy shrine of the creator Viracocha at Cacha. Here the emperor spent some time receiving a vision from the creator god approving the Inca imperial quest. In honor of the deity, the Inca emperor changed his name to Viracocha Inca and became a forceful proponent of the cult of Viracocha.

Throughout his reign, Viracocha Inca apparently had to deal with plots against him by his own kinsmen. Some were dissatisfied with his election to

# EL OTABO íNGA
# VÍRACOCHA·ÍNG

Viracocha Inca, the eighth ruler, as depicted by Felipe Huamán Poma de Ayala. He wears a tunic completely covered with royal *tocapu* designs.

rule, while others were angered by his promotion of the creator god at the expense of the Inca patron Inti the sun god. Late in the life of Viracocha Inca a crisis developed resulting in his overthrow, according to most accounts.

In 1438 a rival expansionist group from the north known as the Chanca threatened the Inca capital at Cuzco. The Chanca were said to have a large, disciplined army fully capable of conquering the Incas and two able leaders named Hastu Huaraca and Tomay Huaraca. Bringing with them their ancestral mummy Uscovilca, they advanced on Cuzco.

Viracocha Inca responded by withdrawing with his appointed heir, Inca Urcon, to a more defensible location at a stronghold above Calca in the Urubamba Valley. A brother of Urcon and younger son of Inca Viracocha named Inca Cusi Yupanqui decided to remain and defend Cuzco against what seemed overwhelming odds. Together with a small but heroic contingent of Incas, he led the resistance to the Chanca attack and ultimately achieved a decisive defeat of the enemy. He claimed that the gods provided his victory by causing the very stones of the battlefield to turn to warriors to aid his cause. Having heroically saved Cuzco, Inca Cusi Yupanqui was in a position to assume the leadership of the Inca state. The generals of the army and other supporters elevated him to the position of Sapa Inca; he was thus crowned and took the new name of Pachacuti Inca. Viracocha Inca was deposed and humiliated, and Inca Urcon was killed. So ended another reign by violent overthrow (Brundage 1963: 72–92).

Not all sources agree that Pachacuti Inca was responsible for saving Cuzco from the Chanca threat. Cobo (1979: 128) credits the entire Chanca war and its successful conclusion entirely to Viracocha Inca. There is some suspicion that Pachacuti took credit for this victory when he rewrote Inca history in order to justify his usurpation of the throne.

**Pachacuti, 1438–1471.** Although it seems that Viracocha Inca was the first ruler to begin the Inca expansion, Pachacuti is most commonly viewed as the creator of the Inca Empire. He is also the first Inca for whom we have relatively secure dates, because at the time of the Spanish Conquest, people whose fathers and grandfathers had served him were still living. The name Pachacuti (sometimes given as Pachacutec; both words mean the same thing and either is correct) suited him well, because in the Quechua language it means "you shake the earth" or "earthshaker" and is also translated as "cataclysm" (*pacha* means "earth," "time," "space" and *cutiy* is the verb meaning "to shake"). For the Incas, a *pachacuti* was an event that overturned the existing order and disrupted the space-time continuum. Andean peoples believed that periodically creation came to an end with a *pachacuti* event and a new age was born.

Pachacuti Inca soon set about living up to his name. He consolidated his power by immediately turning upon those allied and neighboring states that had not fully supported the Incas against the Chanca in their hour of need. He was nearly assassinated by treacherous former allies during this time and used the destruction of these enemies as an example of his power. He then turned his army down the Urubamba Valley to conquer the town of Ollantaytambo, where he later built a major estate.

Having consolidated the near environs of Cuzco, Pachacuti then embarked on his campaigns of conquest. First he turned to the west, conquering the provinces of Vilcas and Soras. From there he moved into the provinces of Aymaraes, Omasayos, Cotapampas, and Chilques. An Inca general named Capac Yupanki was sent to expand the conquests to the north. He conquered the

The ceremonial complex of Sacsayhuaman located on the hill above Cuzco. (Corel)

provinces of Angará, Huanca, and Tarma but apparently exceeded his orders and was executed by Inca Pachacuti for insubordination.

Following these campaigns, Inca Pachacuti found it necessary to personally lead an expedition to quell unrest in the Lake Titicaca Basin. There he put down a revolt by the Ayaviri and went on to conquer the major polity called the Lupaca. The last campaign of Inca Pachacuti was against the Chumbivilca, adding them to the empire in the southwest. At this point in his career, Pachacuti decided to turn over the command of the imperial armies to his son Topa Inca, who continued the conquests (Rowe 1946: 206–207).

Inca Pachacuti retired to Cuzco, where he undertook many other projects. One of the most important was rebuilding the city as a new imperial capital. The chronicler Juan de Betanzos recorded that everyone was forced to evacuate the city and existing structures were razed. Using an architectural model made of clay, Inca Pachacuti made a plan of a city in the form of a puma, or mountain lion. The animal was represented in profile, with the residential blocks of the city forming its body, Sacsayhuaman, the great fortress or temple complex on the hill above Cuzco representing its head, and the confluence of the Tullu and Saphi rivers representing its tail. Between the fore and hind legs of the puma were located the two great plazas of Cuzco, where the highways to the four imperial quarters of the empire, called *suyus*, converged. These enormous spaces lay adjacent to each other on opposite sides of the Saphi

River. On the north bank lay the plaza called Hawkaypata, where serious and solemn ceremonies were carried out. In this plaza were also located the *ushnu* platform, from which the Sapa Inca could preside over the gatherings, and a tower called the Sunturwasi, whose function is obscure. On the south bank was the plaza of Cusipata, where celebrations were held on joyous occasions. Clustered around these plazas were the palaces of the later Inca emperors, and lining the perimeter of the Hawkaypata on three sides were a series of enormous halls called *kallankas*. These provided sheltered spaces in which ceremonies could be conducted in bad weather.

After the old site had been cleared, Pachacuti is said to have measured out the new plan and staked it out on the ground using a cord and his own hands. After the city was constructed, he assigned each inhabitant his own house (Betanzos 1996: 69–73). The city was laid out in a grid pattern, with streets and blocks of houses built in the *cancha* pattern. The whole was divided in accordance with the moiety system into upper (Hanan) and lower (Hurin) Cuzco. The city also featured many important temples, including the Coricancha temple of the sun. Numerous fountains and canals brought water into the center for both practical necessities and esthetic enjoyment.

On the hill above the city lay the puma's head, Sacsayhuaman. It is the largest megalithic structure ever erected in the Western Hemisphere. Built in the famous Inca polygonal style of stonework, its outer walls contain individual blocks that weigh as much as 100 tons. The center of the complex consists of three concentric zigzag walls enclosing a prominence on which three towers were erected. Two of these were square and between them was a circular tower. To the north of these structures is a vast complex of ruins showing that there were once many more buildings and structures of a wide variety of shapes, both rectangular and circular. There were many fountains and canals in this area, as well as many carved *huaca* stones. The function of Sacsayhuaman has been debated for years. There was a battle fought there during the Inca siege of Cuzco as they resisted the forces of Pizarro. The Spaniards therefore thought of the structure as a fortress. Although it may have once served as a fortress and did so during that battle, its function at the height of the empire, when the empire felt no threat to the capital, was surely much more complex. It was likely the site of temples and religious shrines of various cults and residences for Incas. The functions of many of the buildings and architectural monuments of the Inca capital are just beginning to be understood.

Although a magnificent and appropriate capital for the empire of the Incas, Cuzco was never a city in the European sense. It housed only royalty and nobility and religious shrines. There were no markets or centers of commerce. Commoners and foreigners were not permitted to live there and had to leave the city each night. These peoples were housed in satellite communities surrounding Cuzco at a short distance. As a result, Cuzco never grew to the enormous size of the capitals of European empires such as Rome or even as large as some of its key administrative centers in the provinces.

In addition to the city, Pachacuti also undertook many public works, including canals, aqueducts, storehouses, terraces, and highways, as well as a number of private estates. He was very fond of the Urubamba Valley and built estates there at Pisac, Ollantaytambo, and most famously at Machu Picchu.

Among his other achievements Inca Pachacuti was credited with a great amount of social engineering. He is said to have codified Inca law, institutionalized the taxation system, and completely reorganized Inca society. Inca religion was restructured and organized in a hierarchy reflecting the administrative hierarchy, with the emperor at the head. He formalized ancestor worship and invented the institution of the *panaca* to care for royal mummies. He invented an agricultural calendar as well as a religious calendar indicating all of the proper rites and holidays and when they should be observed. In short, Inca Pachacuti was the founding genius and the inventor of the Inca Empire. Clearly he was a great leader, but the number of achievements that can actually be accredited to him is unknown.

Inca Pachacuti lived to a very old age and groomed his successor by installing him as coruler during his lifetime. As was the case with many of his predecessors, however, Pachacuti's first choice did not become the ruler. His favorite son was named Amaru Inca. This young man was much esteemed by all on account of his personal character, and he served a six-year coregency with his father, learning the craft of government. Amaru Inca had one terrible failing from the Inca point of view: he was not an aggressive, competent military commander. At the insistence of the emperor's generals, Amaru Inca was deposed and replaced by his brother Topa Inca (Brundage 1963: 104–105).

*Is it really him or just Inca propaganda?*

**Topa Inca, 1471–1493.** The tenth ruler, Topa Inca, was also known as Tupac Inca Yupanqui. He began his conquests while serving as coregent with his father and is responsible for the greatest expansion of the Inca Empire. A brilliant general, he expanded the empire to the north during his coregency with Inca Pachacuti. The Andean highlands as far north as Quito in modern Ecuador were incorporated as well as the Ecuadorean coast. After spending a period on the coast, he is said to have embarked an army of 20,000 men on a fleet of balsa rafts and sailed out into the Pacific Ocean. Two islands named Ninacumbi and Avacumbi, perhaps in the Galápagos archipelago, were visited by the party before they returned to the mainland (Sarmiento de Gamboa 1999: 135–137). Upon his return, he turned his armies southward and conquered the empire of the Chimu. This feat incorporated the Peruvian north coast and central coast as far south as the Lurin Valley, near the modern city of Lima. It also removed the most serious rival state from contention with the Incas.

Following a brief return to the capital at Cuzco, Topa Inca set out to conquer the south coast of Peru. The valleys from Nazca to Mala were added to the empire, and then Topa Inca returned to Cuzco. Pachacuti was by this time very elderly and had decided to retire.

Topa Inca became the Sapa Inca, or emperor, in 1471 and continued his campaigns toward the east through Paucartambo and into the *montaña*. Taking advantage of his preoccupation, or perhaps as a test of the new emperor's strength, the Colla and Lupaca led a revolt against the Incas in the Lake Titicaca Basin, causing Topa Inca to cut short his invasion of the *montaña*. Turning to face this new threat, the Inca armies marched south. The Colla and Lupaca were subdued and the northern Titicaca Basin was occupied.

Following this revolt, Topa Inca proceeded to invade and annex modern Bolivia. He conquered highland Bolivia and invaded northern Chile, setting the southern boundary of the Inca Empire at the Maule River. Finally, the highlands of northwest Argentina were conquered as well. His final campaign was another incursion into the forested *montaña,* after which he returned to Cuzco to concentrate on administration and to enjoy his estates (Rowe 1946: 206–208).

**Huayna Capac, 1493–1525.** Topa Inca's younger son Titu Cusi Huallpa followed him on the throne, taking the name Huayna Capac. Like his father and grandfather, Huayna Capac was a great general and turned his attention to adding more conquests to the empire. He continued to expand the boundaries of the empire to the north and east, incorporating much of what is now modern Ecuador as well as the northeastern Peruvian Andes. The northern border of the empire was pushed into the southern part of modern Colombia and set at the Ancasmayo River. Compared to those of his father, however, Huayna Capac's conquests were modest, and he met stiff resistance from the Ecuadorean tribes. Their conquest was unexpectedly costly, and it is said that at one point the leaders of the Inca armies revolted against their emperor. Huayna Capac was forced to back down and reconsider his course of action. He managed to weather the revolt through diplomacy, but he had spent so much time on his difficult northern campaigns that the social fabric of the Inca nation began to show severe strains. Huayna Capac's long absence was causing him problems in Cuzco society. Surrogates had had to stand in for him at important festivals and ceremonies, and the people of Cuzco began to feel out of touch with their emperor. A new court had grown up around him at his northern headquarters at Tomebamba in Ecuador that rivaled the official imperial court in Cuzco. Administratively, the empire had also become difficult to govern. Decisions from the emperor took a long time to reach Cuzco and even longer to be disseminated to the rest of the empire. The Inca nobility, having achieved great wealth and power, was in a state of unrest and ferment that would carry over into the next reign. Away fighting in Ecuador, the emperor had little firsthand knowledge of what was going on in Cuzco or other parts of his realm. The empire had grown to a size where it was unwieldy and difficult to control. By 1527 two new crises arose that would be fatal to both Huayna Capac and the Inca Empire. The first was the appearance of the Europeans. Pizarro's second voyage was duly reported to the emperor, who had little or no time to react. The second crisis was the appearance of European-introduced diseases that killed unknown millions in the empire and the Inca Huayna Capac himself, his heir apparent, Ninan Cuyochi, and many of the leading members of the Inca aristocracy (Brundage 1963: 239–266).

**Huascar, 1525–1532.** There was a certain confusion among the Incas about the succession following the death of Huayna Capac. In Cuzco he had left as co-regent a legitimate heir, Huascar, who governed in his absence and expected to ascend the throne as next in line. At the same time, Huayna Capac had found a new favorite, Ninan Cuyochi, among the sons who accompanied him on the Ecuadorean campaigns. Some sources suggest that he intended to remove Huascar from power, but before he could act, both he and his favorite son had died from the European diseases. The vacillation about the succession created even more strain on Inca society, which broke into factions. The armies and generals that had been with Huayna Capac in the north backed another of his sons, Atahuallpa, and soon a civil war broke out between the two brothers and their factions.

The faction in Cuzco crowned Huascar as emperor. The details of his reign that were recorded by the Spanish chroniclers, however, were related by the winning faction in the civil war, which deliberately cast Huascar in a bad light. Juan de Betanzos, who married into the faction of Atahuallpa, was told that Huascar was a drunken lout and womanizer. He also was guilty of something more serious: he had ordered that all of the lands of the mummified dead emperors be given to him, which threatened the base of power and wealth of the former emperors' lineages. In doing so, he alienated the Hanan Cuzco moiety completely (Betanzos 1996: 188–190; Brundage 1963: 267–295). After nearly five years of bloody fighting in which countless Incas lost their lives, the civil war finally ended with the fall of the city of Cuzco in 1532 to the forces of Atahuallpa. Emperor Huascar's reign came to an end, and he was captured and imprisoned.

## INCA RULERS UNDER SPANISH CONTROL

As Atahuallpa, accompanied by his army, moved south to Cuzco from Tomebamba to assume the imperial throne, he was met by the Spanish forces led by Francisco Pizarro at the town of Cajamarca in the northern Peruvian highlands. In a stunning surprise move, Pizarro and his small band of 168 men attacked and captured Atahuallpa in the midst of his huge army. As described in Chapter 3, Pizarro held the emperor captive for nearly eight months, waiting for the ransom that would secure Atahuallpa's release. While he was in captivity, Atahuallpa secretly sent orders to have the Inca Huascar killed. He eliminated his rival but to no avail, since he himself was killed by the Spaniards shortly thereafter in July 1533. With the death of Atahuallpa, the last of the independent rulers of the Inca Empire had fallen. The Incas continued to resist the Spanish for many years thereafter, but the Inca Empire ceased to exist.

### Topa Huallpa, 1533–1533

Francisco Pizarro soon realized that the only way he could hope to control the Inca forces that vastly outnumbered his troops was to control their ruler. Having killed Atahuallpa, he needed to place a new ruler on the throne. Topa Huallpa, a son of Huayna Capac allied with the Huascar faction, was chosen and was an enthusiastic collaborator with the Spanish. As the invading army marched toward Cuzco, this new ruler became ill and soon died. He was likely poisoned by one of the factions competing for the throne (Hemming 1970: 86–96).

### Manco Inca, 1533–1545

Within a few weeks of the arrival of the Spanish army in Cuzco, Pizarro appointed another son of Huayna Capac as ruler. Manco Inca was a member of the Huascar faction in the recent civil war and was eager to avenge the defeat of Huascar by cooperating with the Spaniards. At first Manco Inca was treated with respect. He was crowned with full ceremony and became Sapa Inca, although he was under the control of Pizarro. As time went by, however, the Spanish conquerors began to abuse him and treat him with contempt. The behavior of the Spaniards throughout the empire soon convinced him that his alliance with them was a mistake.

By the fall of 1535, Manco Inca could stand no more abuse and fled the city of Cuzco. He was soon captured and returned to Cuzco, where he was imprisoned and further abused. During this period unsuccessful revolts against the Spanish occurred. In the spring of 1536, Manco Inca finally made good his escape and launched an uprising throughout the country. He laid siege to the city of Cuzco and sent an army to attack the new Spanish capital at Lima. Although nearly successful, these efforts were in the end overcome by the Spanish, and Manco Inca and his forces fell back to the town of Ollantaytambo in the Urubamba Valley. Pursued by the Spanish, he ultimately retreated to the town of Vitcos in the Vilcabamba region far downstream on the Urubamba drainage.

In 1538 Manco Inca led a second major revolt against Spanish forces. This revolt spread all the way from the central Peruvian highlands to the Titicaca Basin and the Charcas area in the south. After a number of victories on the part of the Inca forces, the Spanish rallied, and ultimately this rebellion failed as had the first. Manco fled further into the Vilcabamba region and founded a new capital also named Vilcabamba. Manco Inca ruled his small rebel kingdom for some years while the Spanish authorities tried to find a way to eliminate him or coax him into coming back to Cuzco as a Spanish puppet. Ultimately, he made the fatal mistake of offering refuge to some renegade Spaniards and was assassinated by these men in mid-1544 (Hemming 1970: 100–279).

### Paullu Inca, 1537–1549

Following the escape of Manco Inca from Cuzco, the Spanish authorities replaced him with another, more pliable ruler. Paullu Inca, a brother of Manco Inca, was invested by the Spanish captain Diego de Almagro in 1537. He formally took over as ruler in Spanish eyes, and Manco Inca was formally divested of power.

Although, like Manco Inca, he was abused by the Spanish with public insults and theft of his possessions, he remained steadfastly loyal to the Spanish cause, fighting alongside them and against his countrymen during the rebellions. He adopted Hispanicized dress and customs, converted to Christianity, and ultimately became very wealthy. He became adept at surviving the civil strife among the Spaniards, switching sides as necessary to maintain his position.

After the assassination of Manco Inca, Paullu Inca was much involved in trying to convince the young prince Sayri Tupac, who succeeded Manco Inca, to surrender to the Spanish. On one of his embassies to Sayri Tupac, he became ill and, returning to Cuzco, died within a few days (Hemming 1970: 331–346).

## Carlos Inca, 1549–1572

With the death of Paullu Inca, his oldest son became the next ruler under the Spanish authorities, who believed that the succession should flow from father to eldest son in the European fashion. Carlos Inca was thoroughly Hispanicized and cooperated with the Europeans. He married a Spanish woman and became a wealthy and prominent member of society. His fortunes reversed in 1572, when the Viceroy Toledo, frustrated by the long resistance of the Vilcabamba Inca state, unleashed a plan to stamp out any further resistance by the Incas. Although not involved in any plots or rebellions, Carlos Inca was arrested and tried in the Spanish courts. He was deprived of his wealth and lands and ended up in prison. Ultimately, the king of Spain intervened and Carlos Inca was pardoned and his wealth restored. He lived out the rest of his life as a wealthy landowner in Cuzco and died in 1572 (Hemming 1970: 283–455).

## Sayri Tupac Inca, 1545–1558

Although only a small child at the time of his father's murder, Manco Inca's younger son Sayri Tupac Inca inherited the Inca throne and was cared for by a group of regents. Most of his short life was spent in negotiations with the representatives of the Spanish viceroy, who attempted to lure him back to Cuzco with the object of dismantling the rump Inca state in Vilcabamba. He finally accepted a deal with the Spanish and moved to Cuzco, only to die a short time afterward. There were rumors that he had been poisoned, but nothing was ever proved (Hemming 1970: 279–301).

## Titu Cusi, 1558–1571

When Sayri Tupac Inca emerged from Vilcabamba and moved to Cuzco, he left behind the royal insignia and his older brother Titu Cusi. With the death of Sayri Tupac, he became the next ruler of the Vilcabamba Inca state. A much more aggressive figure, he maintained a guerrilla war against the Spanish for the duration of his reign. He also kept up constant negotiations for surrender, but the Spaniards were always disappointed. Like his brother, he died a mysterious death, falling suddenly ill and rapidly declining (Hemming 1970: 327–417).

## Tupac Amaru, 1571–1572

With the demise of Titu Cusi, the crown passed to his brother Tupac Amaru. For a third time, a son of Manco Inca came to the throne. There would be no further negotiations by either side. The Viceroy Toledo was determined to finally exterminate the resistance of the Incas. A large military expedition was mounted that pursued and captured Tupac Amaru in Vilcabamba in 1572. He was brought back to Cuzco, and after a brief trial, the last Sapa Inca, Tupac

Amaru, was publicly beheaded in the main square of Cuzco, the ancient capital of his people (Hemming 1970: 421–449).

## REFERENCES

Bauer, Brian. 1992. *The Development of the Inca State.* Austin: University of Texas Press.

Bauer, Brian S., and R. Alan Covey. 2002. "Processes of State Formation in the Inca Heartland (Cuzco, Peru)." *American Anthropologist* 104(3): 846–864.

Betanzos, Juan de. 1996. *Narrative of the Incas.* Translated and edited by Roland Hamilton and Dana Buchanan. Austin: University of Texas Press.

Bingham, Hiram. 1948. *Lost City of the Incas: The Story of Machu Picchu and Its Builders.* New York: Duell, Sloan and Pearce.

Brundage, Burr C. 1963. *Empire of the Inca.* Norman: University of Oklahoma Press.

Cieza de León, Pedro de. 1959. *The Incas of Pedro de Cieza de León.* Translated by Harriet de Onis and edited by Victor W. von Hagen. Norman: University of Oklahoma Press.

Cobo, Bernabé. 1979. *History of the Inca Empire: An Account of the Indians' Customs and their Origin Together with a Treatise on Inca Legends, History, and Social Institutions.* Translated and edited by Roland Hamilton. Austin: University of Texas Press.

Hemming, John. 1970. *The Conquest of the Incas.* London: MacMillan.

Hiltunen, Juha J. 1999. *Ancient Kings of Peru: The Reliability of the Chronicle of Fernando de Montesinos; Correlating the Dynasty Lists with Current Prehistoric Periodization in the Andes.* Helsinki: Suomen Historiallinen Seura.

Julien, Catherine. 2000. *Reading Inca History.* Iowa City: University of Iowa Press.

McEwan, Gordon F. 1984. "The Middle Horizon in the Valley of Cuzco, Peru: The Impact of the Wari Occupation of Pikillacta in the Lucre Basin." Ph.D. dissertation, University of Texas, Austin.

McEwan, Gordon F., Melissa Chatfield, and Arminda Gibaja O. 2002. "The Archaeology of Inca Origins: Excavations at Chokepukio, Cuzco, Peru." In *Andean Archaeology,* edited by W. Isbell and H. Silverman, 287–301. New York: Kluwer Academic.

McEwan, Gordon F., Arminda Gibaja, and Melissa Chatfield. 1995. "Archaeology of the Chokepukio Site: An Investigation of the Origin of the Inca Civilization in the Valley of Cuzco, Peru: A Report on the 1994 Field Season." *Tawantinsuyu: International Journal of Inka Studies* 1: 11–17.

Rostworowski de Diez Canseco, Maria. 1999. *History of the Inca Realm.* Translated by Harry B. Iceland. Cambridge: Cambridge University Press.

Rowe, John H. 1944. "An Introduction to the Archaeology of Cuzco." *Papers of the Peabody Museum of American Archaeology and Ethnology,* vol. 27, no. 2. Cambridge, MA: Harvard University Press.

———. 1946. "Inca Culture at the Time of the Spanish Conquest." In *Handbook of South American Indians,* edited by Julian Steward, Bureau of American Ethnology, bulletin 143, vol. 2, 183–330. Washington DC: Smithsonian Institution.

Sarmiento de Gamboa, Pedro. 1999. *History of the Incas.* Translated and edited by Sir Clements Markham. Mineola, NY: Dover. English translation originally published 1907. Cambridge: Hakluyt Society.

Urton, Gary. 1990. *The History of a Myth: Pacariqtambo and the Origin of the Incas.* Austin: University of Texas Press.

Zuidema, Reiner Tom. 1995. *El sistema de los ceques.* Lima: Pontificia Universidad Católica del Perú, Fondo Editorial.

CHAPTER 5

# The Economic Structure
# of the Inca State

The Inca economy, which had evolved out of long-standing traditional patterns, was agriculturally based. It was the production of foodstuffs that fueled the activities of the empire. Herding and animal husbandry were also very significant to the economy, providing not only meat but the raw material for the cloth that was regarded as the most valuable commodity of the realm. The most unusual aspect of the Inca economy was the lack of a market system and money. With only a few exceptions found in coastal polities incorporated into the empire, there was no trading class in Inca society, and the development of individual wealth acquired through commerce was not possible. Local political units were ideally to be as self-sufficient as possible in producing their own basic economic requirements. A few products deemed essential by the Incas could not be produced locally and had to be imported. In these cases several strategies were employed, such as establishing colonies in specific production zones for particular commodities and permitting limited long-distance trade. The production, distribution, and use of commodities were centrally controlled by the Inca government. Each citizen of the empire was issued the necessities of life out of the state storehouses, including food, tools, raw materials, and clothing, and needed to purchase nothing. With no shops or markets, there was no need for a standard currency or money, and there was nowhere to spend money or purchase or trade for necessities.

## SUBSISTENCE PATTERNS

Two basic subsistence patterns had evolved over the millennia preceding the rise of the Inca Empire, which Rostworowski de Diez Canseco (1999: 203–209) distinguishes as "the highland economic model" and "the coastal economic model." These were in large part determined by geography, particularly elevation, and the distribution of resources over the landscape. How one made a living was determined by where one lived. The principal food resources were obtained by growing crops and supplementing the vegetable part of the diet with protein obtained through herding of alpacas and llamas, raising *cuy*, or guinea pigs, and exploiting fisheries in the Pacific Ocean or highland lakes.

### Highland Adaptation

In the arid mountain environment it was common to practice herding and farming together. As elevation increased, the pasturage for camelids was

richer, but at the same time the number of plant species that could be cultivated declined. The mix of herding and farming production varied according
to altitude and access to grasslands. In areas where both were abundantly accessible, very large populations could be sustained.

The challenges of highland farming were many. Highlanders tended to develop self-sufficiency at the household level, with each family unit tending its
own crops and animals. Most highland farming could be accomplished with
the water provided by annual rainfall. However, climatic variations were frequent, and rains could vary considerably from year to year. These fluctuations,
when coupled with a short growing season, made agricultural production un-
certain. Frost and hail were also constant threats to farming success. The resulting crop failures had to be factored into a long-term survival strategy. One
additional difficulty was the nature of the highland soils, which tended to be
thin and fragile and required long fallow periods between crops. Fertilizer in
the form of animal dung could be applied in order to enrich the nutritive value
of the soil, but periods of fallow were still necessary.

The highland peoples employed several strategies to meet these challenges
and ensure long-term survival of the population. Research by John Murra
(1964, 1972) has documented the practice of what he calls "ecological comple-
mentarity," which is also known as "verticality." The idea was to control a variety of ecological niches that were at different altitudes but relatively close to
each other. Each of these environments could be planted with different kinds
of crops that would vary in their vulnerability to the vagaries of pests, disease,
and weather. This not only provided a richer and more varied diet but also
served as a form of insurance against any natural calamity that could wipe out
the total production of the fields.

Another manner of insuring against erratic crop yields was a strategy
termed "energy averaging" (Isbell 1978). The idea was to preserve any surplus
acquired during agriculturally productive years for use during hard times,
thus averaging out the energy supply over a series of years. Special processing
by freeze-drying allowed certain types of potatoes to be preserved as a product
called *chuño*. In similar fashion, the meat of llamas and alpacas could be preserved as a product called *charqui*. Certain grains could also be stored for relatively long periods of time.

Although the ideal situation for highland communities was self-sufficiency
within a limited geographic area, there were some crops and commodities that
could not be locally produced because they required special environments far
distant from the other exploited eco-niches. Murra's (1964, 1972) research has
shown that rather than establish trading relationships with groups occupying
such zones, the Incas developed colonies or enclaves that Murra terms "vertical archipelagos." Working groups were sent to settle in distant environments
to produce specific commodities and ship them back home. These colonies
were in turn supported in their other needs by production from the home area.
Such crops as maize, coca leaves, and tropical fruits that required lower elevations and specialized environments and commodities such as salt and marine
products, including iodine-rich seafoods, were produced in colonies directly

Street vendors sell bananas, melons, and a variety of potatoes, including *chuño* (preserved potatoes), at an open-air market in the mining town of Oruro, Bolivia. (Anders Ryman/Corbis)

controlled by distant highland communities. The colonists were considered to be full members of the home community and retained their rights and privileges within the home community. These discontinuous holdings were widely distributed over the landscape, resulting in what Moseley (1992: 45) observes are geographically extensive and far-flung polities that were only loosely dominated politically.

## Coastal Adaptation

In contrast to the generalized adaptation to the highland environment, peoples living on the Pacific coast of ancient Peru were much more specialized. What has been termed the "maritime-oasis" lifeway depended on economic specialization and reciprocal exchange rather than market exchange (Moseley 1992: 146). Specialization was fundamentally divided between the production of agricultural and marine resources. The vegetable component of the diet could be grown in irrigated fields, while protein was extracted from the Pacific fisheries. In both cases production required specialization that precluded the development of community self-sufficiency. Specific ethnic groups would specialize in one or the other of these modes of production and would exchange their surplus in order to achieve a balanced diet.

The rigors of the maritime-oasis environment made specialization manda-

Fishermen with traditional reed boats on the Peruvian coast. (Omar Torres/AFP/Getty Images)

tory. Coastal-dwelling fishermen required specialized tools to obtain their livelihood. They grew certain specific plants such as reeds for boat building, cotton for making fishing nets, and gourds for net floats that allowed them to efficiently harvest marine life. The wide variety of marine animals also encouraged specialization in specific production such as shellfish, anchovies, large fish, or sea mammals.

Coastal farmers were restricted to the oasis-like valleys of the limited number of rivers that flowed from the highlands and across the Peruvian coastal desert. In this environment, unlike that of the highlands, there is no local rainfall to water the crops. Water from highland rainfall arrived on the coast through natural river systems that were subject to the same vagaries of the highland rainfall that affected the highland farmers. Although the land is fertile, it can only be made to effectively and efficiently produce food and economic crops by means of sophisticated irrigation networks. These systems required hydraulic and engineering specialization in addition to farming expertise in order to function. Construction and maintenance of such systems were labor intensive and required tremendous investments of time and energy in exchange for their abundant output of produce.

Specialization resulted in efficiencies of production that produced surpluses that permitted even more specialization in endeavors not directly related to food production. In some coastal polities there developed specialized artisans and craftsmen dedicated to production of a single commodity. These included metallurgy, textiles, woodworking, ceramics, salt production, dyeing, and beer production. The production and disposition of these commodities were regu-

How is water pumped?

lated by the upper classes that could use them to engage in long-distance trade for profit. The best documented traders are those of the Chincha kingdom who traded northward at least as far as Ecuador using great fleets of ocean-going balsa log rafts. This trade seems to have been motivated by the desire for certain culturally precious objects that were not available locally. Such items would include the red *Spondylus* shells used in many religious ceremonies and for fashioning jewelry and ritual objects used by the lords of the many Andean polities. This trade was difficult and probably sporadic and had a limited overall impact on the economy as a whole (Rostworowski de Diez Canseco 1999: 209–214).

## THE INCA IMPERIAL ECONOMY

In constructing their state, the Incas made use of the economic arrangements that they found already in place. These could be modified as needed by the empire but retained the traditional structural logic of the highland and coastal models. The Incas attempted to extract wealth to form their political economy without seriously disturbing local self-sufficiency. In order to accomplish this, taxes were not collected in money, since there was none, and neither were they collected in kind, that is, payment with commodities or crops. Instead, taxes were collected in the form of human labor in a system operated by the decimal hierarchy of the political administration. Each political officer was responsible for a specific number of taxpayers. Assessments of tax liability then depended on the accurate census information on the number of available able-bodied workers and resources. The labor collected as taxes was devoted to three basic needs of the empire: agricultural production, textile production, and service to the state known as the *mit'a* (Moseley 1992: 65; Rowe 1944).

Not all citizens of the empire were taxpayers. All Incas and other nobles were exempt from the labor tax, as were their *yanacona* servants. Political officers, administrators, and their families were also exempt as long as they held administrative responsibility for more than 100 men. As salary, all of these individuals received allotments from the government warehouses to meet their needs and were entitled to a portion of the labor tax of the people that they administered. They could also be rewarded for their performance of duties with gifts from the emperor consisting of jewelry, cloth or other fine objects, livestock, land, and women from the ranks of the chosen women, the *acllas* (Cobo 1979: 211–212; Rostworowski de Diez Canseco 1999: 188–189).

### Land Distribution, Utilization, and the Agricultural Labor Tax

*France: 3 estates?*

When a new region was incorporated into the Inca Empire, its lands were carefully surveyed and catalogued. The new rulers divided the land into three sections. One part was used in service of the state religion, one part for the service of the emperor, and the remaining part was to provide sustenance for the local population. Ideally these parts would be of equal size, but in practice there were many variations. The size of the people's land allotment needed only to be sufficient for their needs, with no profit or benefit to be had from surplus production. This left all remaining land to be divided between the church and the state, whose shares could be much larger. When there was not sufficient local land to support all three of these objectives, new lands were to be opened and developed through terracing and reclamation projects financed by the state. In the portion left to the people, traditional patterns of land distribution continued to be observed. An annual allotment based on need would be made by the basic social unit, the *ayllu*. Lands were also set aside to be worked for the benefit of chiefs and local leaders. Even the lands of the people were said to belong to the emperor, and they were allowed only to use the land, not to own it. Seed, tools, and fertilizer were provided by the state to work all three portions of the land. The people had only to provide the labor to work these lands and to attend to the lands of the religion first, the lands of the emperor second, and their own lands third (Cobo 1979: 211–214).

In addition to the lands of the people, religion, or state that were set aside in the conquered provinces, individual noble Incas privately owned lands in and around Cuzco and throughout the empire. The most elaborate of the royal and noble estates were those established in the Vilcanota/Urubamba Valley relatively near Cuzco. These include such famous sites as Machu Picchu, Ollantay-tambo, Pisac, and Chinchero, among others. These estates were staffed by *yanacona* and were developed as both a private source of revenue for the Incas and as a country house retreat. The output of these estates provided the necessities for underwriting the costs of rulership. Emperors were expected to be generous and to publicly display their generosity with feasts and drinking bouts and the distribution of valuable goods. Since the ruler inherited none of his predecessor's wealth, he had to generate his own. The lands of the estates continued in his possession after his death and supported his lineage corporation called the *panaca* in perpetuity. Over the course of several reigns, all of the best and most productive land in the Cuzco area was seized by one or another of the emperors and was effectively removed from the state economy. By the reign of the last emperor, this was to cause friction among the Inca nobles.

One other class of landowners comprised individual *huacas,* or religious shrines. *Huacas* were sometimes treated the same way as people; wishing to reward a *huaca* for its service or support, the Incas sometimes granted it lands and people to work them. Depending on the size, fame, and prestige of the *huaca,* these estates could be large and substantial. The products of the *huacas'* estates went to maintain their shrines, provide offerings, and sustain their priests and priestesses. Major shrines such as Pachacamac on the Pacific coast were extremely well endowed with wealth and income rivaling that of human lords (Rostworowski de Diez Canseco 1999: 89–90).

### Livestock and Herding

One of the greatest resources in the Andes was the vast herds of camelids, llamas and alpacas that were domesticated long before the time of the Incas. Ownership was, in theory, monopolized by the Inca state, which owned vast herds that grazed in the *puna,* the high plateau of the southern Peruvian and Bolivian highlands. Each province was assigned its state-owned herds. The

Communism?

Llamas, Arequipa, Peru. (Corel)

wool produced by these herds was collected by the state and issued to labor-tax payers to turn into state-owned cloth. Religious institutions also apparently held vast flocks of animals. These provided sustenance to the priests and *acllas* as well as sacrificial animals for numerous religious rites. John Murra (1980: 50–51) points out, however, that there was considerable evidence of private ownership of llamas and alpacas. Animals were granted to individuals as gifts from the state as a reward for services. It also appears that communities owned flocks of animals that were held and redistributed in the same pattern as that of land holdings.

Economically, camelids were important for a number of reasons. Live animals, although too small to use as human transport, could be used as pack animals to carry loads of about ninety pounds. Llamas used as pack animals were essentially self-sufficient, because they could graze on whatever grasses they found along their journey, making it unnecessary to carry fodder. Camelids were also the most important fiber source for the production of the cloth that permitted humans to live in the cold high Andean environment. Llama wool was coarse and was generally used for sacking and rope. The much finer wool of the alpaca was spun into yarn for the manufacture of clothing. The nondomesticated vicuña was also hunted for its exceptionally fine wool. The animal could be sheared without harm and then released back into the wild until the next hunt.

Slaughtered animals were sources of meat, leather, and tallow. Llama meat could be preserved for long periods by freeze-drying it into *charqui*. The leather was used for a variety of products, including footwear, weapons such as bolas, and was made into ropes. Sinew taken from the animals was used in place of nails and screws to fasten tools and agricultural implements together.

## The Textile Tax

The single most important material good in the ancient Andes was cloth. Large amounts of this high-value commodity were required in order to keep the state functioning. It served a variety of purposes: clothing the populace, functioning as a marker of ethnicity and rank, providing storage and transport containers, and serving as a high-value prestige good that could be used by the authorities to compensate and reward the service of their people. Quantities of cloth were also sacrificed in religious ceremonies.

In order to secure the quantities of cloth that were necessary, the state exacted a cloth production tax. This was a variation of the labor tax in which the state provided the households of commoners with the raw materials, cotton and wool, and fibers of various types. These materials were transformed into an assigned allotment of cloth through the laborious processes of spinning, dyeing, weaving, and plaiting to produce yarn, cloth, and cordage. Hundreds of thousands if not millions of yards of thread were required, and Andean women were rarely without their drop spindles that allowed them to spin while walking about and attending to their other duties.

Because of the needs of the empire for vast quantities of the finest cloth, the production of household taxpayers was supplemented by that of weaving specialists. These specialists were of two types. In areas where the natives were famous for the quality of their cloth, male specialists were put to work producing fine cloth in quantity and were exempt from all other duties or taxes. This cloth ended up stored in large quantities at state installations, from which they could be distributed as needed. A second source of fine cloth was the *acllas*, the chosen women who were kept in conventlike *aclla wasi* throughout the realm. These institutions and their women became virtual factories for the finest cloth used by the emperor and for religious sacrifice (Cobo 1979: 223–226; Murra 1980: 65–81).

## The Mit'a Labor Tax

The Inca Empire needed labor not only for producing food and cloth but also for staffing large state projects. This service to the state was called the *mit'a* and those who were performing it were called *mitayoq*. The state's needs included the raising of large armies to defend and expand the frontiers as well as to control rebellious provinces. Monumental public works were also labor intensive, and thousands of workers were needed to build and maintain canals, roads, palaces, temples, and administrative centers. Other industries that required large labor pools were quarrying and mining.

In order to meet the labor needs of the empire, the Inca government systematically drafted taxpayers to perform labor service. Great care was taken to equally distribute the labor-tax burden throughout the empire. The idea was to take only a few men from each administrative unit. By keeping sufficient labor at home, the units could maintain agricultural output and not disrupt the

Weaver in Cuzco. (Corel)

economy. Those staying behind worked the fields of those performing *mit'a* so that they were not at a disadvantage. In cases of especially difficult or burdensome activities, the men were rotated at shorter intervals so as not to cause them harm or exhaustion. For this reason, men working in the mines or at other difficult or dangerous jobs performed a shorter term of labor, thus making these tasks seem less burdensome. People performing their *mit'a* service had only to provide their labor. Tools, weapons, food, drink, and other necessities were provided by the government. Sometimes *mit'a* service could also provide a means of improving one's status or at least a way to obtain valued commodities. People performing outstanding service, such as being part of a victorious army, were often rewarded with cloth and other goods. Although the *mit'a* service was a form of coerced labor, the Incas were clever enough to protect their assets by not overburdening their workers and by rewarding them through this form of asymmetrical reciprocity. The underlying ideology was that of a reciprocal exchange. The state provided for the worker in exchange for the labor the worker gave the state. The state reaped the added bonus of keeping idle hands too busy to contemplate revolts (Cobo 1979: 231–234; Rowe 1946: 267–268).

## REFERENCES

Cobo, Bernabé. 1979 [1653]. *History of the Inca Empire: An Account of the Indians' Customs and their Origin Together with a Treatise on Inca Legends, History, and Social Institutions.* Translated and edited by Roland Hamilton. Austin: University of Texas Press.

Isbell, William H. 1978. "Environmental Perturbations and the Origin of the Andean State." In *Social Archaeology: Beyond Subsistence and Dating,* edited by C. Redman et al., 303–313. New York: Academic.

Moseley, Michael. 1992. *The Incas and Their Ancestors.* New York: Thames and Hudson.

Murra, John V. 1964. "Una apreciación etnológica de la Visita." In *Visita hecha a la Provincia de Chucuito por Garci Diez de San Miguel en el año 1567.* Documentos regionales para el etnología Andina I: 419–444. Lima: Casa de la Cultura.

———. 1972. "El 'control vertical' de un máximo de pisos ecológicos en la economía de las sociedades andinas." In *Visita de la Provincia de León de Huánuco en 1562, Iñigo Ortiz de Zúñiga, visitador,* vol. 2, edited by John V. Murra, 427–476. Huánuco, Peru: Universidad Nacional Hermilio Valdizán.

———. 1980. *The Economic Organization of the Inca State.* Greenwich, CT: JAI.

Rostworowski de Diez Canseco, Maria. 1999. *History of the Inca Realm.* Translated by Harry B. Iceland. Cambridge: Cambridge University Press.

Rowe, John H. 1944. "An Introduction to the Archaeology of Cuzco." *Papers of the Peabody Museum of American Archaeology and Ethnology,* vol. 27, no. 2. Cambridge, MA: Harvard University Press.

———. 1946. "Inca Culture at the Time of the Spanish Conquest." In *Handbook of South American Indians,* edited by Julian Steward, Bureau of American Ethnology, bulletin 143, vol. 2, 183–330. Washington, DC: Smithsonian Institution.

CHAPTER 6

# Social Organization and Social Structure

The empire over which the Incas ruled was composed of dozens if not hundreds of different ethnic and tribal groups, many with distinct languages. Of all these peoples, only a very few were considered to actually be Incas, since membership in the Inca caste was based on blood relationships. The Incas are believed to have been a very small group; estimates of their numbers range from 15,000 (Brundage 1967: 30–32) to 40,000 (Moseley 1992: 9). It was this small group of kindred that ruled over the much larger population of the empire.

The empire itself was divided into four parts called *suyus* in Quechua, and the name given to the empire as a whole by the Incas was Tawantinsuyu, meaning "four parts together" but often translated by writers as "The Land of Four Quarters." Each *suyu* was subdivided into a number of provinces. Census records for the empire were compiled by province and *suyu*.

## ESTIMATING THE POPULATION OF THE INCA EMPIRE

Determining the number of people populating the various provinces subject to the Inca Empire before the Spanish Conquest is extremely difficult for a number of reasons. While the Incas kept very careful and exact census records for their empire, the figures were kept on perishable media, such as the famous knotted cord system called the *quipu*. Even if the recording device itself survived, it could not be read without the knowledge of its contents and the intent of its original makers. The huge number of deaths resulting from the European plagues, the Inca civil war, and the Spanish Conquest caused a demographic collapse in the Andes of startling proportions. So many people died that the preconquest population could not be easily or reliably estimated from the numbers of survivors. Numerous attempts have been made to reconstruct the population figures for the Inca Empire, but the results have varied widely.

### Inca Census Records

In his account of the Incas, Pedro de Cieza de León (1959: 177–178) records with much admiration how the Incas kept records of their population. Each province was required to give an annual report of births and deaths and an account of the numbers of individuals available for certain kinds of tasks. For the empire to run efficiently, it was necessary for the rulers to know how many

A *quipu*, the knotted cord device used by the Incas for keeping accounts.
(Werner Forman/Corbis)

taxpayers there were, the number of able-bodied men available for military service, and the numbers of children and elderly. All of this information was recorded on the knotted cords of the *quipu* and carried from the provinces to the capital. The *quipu*, however, could only be read by someone who knew what it contained and to what its different cords and knots referred. With the deaths of so many, the knowledge of how to interpret individual *quipus* was lost forever. There is no surviving record of how many people the Incas counted in their empire.

## Modern Population Estimates

Modern scholars have used a variety of methods to estimate the population of the Inca Empire. In his book on the demographic collapse of the conquest-era Peruvian population, Noble David Cook (1981) explores these methodologies, which have included evaluations of the numbers of people that the land could support, archaeological studies, depopulation ratio studies, estimates based on social organization, models based on disease mortality, and projections based on census data taken after the conquest.

The ecological model for determining population uses studies of the carrying capacity of the land of ancient Peru. This approach can determine the maximum potential size of the population based on how much food could be produced. However, in order to make that determination, detailed knowledge of the ecosystems and the amount of land involved is required. For highland Peru, this information is only slowly becoming available. Using what data he had, Cook (1981: 108) estimated a total population of 13.3 million persons as the maximum supportable population of the Inca realm.

Archaeologists have had little success in attempting to estimate the population of the Inca Empire. The field of Andean archaeology is too new and too few areas are known well enough to draw any reliable conclusions.

Estimates of the population based on depopulation ratios have been used by a number of scholars in the twentieth century. This methodology is based on sampling areas where there exists some information on the size of the preconquest population that can be compared with Spanish census data taken after the conquest. A ratio of change can be established and applied to the whole of the area.

Perhaps the most influential use of this methodology was the study done by John Rowe (1946: 184–185). Rowe found that there were estimates of the preconquest populations for only five provinces: Rimac, Chincha, Yauyos, Huancas, and Soras. These estimates were based on a variety of information preserved in the Spanish chronicles and could be compared to the figures for these provinces from the census of 1571 taken by the Spaniards. From this, Rowe derived a 4:1 ratio of change, which led him to calculate a total population for the Inca Empire of about 6 million people.

Another attempt at determining a depopulation ratio was made by Henry Dobyns (1966), which yielded a very different result. Using information from the entire Western Hemisphere, not just the Andean region, he calculated a ratio for depopulation of 25:1. This yielded a population estimate of 37.5 million for the preconquest Andean area.

Falling between these two extremes, two other scholars derived different and sometimes multiple ratios for differing parts of the Andean area. They used the same basic methodology comparing preconquest estimates and postconquest Spanish census data. C. T. Smith (1970: 456–459) calculated a population of a little over 12 million people for the Andean region. Nathan Wachtel (1977: 89–90) calculated approximately 10 million inhabitants. All of these studies have been criticized as being imprecise for methodological reasons. It is clear that there is no general agreement in numbers produced by this methodology.

Since the Incas organized their population in decimal units for the purposes of administration, another approach to estimating population consisted of determining how many people these decimal units contained and adding them together to arrive at the total. Philip Ainsworth Means (1931: 296) concluded that each of the four quarters, or *suyus*, of the empire contained at least twenty provinces, each with populations between 200,000 and 400,000 people. Adding them all together, he estimated the total population for the Inca Empire at 16 million to 32 million people. This estimate requires that an exact number of people remain constant in each administrative unit. Cook (1981: 57–58) has observed that it would have been exceedingly difficult in practice for the Inca to have maintained these constant numbers. Because of variations in births, deaths, and population densities by region, constant shifting of populations would have been required in order to keep all units with uniform numbers. It is likely that the system employed by the Incas was idealized at certain decimal figures, but in reality there was probably much variation.

Modern epidemiology has allowed scholars to devise yet another means of estimating pre-Columbian populations for Peru. Models based on the mortality rate of the epidemic diseases brought by the Europeans to the Americas can provide a basis for calculating the preconquest population. The difficulty with this approach is that all of the variables cannot be controlled. Accurate data on sixteenth-century mortality rates for specific diseases is not available for Peru, nor are there data reflecting evolutionary changes in either the humans or the disease that would alter the rates of death and resistance. The estimates produced by Cook using this methodology and acknowledging its limitations range from 3.25 million to 8 million people (Cook 1981: 59–74).

Cook, in his study of the population issue, finally suggests that the most reliable calculation of the ancient population of Peru can be achieved by using mathematical formulas that have been constructed to project census figures from years in which a census was conducted to years in which a count was not made. This method makes use of the census data from the early Spanish colonial period to derive rates of change that can be projected backward in time to the late Inca period. He projects the population to have been between 4 million and 14 million people for the year 1520 (Cook 1981: 75–107).

Given the complexity of the population problem and the limitations of all the methodologies used by various scholars, it seems unlikely that we shall ever be able to determine an accurate population figure. Nevertheless, these attempts have helped narrow the range of estimates. Most modern Inca scholars seem to accept and work with figures ranging between 6 million and 14 million people.

## THE SOCIAL ORGANIZATION OF INCA CIVILIZATION

At the local level Andean society was fundamentally kin based and typically organized under a hereditary ruler called a *curaca*. Each polity was organized into two parts, upper and lower halves, with a *curaca* presiding over each half, or moiety. Thus there would be dual *curacas* over every political division. One of these two paired hereditary rulers always took precedence over the other and was the highest authority. In turn, each of these officers had an assistant, so there were actually four officers governing each group. This dual organization principle was characteristic of all Andean institutions. Over this structure the Incas imposed a strict system of stratified classes. The local *curacas* varied in terms of their power and prestige depending on the size of the groups over which they ruled, and this dictated their rank within the Inca system. They were considered to be nobles by the Incas, were incorporated into the imperial class system, and usually continued in the offices they held prior to the Inca conquest in order to manage their traditional groups.

### The *Ayllu*

In the Inca world, the vast majority of people lived in small communities widely scattered over the landscape. Individuals living in these communities were organized into extended kin groups called *ayllus*. The term *ayllu* is a bit confusing, since the Spanish sources use it to describe a number of different-sized social units, from a single lineage to a grouping of several extended families or even moieties. *Ayllus* were named entities and were in theory kin groups descending through the male line that practiced endogamy (marriage only within the group). The *ayllu* collectively owned a specific territory and water rights and annually redistributed the land among the membership on the basis of need. The binding tie among the people of the *ayllu* was their theoretical common descent from a mythical ancestor who originally was granted ownership of the land and water by supernatural powers at the moment of the creation of the world. *Ayllu* members had a large number of reciprocal obligations to each other, which provided the impetus for cooperation in tasks requiring collective action, such as plowing, harvesting, and building and maintenance projects. This obligation for labor exchange is referred to as *ayni* in Quechua. A parallel concept is *mink'a*, which refers to calling upon exchange partners to perform labor that is owed. *Ayllus* also provided work groups for the lands of the local *curaca* and the labor tax of the Inca rulers and state religion (Rowe 1946: 253–255). A province, community, or town (called a *llacta* in Quechua) would be composed of a number of *ayllus*. These would ideally be divided into groupings called *saya* and often, but not always, followed a moiety organizational system that grouped them in pairs. Thus many Andean communities, including Cuzco, were composed of two parts: Hanansaya, the upper moiety, and Hurinsaya, the lower moiety (Rowe 1946: 255–256). All classes, including the royalty, maintained this *ayllu* structure and were divided into *saya*.

## THE SYSTEM OF SOCIAL CLASSES

The empire of the Incas contained a rigid class structure consisting of a division between rulers and the ruled. Upward mobility was extremely difficult. The system of social classes was strictly maintained and privileges and outward signs of status were jealously guarded through sumptuary laws. The

classes were (1) commoners, (2) *curacas*, who ruled directly over the commoners, and (3) noble (*hahua*) Incas and royal (*capac*) Incas, who ruled the empire.
There were additionally special classes of people called *yanacona, aclla, camayos,* and *mitimas.*

### The Common People

The great masses of people in the Inca empire were commoners with little
wealth and almost no political power. They subsisted primarily as farmers and
herders. They were referred to as the *runakuna* (people), and the heads of their
households, upon marriage, were called *hatun runa* ("big man"). These *hatun
runa* were responsible for their households and were the basic taxpaying unit.
They were the principal source of labor and wealth production for the state. As
such, their value was keenly felt by their lords and rulers, who made sure that
they were well kept. Commoners had few rights or privileges, but the Inca
government made sure that they were efficiently governed and cared for by
their *curacas.* All major decisions in the lives of commoners were made by their
overlords. Commoners were even forbidden to look at the highest-ranking Incas and were not allowed to leave their home communities or enter major
towns or cities without special permission. Inspections were made by the authorities to ensure that commoners did not own gold or silver, had no more
than ten head of livestock, and were not wearing valuable clothing. The people
were told what to eat and whom to marry, and they did not even control the
lives of their children (Cobo 1979: 239–243).

### *Curacas*

The *curaca* class was a lower, provincial nobility made up of all of the administrative officials charged with governing a hundred or more people in the decimal administrative system. This class was hereditary and so passed on to succeeding generations. Hereditary rulers of groups conquered by the Incas were
admitted to this class. The *curacas'* job was to govern and administer the people under them, making sure that all of the rules of the Inca state were followed and enforced. Besides performing administrative duties, *curacas* acted
as judges for all kinds of trials and disputes that fell within their jurisdiction.
The privileges enjoyed by the *curacas* included exemption from taxation, a
paid salary, assigned servants based on the number of subjects ruled, and the
right to be carried in a hammock or litter. They could also be rewarded for outstanding service with secondary wives, lands, animals, fine cloth, and gold or
silver objects (Cobo 1979: 198–202, 208–210; Rowe 1946: 261).

### Hahua Incas and Capac Incas

The meaning of the term "Inca" was never completely understood by the
Spaniards. They often supposed it to be a title, like the word "king." It may
have been an ancient title handed down from previous generations. It is curious that the term is first used by the sixth ruler, Inca Roca, and so may have
been introduced during his reign. It is also possible that it was a family or personal name that came to mean "ruler" in much the same way that Julius Cae-
sar's last name came to mean a Roman ruler.

The Incas themselves were divided into two classes based on blood and privilege. The emperor and other royalty came from a class of people related by blood called Capac Incas. *Capac* is a term of great honor whose meaning is somewhat unclear. The chronicler Juan de Betanzos (1996: 123) states that *capac* is a title higher than a king. However, the term was also applied to foreign kings of various groups that the Incas fought and conquered (see Julien 2000: 23–48 for detailed discussion of *capac* status and its meaning). The Capac Incas were a class of people related by blood who were believed to have descended from the Inca founder Manco Capac. These were the pure ethnic Incas, and as such, they held all of the highest posts in the empire. The males wore insignia consisting of very large ear ornaments called earplugs placed in the lobes of their pierced ears. They also wore their hair very short.

As the empire rapidly expanded, beginning with the reign and conquests of Pachacuti, there soon were not enough Incas to fill all of the critical posts in the government. In order to solve this problem, Pachacuti decided to make Incas out of all of the nearest neighboring groups to Cuzco who spoke Quechua. These were known as the Hahua ("outer") Incas. They are also referred to as Incas by privilege or adoption. These groups were organized into ten *ayllus* based in Cuzco; half of the group was assigned to Hanan (upper) Cuzco and the other half assigned to Hurin (lower) Cuzco. They were also granted the right to wear the large earplugs marking them as Incas. Both kinds of Incas were referred to as *pacayoc,* meaning "those with earplugs." The Spaniards referred to them as *orejones,* meaning "big ears." The principal difference in privileges between these two groups was that only Capac Incas could become emperor and rule the land (Rowe 1946: 261).

### The Sapa Inca

At the apex of this system stood the emperor who came from the Capac Inca line. As a direct descendant of Manco Capac, he held ultimate authority in the empire. He was also a son of the sun god Inti and therefore semidivine. The title Sapa Inca set him apart from the other royal Incas and meant "unique or only" Inca. The emperor is reported to have carried himself with great dignity. He spoke in low tones, was carried in an elaborate litter, and held court from behind a screen of cloth. No one was allowed to look him in the face, and all those approaching him on business, even nobles, had to remove their shoes and carry a token burden on their backs. He was constantly attended by serving women and enjoyed the greatest of luxury in all things. Like the nobles, he had one principal wife and numerous secondary wives and concubines. In the later reigns, it was the custom to have the emperor marry a full sister in order to keep the Capac Inca bloodline intact (Cieza de León 1959: 185–187; Cobo 1979: 142, 244–250).

### The *Panacas*

The *panaca* was an institution peculiar to the royal Incas. It was composed of the descendants of a reigning emperor but excluded the ruler himself. In effect, the *panaca* formed a sort of royal *ayllu*. The purpose and function of this organization was to preserve and protect after his death the emperor's mummy and his *huaoque* image, which was a statue that could stand in for the Sapa Inca at ceremonies when the ruler needed to be elsewhere. The *panaca* was also responsible for preserving and celebrating his memory and the historical events of his reign in the form of oral histories and songs. The members of this organization made sure that the royal mummy was wined, dined, and kept comfortable and that he participated in the social life of the empire and expressed his opinions. The members of a *panaca* also acted as stewards of the palaces, royal estates, *yanacona,* and other sources of wealth accumulated by the emperor during his life. None of this wealth was passed on to the next ruler but was kept perpetually in the care of the *panaca.* These organizations formed the social elite of the aristocracy. They were extremely powerful politically on account of the wealth that they controlled as well as their blood ties to a ruler. Selection of a new emperor was negotiated among the *panacas,* and no emperor could effectively rule without their advice and consent.

By the time of the Spanish Conquest, there were eleven *panacas.* In a system of reverse seniority, the most important and powerful was that of the most recently deceased emperor. Each *panaca* was named and assigned to either Hanansaya or Hurinsaya of Cuzco.

## Yanacona

A special class of people outside of the normal hierarchy but still subject to the nobility was the *yanacona.* As Rowe (1982) indicates, the status of *yanacona* was never exactly understood by the Spaniards. They tended to classify them as servants, but they were not just ordinary servants. In fact, becoming a *yanacona* was one of the very few paths to upward mobility in the Inca Empire. *Yanacona* were recruited from the best and most able people in the provinces of the empire. They were assigned jobs and positions that required skill and ability and were sometimes of great importance. Some *yanacona* were even appointed to positions as *curacas.* Since *yanacona* operated outside of the reciprocal labor system, their labor could be used by the emperor without having to request it through their native lords, and no reciprocal obligation to these lords was therefore engendered. As a class they owed their loyalty to and received their support from individual nobles or emperors and sometimes were attached to institutions such as temples or royal estates. *Yanacona* severed all ties and reciprocal obligations to their native communities. They also received the privileges of exemption from taxes and the authority of their native *curaca,* and their children could inherit *yanacona* status (Rostworowski de Diez Canseco 1999: 176).

## Acllas

Another class operating outside of the regular social hierarchy were the so-called chosen women, or *acllas.* Each year the emperor sent out to the provinces royal inspectors called *apupanaca* to collect the tribute to be paid to the state in the form of young girls. From each village in each province the most beautiful young women between the ages of ten and twelve years were selected. Being selected was considered a great honor and represented a path of upward mobility in Inca society. These girls were taken to Cuzco and di-

Women in traditional ceremonial dress performing during a celebration of the Inca winter solstice festival, Inti Raymi. (Keren Su/Corbis)

vided into several classes based on their social standing, skills, and beauty before being assigned to the *aclla wasi* (house of chosen women) in Cuzco or the provinces.

The highest-ranking category consisted of young women of Inca blood who were consecrated to Inti, the sun god. These young women became virgins of the sun and were called *mamacona* or *yurac aclla*. They never married, and violation of their chastity would be punished by death. They were consecrated and sometimes married to one or another of the gods and spent their days tending the temples. The next-ranking class was called *huayrur aclla*. These were the most beautiful girls, and from this group were selected the secondary wives of the emperor. A third class of young women was called *paco aclla*. These girls were used by the emperor to reward *curacas* and other important officials with wives. The next class was called *yana aclla* and consisted of the least desirable girls, who became servants. One other class was called the *taqui aclla*; its members were selected for their talent in playing music and singing. Their job was to entertain at festivals and feasts of the royal court. Most *acllas*, when not engaged in special duties, spent their days weaving fine cloth and making *chicha* for use at court (Cobo 1990: 172–174; Rostworowski de Diez Canseco 1999: 176).

## Camayos

Specialists in management or in a particular trade (such as metalsmiths or potters) or in other skills (such as engineers) were classed as *camayos*. These people worked directly for a ruler or noble and, like the *yanacona*, were exempt from labor tax and service in the army and were also removed from the authority of their local lords. They were responsible only to the lord for whom they worked and moved to live in whatever place he directed (Rowe 1982: 102–105).

## Mitimas

The *mitimas* were family groups governed by their own ethnic leaders who were sent from their place of origin to another place in the empire to fulfill a specific mission. Although removed from their origin places, these people still maintained the reciprocal ties and obligations to their kinsmen in their home region. The tasks performed by the *mitimas* varied considerably. Some were sent as colonists to newly opened regions. Others were transplanted to areas needing a garrison or where the loyalty of the indigenous population was questionable. Still others might be sent to exploit a particular eco-zone and grow particular crops or work on a special construction project. Rebellious groups could also be sent away from their native land as punishment and moved into areas where they would be surrounded by people loyal to the state. It was possible to be both a *camayo* or a *yanacona* and a *mitima* at the same time (Rostworowski de Diez Canseco 1999: 173–174; Rowe 1982: 105–106).

## LIFE UNDER INCA RULE

The lives of the citizens of the Inca Empire were tightly controlled by the state. The people were not free to make their own life decisions, although those of the Inca class had more say than most in what happened to them. Much has been made of the Inca civilization's policy of taking care of its citizens. Some have argued that the Inca state represents a socialist empire (Baudin 1928). In fact, a better analogy would be that the state was like the farmer or herder who takes good care of the animals that provide his income. Commoners were taken care of out of practical necessity rather than benevolence. Unlike a socialist system, everything in the state was owned by the ruling Inca class.

## Age Grades

Society under the Incas was organized into a series of age grades. Membership in a particular grade indicated what tasks could be expected of the individual. The ability to work governed the assignment of grade and transition through the graded system rather than actual chronological age. The purpose of the grades was to give the government census takers an idea of the condition of their workforce and how much output could be expected, as well as the numbers of nonproductive citizens that would have to be supported. There were ten standardized and named age grades for each sex, which encompassed the whole life cycle, much as today we classify people as infant, child, adolescent, young adult, middle-aged, and so on (Huamán Poma de Ayala 1978: 54–59; Rowe 1946: 256, 1958: 514–516).

## The Life Cycle

In describing Inca culture, the Spanish sources often do not distinguish between the practices of the Incas themselves and the ordinary people. As mentioned earlier, the empire was composed of millions of people belonging to numerous tribes and ethnic groups, each of which had its own customs and practices. If the people in any particular place were observed by the Spanish chroniclers as doing something in a particular way, it could be attributed as standard practice to the whole population. Therefore, we must assume that the Inca rulers living in luxury did not behave exactly as the ordinary people did in many aspects of their lives and that there were some variations in practice among the various cultures incorporated into the empire.

**Birth and Childhood.** Bernabé Cobo tells that women gave birth unattended by midwives. Prayers asking for a successful delivery would be said by the expectant couple when the mother went into labor. After the birth, the mother went to the nearest stream and washed herself and the baby regardless of the weather or temperature. The child was then placed in a cradle, four days after birth, with no particular care given to keeping it clean (Cobo 1990: 200–201). Garcilaso de la Vega (1966: 212) describes rather rough treatment of babies, saying that they were deliberately left exposed to the dew and night air, washed in cold water, and never held by their mothers. The idea was to produce tough, strong individuals. It is difficult to reconcile this account with that of the Inca Pachacuti tenderly receiving the infant Huayna Capac and taking him in his arms as reported by Juan de Betanzos (1996: 122–123). The Incas no doubt loved their children as much as any other people. It seems likely that in response to the high infant mortality rates of ancient populations, there was a tendency to try not to become too attached to the infant until there was a reasonable expectation that the child would survive. This is perhaps reflected in the fact that children were not named until they were more than a year old and weaned from the mother's breast. On this occasion, the child's hair and finger-nails were cut for the first time in a ceremony called *rutuchicoy*. In this cere-mony, the child was given the name it would use until reaching maturity. Gifts were presented by the child's relatives, and a party was held (Cobo 1990: 201–202; Rowe 1946: 282).

**Puberty Rites.** Upon reaching the age of about fourteen, boys took part in a ceremony called *huarachicoy* that was held once a year during the December festival of Capac Raymi. The boys participated in many rituals, including llama sacrifices, dancing, drinking, and a foot race. They received their breech-clouts (*huara*) and weapons as well as their permanent names. Finally, after their ears were pierced to receive the ear-spool insignia of the Incas, the boys officially became warriors.

The equivalent ceremony for girls was called the *quicuchicoy* and was cele-brated at their first menstruation. After a three-day fast, the girl was washed by her mother and dressed in fine new clothes and sandals. Her relatives held a feast at which the girl was presented with gifts and received her permanent name from her most important uncle (Cobo 1990: 202–203).

These elaborate rites were held for the Inca class. Those of the common peo-ple would have been much less elaborate and would not have included the ear-piercing ceremony for the males.

**Kinship and Marriage.** The dual organization seen in other aspects of Inca culture also dominated kinship and relationships between males and females. Although males and females were viewed as complementary parts of a greater whole and had considerable equality in Inca culture, access to political power and natural resources were generally controlled by men. As with the moiety divisions of communities and the dualistic worldview of Andean peoples, males and females were essential complementary halves of a larger whole. However, one of the dual parts of every whole ranked higher than the other. In gender relations, men ranked higher than women.

Following this concept of balance and duality, kinship terminology was gen-erational and dependent on the sex of the person using it. A brother referring to his sister or a female cousin would use a different term (*pana*) than a woman would use in referring to her sister or female cousin (*ñaña*). A woman would call her brother or male cousin *tora*, and a man would call him *huaoqui*. Fathers and mothers used different terms to refer to their children (for a complete dis-cussion of Inca kinship terminology, see Rowe 1946: 249–252).

In the endogamous *ayllu*-based society, marriage had certain restrictions and strict rules regarding what would be considered incest. Commoners were al-lowed only one wife at a time, and this wife was decided upon and given by the state. An official of the state would travel through the provinces once each year and pair up all of the eligible young men and women. Commoner men could not take a wife of their own accord without the sanction of the state. The ideal was marriage within the *ayllu*, but certain restrictions were applied. Mar-riage and sexual relations were prohibited between anyone in a direct bloodline of descent, including between parents and children, grandparents and grandchildren, and brothers and sisters. The penalty for violation of the incest ban for all classes was death. The only exception that occurred was the practice instituted by Topa Inca of having the emperor marry his full sister. The incest ban did not, however, include first cousins. With permission of the authorities, it was apparently common for first cousins to marry.

Nobles were allowed to have more than one wife, and depending on their status, it could be a large number of wives. Of these, however, only one would be the principal or legitimate wife and the others were considered to be concubines. In the case of death of the legitimate wife, none of the concubines could rise to fill the position of principal wife but instead another principal wife would be given to the man. Although ranking men could gain additional wives as booty in war, more often they received them from the emperor as compensation for some service performed for the state.

Marriage ceremonies varied throughout the provinces of the empire. For the Incas in Cuzco, it is recorded that a solemn ceremony was performed only in the case of marriage to a principal wife. The groom and his family would go to the house of the bride's father and she would be given to him. As a token of the groom's acceptance of the bride as his wife, the groom would place on her right foot a sandal made of wool if she were a virgin and made of grass if she were not. He would then take her by the hand, and relatives from both families accompanied the couple to their new home. Once there, the bride presented the groom with a fine wool tunic and a headband with a metal ornament, which the groom immediately donned. Next the bride's female relatives lectured her on her duties as a wife, and the groom's male relations gave advice on his duties as husband. Gifts were then presented by members of both families and a celebratory feast was held (see Cobo 1990: 204–210, for a discussion of marriage customs).

**Adulthood and Old Age.** There is little information available about the lives of ordinary people in the Inca empire. With marriage, people became fully adult members of society. A man became a *hatun runa* and a taxpaying head of a household. With this social status came the obligation to perform labor tax and service in the military in addition to participating in the web of *ayni* obligations to relatives and community. Both men and women shared the labor in the agricultural fields jointly, participating in activities such as plowing and harvesting. During the agricultural dead season, between harvest and planting, men might go off to war or perform their labor taxation. Women sometimes accompanied their men in war in order to take care of them. Women also maintained the household, prepared the food, and looked after the children. As one got older and was less physically able, one shifted through age grades requiring less hard physical work. Finally, in extreme old age, no work was expected.

## Education and Training

For most citizens of the Inca Empire, there was no formal education. Children of commoners learned life skills by watching and helping their parents and other members of their families and communities. They also would have relied on family members to instruct them on the basics of religion and social behavior. All males were expected to render military service and would also have received basic training in weapons and fighting.

A more formal education was reserved for the upper classes. As Hiltunen has pointed out (1999: 90), upper-class men and women received higher education in different institutional settings. Women would have been formally educated in greater numbers than men because they received their training in the houses of the chosen women, or *aclla wasi*, of which there were possibly as many as forty throughout the empire. In these *aclla wasi*, the chosen women were educated in skills of weaving fine cloth used for the emperor's wardrobe and that of his wife. Fine cloth was also made by them to be used in sacrifices and for other state purposes. They were also trained in cooking and preparing the corn beer called *a'qa* (also known as *chicha*) for the royal household. In addition to practical skills, these women would have been schooled in the requirements of religious service for the temples (Cieza de León 1959: 146; Garcilaso de la Vega 1969: 195–203). It is most probable that upper-class women who were not *acllas* also received this type of training as well as lessons on deportment, etiquette, and social skills.

The formal education of **upper-class males** was said to take place in an institution located in Cuzco called the *yachaywasi*, or house of learning. There was only one of these schools serving a much smaller number of students than the *aclla wasi*. Entering the school at an age between eight and ten years, boys pursued a four-year curriculum, graduating just in time for their *huarachicoy* (coming-of-age) ceremony. The first year of study was devoted to the Quechua language. Oratory was prized by the Incas, and important men were expected to speak well. The second year was devoted to religious studies, and the third year to learning to tie and interpret the knotted cords of the *quipu* recording device. In the fourth year, Inca history was studied. The *yachaywasi* school was conducted by instructors who held the title of *amauta*, which means "wise man." Those who attended were the sons of Inca nobles and important provincial *curacas*. The purpose of this course of instruction was to teach practical skills of statecraft but also to indoctrinate the future leaders of the state with the official Inca ideology (Murua 1946: 169–170). Some scholars have speculated that the structure of this school was possibly more along the lines of an apprenticeship served until sufficient knowledge was acquired. The four-year curriculum sounds to some a bit too European in structure to be an accurate reflection of Inca practice (Rowe 1982: 95). In any case, the jobs for which the young nobles were being prepared were very complex and would have required considerable training.

## Social Expectations

Free will and independent thought were not encouraged by the Inca state. Andean culture in general relied on collective action and cooperation even at the household level. Everyone within the empire lived within a rigid set of expectations. Although the *curacas* and nobles had a greater degree of freedom of action than the commoners, it could be exercised only within specified limits. Even the emperor himself was expected to function within a certain set of norms, and his failure to comply could lead to mutinies or even his overthrow. One famous case involved the emperor Huayna Capac failing to uphold his obligation of reciprocal generosity with his army generals during the war against the Cayambis in Ecuador. Failing to receive the gifts and honors due them by custom, his generals in anger took their armies from the battlefield and returned to Cuzco. Only after receiving their due did they return to the field and fight under the command of the emperor (Rostworowski de Diez Canseco 1999: 44–45). The emperor Huascar's failure to observe established norms, particularly his interference in the cult of the mummies and the power of the *panacas* before and during the civil war with Atahuallpa, resulted in many defections from his cause and contributed greatly to his losing the war (Brundage 1967).

Achieving the status of *hatun runa* upon marriage brought numerous obligations to family, *ayllu*, and the state. To the family and *ayllu* were owed the labor of *ayni* and other reciprocal obligations of hospitality. To the state was owed military service, the working of state lands, and the *mit'a*, a fixed period of labor that was performed as the payment of tax. The welfare of the community exerted considerable social pressure on people to perform their obligations correctly. Strict account was maintained of labor owed, and sloth and laziness were not tolerated since the whole community could be affected. Society expected its citizens to be upstanding and moral, and it forbade lying, cheating, and stealing.

The nobility also carried numerous obligations but were exempt from paying labor taxes. Nobles were expected to display generosity to the commoners who labored under them. At a minimum, they provided food and drink, and other rewards were doled out as merited by individual cases. The nobles were also responsible for the welfare of the people serving under them and could be severely punished for failing to efficiently administer their populations. Although not required to pay taxes, nobles were obligated to the state in other ways. They served in the officer corps of the army in times of war or in other governmental posts where the empire needed their talents. Morality was said to be more strictly enforced for the upper classes (Rostworowski de Diez Canseco 1999: 150–154; Rowe 1946: 260–261).

## The Inca Legal System

Inca law was based on custom and tradition as well as the wishes of the emperor. There was no written code, but as with all important sets of information, the law was kept in memory aided by the use of *quipus*. In this system nobles were distinguished from commoners. Nobles received lesser punishments, since it was believed that they suffered greatly from the public humiliation of being even lightly punished. The emperor served as the supreme judge of the system. When he was present, cases were tried before him. Otherwise governors and *curacas* filled the role, their rank depending on the status of the litigants. Trials were held with witnesses confronting the accused, and arguments were heard regarding guilt or innocence. The judge then rendered his verdict and meted out punishment if the accused were to be found guilty.

Punishments were severe. The death penalty was prescribed for numerous offenses, especially killing, murder, and disobedience to the Inca. It was also used for traitors, men who violated the virgins of the sun, and those who destroyed state property. The death penalty was carried out in a variety of ways, including hanging by the feet, stoning, beating to death, or throwing the condemned off a cliff. The ultimate in capital punishment was inflicted for particularly heinous crimes such as treason or rebellion. The victim was thrown into an underground pit, called a *sankacancha*, containing pumas, bears, jaguars, or poisonous snakes.

The death penalty could be carried out only with the express permission of the Inca emperor. A *curaca* could not arbitrarily kill one of his subjects but had to ask permission of a higher authority. Without this permission, the *curaca* was punished with death, torture, or removal from office.

A lesser punishment called *hiwaya* was used in cases where death was not warranted on the first offense. It consisted of dropping a stone on a person's back from a height of about 1 meter. This could be fatal and even if survived was considered a severe public humiliation. Torture and banishment were also used on occasion. Someone who stole food out of necessity, however, was mildly punished on the first occasion, and the *curaca* responsible for him could be punished for not taking care of his people.

Although a few individuals seem to have been imprisoned, especially while awaiting trial or as prisoners of war, the Incas did not build large prison facilities. The *sankacancha* structures at Wimpillay and Arahuaya in Cuzco that are described by the Spanish as prisons seem to have been used as an extraordinary method of execution rather than for incarceration. Justice was swiftly meted out to the guilty, and the infliction of punishment did not disrupt the normal routine. Indeed, the justice system was so efficient that the Spaniards frequently remarked on the very low crime rate in the Inca Empire (Cobo 1979: 203–207; Rowe 1946: 271–272).

## INCA TOWNS AND CITIES

The Inca Empire contained numerous settlements of various sizes, ranging from those large enough to be called cities to small hamlets of a few houses. The bulk of the population was scattered across the landscape in small isolated hamlets that were located for the convenience of access to the agricultural fields. Larger accumulations of people resulted in areas where resources were concentrated. On the Pacific coast and the shores of Lake Titicaca, people lived in fishing villages. In some of the larger fertile valleys with expanses of good land, both in the coastal valleys and in the highlands, urban centers or towns developed and had existed for centuries before the Incas came on the scene. To these preexisting settlements the Incas added their own large urban centers. Throughout the Andes, most urban centers served as ceremonial centers and as residences for the ruling elite. Cities in the European sense as centers of

Pachacuti's royal estate at Machu Picchu. (Gordon F. McEwan)

trade and commerce did not exist. Inca imperial administrative centers were peculiar in that they were built to a master plan and served the sole function of administration. In places where centers already existed, the Incas would make use of what they could and add any additional structures and changes that they thought necessary. However, in some areas, there were no large urban centers to suit the Incas' purposes, so new cities were built from scratch. Many of these centers, since they had no other purpose except to serve the administrative needs of the Incas, were abandoned and depopulated following the Spanish Conquest.

Even the royal capital of Cuzco was not a city in the European sense. Instead, it served solely as a ceremonial center and place of elite residence for the nobility and royalty (Rowe 1967: 59–76).

One other type of settlement also deserves mention. These are the royal estates and the estates of the nobility that were scattered throughout the country. The most famous of these is the site of Machu Picchu, the so-called lost city of the Incas. In fact, it was neither a city nor lost. Instead it was a royal retreat for the Inca Pachacuti. These estates were designed to be relatively self-sufficient and were staffed by *yanacona* so that their owners did not have to repay agricultural labor with reciprocity. Not only did they provide a place of relaxation,

Urubamba River valley (The Sacred Valley of the Incas). (Gordon F. McEwan)

but they also generated agricultural and other types of wealth. It was not uncommon for an Inca ruler to own numerous estates, the favored locations being the so-called Sacred Valley of the Urubamba and other places near Cuzco.

## REFERENCES

Baudin, Louis. 1928. *L'Empire socialiste des Inka*. Paris: Institut d'Ethnologie.

Betanzos, Juan de. 1996. *Narrative of the Incas*. Translated and edited by Roland Hamilton and Dana Buchanan. Austin: University of Texas Press.

Brundage, Burr. 1967. *Lords of Cuzco: A History and Description of the Inca People in Their Final Days*. Norman: University of Oklahoma Press.

Cieza de León, Pedro de. 1959. *The Incas of Pedro de Cieza de León*. Translated by Harriet de Onis and edited by Victor W. von Hagen. Norman: University of Oklahoma Press.

Cobo, Bernabé. 1979. *History of the Inca Empire: An Account of the Indians' Customs and their Origin Together with a Treatise on Inca Legends, History, and Social Institutions*. Translated and edited by Roland Hamilton. Austin: University of Texas Press.

———. 1990. *Inca Religion and Customs*. Translated and edited by Roland Hamilton. Austin: University of Texas Press.

Cook, Noble David. 1981. *Demographic Collapse: Indian Peru, 1520–1620.* Cambridge: Cambridge University Press.

Dobyns, Henry F. 1966. "Estimating Aboriginal American Population: An Appraisal of Techniques with a New Hemispheric Estimate." *Current Anthropology* 7: 395–449.

Garcilaso de la Vega, El Inca. 1966. *Royal Commentaries of the Incas and General History of Peru, Parts One and Two.* Translated by Harold Livermore. Austin: University of Texas Press.

Hiltunen, Juha J. 1999. *Ancient Kings of Peru: The Reliability of the Chronicle of Fernando de Montesinos; Correlating the Dynasty Lists with Current Prehistoric Periodization in the Andes.* Helsinki: Suomen Historiallinen Seura.

Huamán Poma de Ayala, Don Felipe. 1978. *Letter to a King: A Peruvian Chief's Account of Life under the Incas and under Spanish Rule.* Translated by Christopher Dilke. New York: E. P. Dutton.

Julien, Catherine. 2000. *Reading Inca History.* Iowa City: University of Iowa Press.

Means, Philip Ainsworth. 1931. *Ancient Civilizations of the Andes.* New York: Scribner's.

Moseley, Michael. 1992. *The Incas and Their Ancestors.* New York: Thames and Hudson.

Murua, Martín de. 1946. *Los origines de los Inkas.* Lima: F. Loayza.

Rostworowski de Diez Canseco, Maria. 1999. *History of the Inca Realm.* Translated by Harry B. Iceland. Cambridge: Cambridge University Press.

Rowe, John H. 1946. "Inca Culture at the Time of the Spanish Conquest." In *Handbook of South American Indians,* edited by Julian Steward, Bureau of American Ethnology, bulletin 143, vol. 2, 183–330. Washington, DC: Smithsonian Institution.

———. 1967. "What Kind of Settlement Was Inca Cuzco?" *Ñawpa Pacha* 5: 59–77.

———. 1982. "Inca Policies and Institutions Relating to Cultural Unification." In *The Inca and Aztec States 1400–1800,* edited by G. Collier, R. Rosaldo and J. Wirth, 93–117. New York: Academic.

Smith, C. T. 1970. "Depopulation of the Central Andes in the 16th Century." *Current Anthropology* 11: 453–464.

Wachtel, Nathan. 1977. *The Vision of the Vanquished.* Translated by B. Reynolds and S. Reynolds. New York: Barnes and Noble.

CHAPTER 7

# The Political Structure
# of the Inca State

The Inca nation, known by the Incas as Tawantinsuyu ("four parts to-gether"), can be described politically as an imperial state ruled by an ab-solute despot. States are internally specialized organizations having three or more decision-making levels within a centralized administrative hierarchy. The criteria used in anthropological definitions of the state commonly include the concentration of economic and political power, monopoly of force, organi-zation along political and territorial lines, and differential access to resources based on status (Adams 1966; Fried 1967; Service 1962; Wright and Johnson 1975: 267; Wright 1977). An empire is a type of state that exercises political and economic control over other polities throughout a broad geographic area, often through the use of force (Schreiber 1992: 3–6).

As is the case with Inca state ideology, archaeological evidence indicates that many elements of Inca political structure were the products of millennia of cul-tural experience stretching back to the founding of civilization in the Andes. The fundamental principles of Inca political structure are the same as those governing basic peasant social organizations in the Andes: the reciprocal obli-gations between the people, their basic social group (the *ayllu*), and their local lords. The empire of the Incas was erected on this ancient foundation of recip-rocal obligation.

## INCA GOVERNMENT

The Incas conceived of their empire as being composed of four areas that united physically at their capital Cuzco. Highways radiated outward from the central plaza of Cuzco connecting these four quarters of the Inca world. Al-though quite different in size, each of these four sections, called *suyus*, were conceptually equal. Viewed from Cuzco, to the northwest was Chinchaysuyu, to the northeast Antisuyu, to the southeast Collasuyu, and to the southwest was Contisuyu. Administrative organization of the empire was centered at Cuzco, where resided the head of state, the Sapa Inca, and the highest officials of the land.

Each of the *suyus* was in turn subdivided for the purposes of governance into numerous provinces called *wamani*. The composition of the Inca provinces is believed to have reflected to a large degree the pre-existing tribal and lin-guistic divisions in the Andes. No exact list of the Inca provinces has survived,

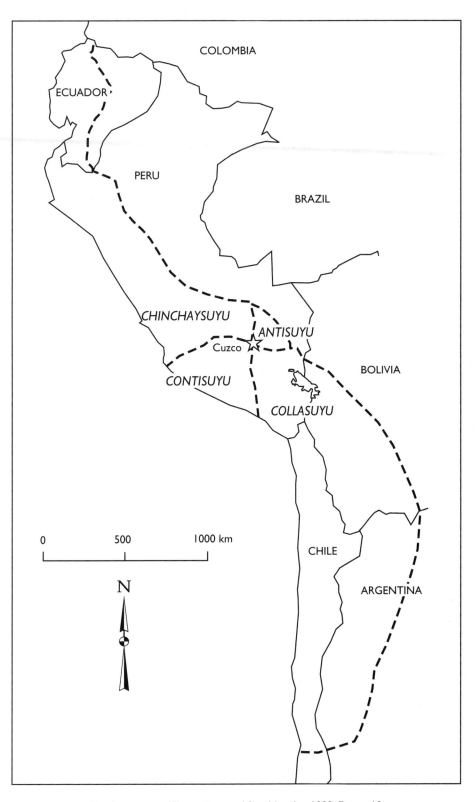

The four *suyus* of Tawantinsuyu. After Moseley 1992, Figure 10.

but John Rowe has been able to reconstruct an extensive partial list based on the early written sources. He identifies 48 provinces in the Andean highlands and 38 provinces on the coast (Rowe 1946: 185–192).

At the head of the state was the emperor, or Sapa Inca, who was, by the time of the Spanish Conquest, an absolute ruler and the ultimate authority, claiming a divine mandate to rule. Directly under the emperor and forming an advisory council were the governors of each of the four *suyus*, who were called *apu*. Individuals holding this rank would have been close relatives of the ruler, usually brothers, cousins, or uncles.

Each province within the *suyu* was headed by a governor called *tocricoq*. This governor was appointed on the basis of administrative ability and was almost always an ethnic Inca. The governor had broad powers in both judicial and administrative areas and was assisted by accountants called *quipocamayoc* and trusted officers called *michoq* (Rowe 1946: 262; Schaedel 1978: 300–306). The citizens of each province were required to wear a distinctive headdress and hairstyle so that they could be easily identified by the authorities (Cobo 1979: 196; Rowe 1946: 262).

Ideally each province was subdivided into two sections, or *saya*, reflecting the dual divisions of a moiety system. However, some provinces had such large populations that it was necessary to divide them into three *saya*, because no division should contain more than 10,000 taxpayers. Finally, the *saya* divisions themselves were divided into *ayllus* based on the existing kin-based *ayllus* of the inhabitants (Rowe 1946: 262–263).

## INCA DECIMAL ADMINISTRATION

One of the most famous aspects of the Inca Empire is its decimal organization of administration. Serving under the provincial governor were a hierarchy of administrators called *curacas*, whose status varied with the number of taxpayers for whom they were responsible. These offices were filled by the provincial nobility and were hereditary. The *hunu curaca* were responsible for 10,000 heads of households; *piska waranga curaca* were responsible for 5,000 heads of households; the *waranqa curaca* were responsible for 1,000 heads of households; the *pisca pachaca curaca* were responsible for 500 heads of households; and the *pachaca curaca* were responsible for 100 heads of households. Beneath these positions were two levels of nonhereditary officers: *pisqa chunca camayoc*, who were responsible for fifty heads of households, and *chunca camayoc*, who were responsible for ten heads of households. These numerical categories were idealized, since as a practical matter, it was extremely difficult to maintain a perfect numerical balance of the population in all provinces and at all times.

In addition to maintaining good order and Inca authority, the principal function of the provincial administration was to oversee the collection of taxes in the form of labor service. This decimal division of responsibility made it easier for the provincial governors to accurately record and efficiently distribute the exaction of labor.

One other class of government officials were the royal inspectors, known as *tocoyricoq*, which means "he who sees all." These inspectors were chosen from close family members of the ruler and traveled the empire checking on how well administrators were performing their jobs. Sometimes they would be sent anonymously or in secret so that the emperor could spy on his state officers (Rowe 1946: 264).

## ADMINISTRATIVE INFRASTRUCTURE

In order to expand the empire and to allow it to operate efficiently, the Incas had to build an enormous infrastructure. The most important elements of the infrastructure were the royal highways, administrative installations, storage facilities, terraforming, and hydraulic works. At the beginning of their expansion, the Incas had the use of some infrastructural elements left over from the previous empires of Wari and Tiwanaku. The Valley of Cuzco already contained an elaborate, well-engineered canal system, as did many other areas heavily occupied by the earlier empires. It is also apparent that the core of the highway system was already in place, since all of the major Wari administrative sites are located on the later Inca highway. This gave the Incas an advantage at the outset of their conquests, but they soon outstripped the existing facilities and had to expand the infrastructure as they conquered areas outside of the domain of the older empires.

### The Inca Highway

One of the most important elements in the success of the Inca Empire was the remarkable system of highways extending for at least 40,000 kilometers (Hyslop 1984: 224). For the empire to operate, it was essential to be able to move goods and people rapidly from place to place. An all-weather road was particularly important for the rapid movement of the army when it campaigned to expand the empire and when it needed to be moved to suppress rebellions. This system also served as a communications network linking all of the many provinces of the empire to a central command system.

The imperial highway system, called the Capac Ñan, comprised two main trunk roads that ran roughly north-south. One was the coastal route from Tumbes on the Peruvian north coast extending all the way south to Talca in modern Chile. The other was the highland route, which extended from Quito in modern Ecuador to Mendoza in modern Argentina. These two trunk roads were cross-connected by a network of shorter highways that linked all of the Inca provincial centers into one large system. Use of this highway system was restricted to those on official imperial business. Commoners were not allowed to travel on it without special permission.

The construction of the roads varied from place to place depending on the circumstances of the terrain. The width of the highway varied from 1 to 4 meters. The surface treatment ranged from fine paving stones on one extreme to natural dirt surfaces on the other, depending on the climate and terrain to be crossed. Because there were no wheeled vehicles, Inca roads often rose precipitously, climbing steep slopes with long flights of steps or making use of extensive switchbacks to gain altitude over relatively short distances. Where the ground was marshland or bog, the Inca engineers built raised causeways.

Inca paved highway near Machu Picchu. (Gordon F. McEwan)

Drainage was achieved through gutters and culverts, and often low walls delimited the margins of the road to keep it free of wind-borne sand and other obstacles (Hyslop 1984). Tunnels and retaining walls were frequent features of the road as it crossed steep and mountainous terrain.

Bridges were a vital part of the highway system, and without them, the highways would have been useless. In the steep canyons and rugged terrain of the Andes, rivers tend to be swift and very difficult to cross. Bridges of various

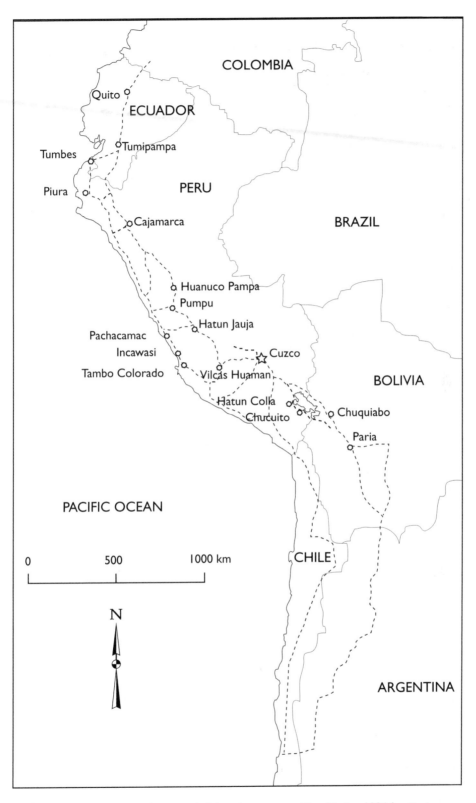

The Inca highway system and major administrative centers. After Hyslop 1984 frontispiece and Hyslop 1990 frontispiece.

An Inca suspension bridge. (Felipe Huamán Poma de Ayala)

types were constructed and carefully maintained by the Incas. The most famous are the suspension bridges constructed of rope that was made from *ichu*
grass. Bridges of this type were up to 20 meters long. These bridges required
specialists for their construction and maintenance and had to be reconstructed
on an annual basis. Usually near the crossing was a small community that had
the specific task of keeping the bridge. Bridges crossing shorter distances and
more placid waters could be made of pontoon rafts, wood beams, or even

stone slabs. One other method commonly used to cross rivers was a device called an *oroya*. This consisted of a basket suspended under a cable that spanned the river. A passenger sat in the basket and was pulled along the cable crossing the water. Construction and maintenance of the roads were the responsibility of the communities nearest where it passed. Each community was responsible for its segment of the highway as part of its labor tax, and in this way the work was distributed over a large segment of the population, with no one community being burdened with too much (Cobo 1994: 231–233).

An important feature of the royal road system was the presence of *tampu* stations, located approximately every 22 kilometers along the road. According to Cieza de León, the rate of travel for official parties of high rank that were not on urgent business was about 20 kilometers a day; the *tampu* were thus placed at intervals of about a day's travel. *Tampus* varied depending on their location, but all provided lodging, food, and supplies for those traveling on official business (Cieza de León 1957: 105). Thus anyone traveling the state highways was always provided for on their journey.

The Inca postal system was intimately tied to the highway system. Relay runners called *chasqui* were stationed along the road at intervals of about 1.4 kilometers. The swiftest-running young men from the nearest communities performed this duty as labor service and served a term of one month. They were stationed in pairs at small stone houses along the highway and took turns keeping watch for approaching messengers. A message could be relayed verbally or carried on a *quipu* passed from one runner to the next. Small amounts of goods could sometimes be carried, and it is said that the Sapa Inca could dine on fresh fish from the Pacific Ocean brought to him in less than two days (Cobo 1979: 228–230). The speed of this system has been estimated at about 240 kilometers a day (Rowe 1946: 231).

## Administrative Facilities

The Incas built provincial capitals throughout the empire that served as the local seats of government and religious centers. The governor and officials of the state religion resided there and conducted state business. Stored at these centers were huge quantities of food and material goods that were used in public ceremonies of reciprocity and also to supply the army when it passed through. Each of these centers was equipped with a stagelike platform structure, called an *ushnu*, which was situated in a large plaza. The *ushnu* and plaza provided a venue for conducting large-scale public ceremonies when the Inca emperor or other high officials were present. These settlements were named for the province in which they were located; the prefix Hatun was added to the province name. Thus, for example, the name of the capital of the Colla province was Hatun Colla.

The ceremonies of administration carried out in the provincial centers were larger versions of the reciprocal rituals of the local *curacas* and their subjects. In the early days of the empire, the ruler was required by the custom of reciprocity to formally request the aid of local *curacas* for whatever project he had in mind. This request took the form of elaborate feasts and entertainment accom-

A *chasqui* or runner in the Inca postal system. (Felipe Huamán Poma de Ayala)

panied by much drinking and the giving of fine presents. Only after a conspicuous show of generosity could the ruler make his formal request and expect it to be fulfilled. After receiving the food, drink, and gifts, the *curacas* were reciprocally obligated to lend their support to whatever the Inca ruler wanted done. As the empire expanded, this traditional exchange ceremonial became increasingly impractical. The Inca emperor found it impossible to meet with each local *curaca* in order to carry out the ritual obligations of feasting and drinking.

As the power and wealth of the empire increased, the Inca ruler could command rather than ask for aid from his subjects. Nevertheless, traditional practices had to be observed in order to cement the loyalty of the provincial lords to the emperor. To facilitate this problem, large regional administrative centers were built along the royal highway at Tumibamba, Cajamarca, Huánuco Pampa, Pumpu, Hatun Xauxa, and Vilcashuaman north of Cuzco. To the south of Cuzco were the great centers of Chucuito, Hatun Colla, Chuquiabo, and Paria. On the coast were the centers of Tambo Colorado and Incawasi. Ranking below these large administrative centers in the hierarchy were at least three other levels of smaller provincial centers.

These planned centers provided a place where large numbers of the regional lords could be convened in order to renew their reciprocal ties with the Inca ruler or his representatives. Not only was a suitable space required to hold this ceremony, but facilities were also needed for storing the massive quantities of gifts to be distributed. Facilities were also needed to produce maize beer, prepare food, and house those who did this work. The best known and most studied of these centers is at Huánuco Pampa in the north highlands. It consisted of more than 4,000 structures arranged around an immense plaza. The entire complex covered approximately 2 square kilometers. Located nearby on the hillsides to the south were more than 700 storage houses arranged in neat rows. These contained the vast quantities of goods needed for the displays of public generosity. This center could probably accommodate as many as 15,000 people at one time and rivaled the capital at Cuzco in terms of size. Because it was used only periodically, the permanent population was likely much smaller, with most people staying for relatively short visits to attend ceremonies and perform duties (Morris and Thompson 1985).

## State Storage Facilities

An important strategy used by the Incas to ensure the smooth operation of their empire was the concept of energy averaging (Isbell 1978). By storing surpluses, the state could average out the availability of food energy in years of meager production because of weather or pests. To average energy at the state level, a huge infrastructure of storage facilities was required. Each state administrative center was accompanied by a state storage facility. Storage centers were also constructed at state-owned farms, temples, and royal estates, as well as at each *tampu* along the royal highway.

Storehouses were called *qolqas* by the Incas and were built in a variety of styles and sizes. In his study of Inca state storage, Morris (1967) notes that *qolqas* varied in design by region and describes both circular and rectangular single-room freestanding stone buildings that were specially constructed for this purpose at major Inca centers at Huánuco Pampa and Jauja. Another kind of *qolqa* consisted of long, narrow stone buildings that were subdivided into smaller rooms by means of cross walls. This type of *qolqa* has been described at the royal estate of Ollantaytambo (Protzen 1993: 111–136) and at various locations around Cuzco (Kendall 1985; McEwan 1987; Niles 1999). Normally, *qolqas* were laid out in neat rows, with access lanes running between the rows. *Qolqas*

Inca storage structures, or *qolqa*, at the royal estate of Ollantaytambo. (Gordon F. McEwan)

were carefully sited on slopes in dry areas with good drainage that allowed the prevailing winds to blow through them, which helped to preserve any perishable contents from dampness. Goods were said to be stored for years at a time without damage.

The contents of the storehouses varied from region to region but included an amazing variety of products according to the Spanish chronicles. Agricultural surplus was one of the main commodities stored. Dried maize (corn), quinoa, *chuño* (freeze-dried potatoes), beans, other vegetables, and seeds were stored in mass quantities. Stores of clothing included tunics, blankets, shawls, and sandals of several types. Fine cloth, coarse cloth, bags, tents, and the raw materials for making cloth, such as wool, cotton, and feathers, were also stored in abundance. Metal objects, tools, and weapons were another class of stored commodities. Storerooms were filled with spears, slings, darts, clubs or maces, shields, and knives, as well as agricultural tools like hoes and *chaquitaqlla* (foot plows). Valuable items were also stored in great quantity, including gold and silver vessels and jewelry, beads, and shells (Cobo 1979: 218–222).

The capacity of the storage system was staggering. An estimate for the Mantaro Basin, which contained a major administrative center at Hatun Jauja, suggests that there were 2,753 *qolqa* in this area. Their capacity would have been around 170,000 cubic meters (Browman 1970; D'Altroy 1992, 2002: 281; Morris 1967).

Careful records were kept on the knotted cords of the *quipu* that could tell an Inca official at any time exactly how much of what commodity was stored in each of the storehouses. There records in turn would be sent to Cuzco so that the emperor could keep track of all of this wealth and have products moved from region to region depending on needs that arose.

## Terraforming and Hydraulic Works

Being agriculturally based, the Inca Empire invested heavily in farming infrastructure. In the steep Andes mountains, where good farming land was scarce, the Incas devoted huge amounts of energy and resources to create new fields through the construction of agricultural terraces. Building of these terraces required an extensive knowledge of civil and especially hydraulic engineering. Some of this technology may have been inherited from earlier cultures, but none of the earlier cultures seems to have built terraces on the huge scale of the Incas.

Terracing served a number of functions. It created new lands for agriculture, stabilized steep slopes and prevented erosion, and provided level ground on which to build. The Incas were not content, however, to simply make utilitarian terraces. Many of their most impressive terraced sites are works of landscape architecture famous throughout the world. Sites such as the royal estates of Machu Picchu, Chinchero, Pisac, and Ollantaytambo were all built on terraces, some of which seem to cling to impossibly steep hill sides. Cuzco itself and almost all major highland sites were heavily terraced, and some sites such as Amarupata in the Valley of Cuzco and Inti Pata near Machu Picchu consisted solely of elaborate terrace works.

Terracing was a very sophisticated technology. On the surface what is most visible are the stone retaining walls, but beneath and within their confines are elaborate foundations. Excavations at Machu Picchu have revealed how the terraces were made. After the retaining walls were constructed on sturdy foundations or bedrock, the terraces were filled first with a layer of medium gravel and then with a layer of fine sand and gravel. Finally, a cap layer of topsoil ranging from 50 centimeters to 1.5 meters thick was placed on top of the sand and gravel layer. The topsoil was carried up to the terraces from lower elevations such as river bottoms. The resulting terrace provided well-drained rich soil and a level surface for growing crops (Wright and Valencia 2000: 39, 47–52). One other aspect of the construction of the terraces was essential for growing frost-sensitive crops such as maize. The stone retaining walls absorbed heat from the sun during the day and radiated heat during the night. This could often be enough to prevent temperatures on the terraces from dropping below freezing.

In addition to good soil and sunlight, the other major requirement for growing crops was a reliable supply of water. In the high Andes, it is possible to farm

Inca terraces at Wiñay Wayna. (Gordon F. McEwan)

using rainwater alone, but the climate is such that rainfall is not consistent and reliable from year to year. To insure against weather fluctuation, the Incas watered many of their terraces through elaborate and sophisticated canal systems. Similar systems were used to supply fresh drinking water and to remove sewage and waste from major Inca settlements. Although there was abundant water in most highland rivers, the riverbeds are so steeply cut that it is impossible to channel water through canals, because the elevations where it is needed are much higher than the rivers. Water was generally collected from high-altitude springs and channeled through stone-lined canals. The canals brought the water at a controlled flow rate to the fields or other locations where it was needed. Reservoirs were built to control and store water in the hydraulic systems. Often these canals carried water for many kilometers passing over very large stone aqueducts as they crossed the steep Andean terrain. Water for daily human needs was accessed by means of stone fountains connecting to the canal system. These were often beautifully carved stones set up to make a water jet and cache basin surrounded by low stone walls. The jetting stream of water could be used to fill jars and other containers, while the basin provided water for washing. Not only did the water systems have utilitarian functions, they were an important aesthetic element in Inca landscaping and site planning.

Stone Retaining Wall
with 5% Batter

Zone A - Soil

Zone B - Fine Sand &
Gravel

Zone C - Medium
Gravel

*The agricultural terraces were constructed to provide good subsurface drainage. Much of the rainfall percolated downward to the permeable zones beneath.*

A cross section of a terrace. (Kenneth R. Wright and Alfredo Valencia Zegarra, *Machu Picchu: A Civil Engineering Marvel,* American Society of Civil Engineers, 2000)

Inca fountain at Ollantaytambo. (Gordon F. McEwan)

Inca aqueduct at the site of Tipon. (Gordon F. McEwan)

In addition to terracing and building canals, the Inca undertook other major civil engineering projects. Rivers were canalized by constructing stone banks that straightened and controlled meandering or braided rivers and prevented flooding. This allowed the opening of great tracts of bottomlands for agriculture. An impressive example of this technique can be seen in the Urubamba Valley between Pisac and Ollantaytambo.

## THE INCA ARMY

As an empire based on conquest, the Inca state depended on its military power for its very existence. Warfare was a primary occupation for both the ruler and the highest-ranking nobility. All young Inca males were trained in the military arts as part of their basic education. Each ruler was expected to expand the empire and demonstrate success in war as evidence of his fitness to rule. A second motivation for war resulted from the system of split inheritance that applied to the royal succession. When a new Sapa Inca was crowned, he inherited only the office and titles. His predecessor, although deceased, retained all of the wealth acquired during his reign, which was controlled and managed by his *panaca*. The mummified former emperors continued to live in their palaces, enjoy their numerous estates, and participate in Inca political life. To successfully carry out his reign, the new emperor had no choice but to expand the empire in order to generate the wealth necessary for him to exercise power (Conrad 1981). One other consideration was that by constantly expanding the frontiers by conquest, the ruler could keep his most dangerous internal opponents occupied and at a distance from Cuzco. Generals in the Inca army came from the ranks of the highest-status male Incas: the emperor's brothers, uncles, and sons. These were all people who might have a legitimate claim to the throne and who were therefore potential rivals. Sending them out on campaign was a double-edged sword, since their successes on the frontier might also embolden them to revolt. In one famous case, the Inca Pachacuti executed his general Capac Yupanki because his successes were so great as to threaten the power of the throne (Rowe 1946: 206).

## Size and Organization

The size of the Inca armies was astonishing even by modern standards. Sources disagree on exact numbers, but all agree that armies numbering between 35,000 and 140,000 men were raised on various occasions, with several large armies being in the field at once. Maneuvering a body of men this large requires phenomenal organizational ability, especially in the area of logistics. Raising such large numbers of men without seriously disrupting the rest of Inca society and the economy required extreme care in planning. The highest-ranking officers of Inca armies were more or less professional soldiers and came from the ranks of the Incas themselves. All generals and top commanders were Capac Incas or Hahua Incas, who as such held the ruler's confidence. Lower-ranking officers would have been drawn from the traditional tribal *curacas*. The fighting men were drawn from the masses of the *hatun runa* and participated as part of their labor tax obligation. They were provided only with food, clothing, and arms as payment. In order to keep production stable while so many men were occupied on military campaigns, only a few men from each *ayllu* were drafted so that their kinsmen could easily work their lands for them in their absence. On long campaigns, personnel could be rotated to spread the hardship more evenly (Cobo 1990: 215).

Within the army, divisions of different sizes were organized based on ethnic origins. Men speaking the same language and sharing the same cultural background served together in the same units. The organization of the different-sized divisions within the army more or less paralleled the social organization governing taxpayers. The commanders of these units were referred to by the number of men under them. Groups of ten men were formed under an officer called *chunca camayoc*. Groups of fifty were led by *pisca chunca camayoc*. Leaders of 100 men we called *pachaca camayoc*, and leaders of 1,000 were *waranqa camayoc*. An *apu*, assisted by an *apuratin*, led 2,500 men, and a *hatun apu*, assisted by a *hatun apuratin*, led 5,000. The largest division was 10,000 men, commanded by a *hunu curaca*. Above this level were the army commanders. Typically there were dual commanders. The commander of a field army was called *apusquipay* and was assisted by a deputy commander *apusquipratin*. This dual command was in keeping with the logic of the division of Inca society into *saya* of *hanan* and *hurin*.

One other division of the army that was of paramount importance to the ruler was the emperor's personal guard. This was a body of men numbering perhaps 5,000 that was made up of ethnic Incas highly skilled in the arts of war. These Inca troops were in later reigns supplemented by soldiers from groups who had resisted the Incas' advance most fiercely and won their respect. Inca Huascar, for example, used Cañari and Chachapoya soldiers in his bodyguard. When on campaign, the emperor was always surrounded by these heavily armed highly trained troops. Units were placed in marching order depending on their reliability and how long they had been under Inca dominance. Troops from the most recent conquests were placed in the front of the line at the greatest distance from the Inca ruler (D'Altroy 2002: 219; Espinosa Soriano 1980: 175; Heath 1999: 89).

Discipline within the Inca armies was said to be very strict. Movement was exclusively on foot except for the highest-ranking generals and the emperor, who were carried in litters. On the march the men were kept in ranks and closely supervised. Looting, pillaging, and straggling were not tolerated. Cowardice or flinching in the face of the enemy could be punished by death (Hemming 1970: 35; Rowe 1946: 278).

## Weapons, Equipment, and Logistics

Inca armies employed a variety of weapons for both long-range and hand-to-hand fighting. Since they did not employ heavy artillery of any sort or use siege engines, all of their weaponry could be classed as light armaments. The choice of weapons for any particular unit was based on the traditions of the ethnic group of which it was comprised. Cobo (1994: 218) recounts that there were whole units equipped with a single type of weapon; thus there were squadrons of archers, slingers, spearmen, and so on.

For long-range combat a variety of weapons was available. Slings were perhaps the most common. These were made of wool, grass rope, or leather and could be used to fire a stone about the size of a hen's egg with great accuracy. Bows and arrows were used by some units, and others used spear throwers and darts. At a somewhat closer range, bolas were used to entangle the legs and feet of the enemy. Bolas consisted of several weights of stone or metal that were attached to individual cords. All of the cords were tied together at their ends and the whole device was spun and thrown in such a way as to wrap around feet and legs of the target. Another tactic was to throw or roll stones down from a high position onto attackers.

For close-quarters combat, the preferred weapon was a short club called a *champi*, about 60 centimeters to 1 meter long with a heavy weight on one end. This type of weapon has been called the star-headed mace, since the weights of bronze or stone were shaped like doughnuts with five or six projecting knobs on their perimeter, making them resemble an asterisk or star shape. Another type of club, called a *macana*, was made of the very hard wood of the *chonta* palm. This weapon was shaped like a sword, was about 1.2 meters long, and had a maximum width of 10 centimeters. Its edges were sharpened, and it was wielded with two hands like a European broadsword. Battle-axes, axe-mace combinations like European halberds, and spears with metal points were also used in hand-to-hand fighting.

The battle equipment of Inca soldiers included more than weapons. Soldiers wore tunics and sandals much like their everyday wear. A type of armor was made from quilted cotton and by wrapping lengths of cloth around the body to help absorb blows. On their backs, warriors wore small round shields made of woven palm-wood slats and cotton. They also carried a larger rectangular shield that was covered with decorated cloth that extended below the shield itself as a banner. The soldiers' heads were protected with helmets of wood or plaited canes that were strong enough to withstand heavy blows from an opponent's weapon. Over their defensive armor, the soldiers wore their finest clothing and ornaments, such as they wore on holidays and festivals. Depending on the status of the warrior, metal discs about 15 centimeters in diameter called *canipu* were worn. Made of copper, gold, or silver, these were worn on both the front and the back of the tunic as a military decoration indicative of skill and bravery. Knees and ankles were also decorated with colorful fringes tied around the legs (Cobo 1990: 215–219; Rowe 1946: 274–276).

The art of military logistics was highly developed in the tightly organized Inca Empire. In order to move and supply such large armies, the Incas provided for enormous caches of food and weapons to be stored at key administrative centers and at *tampu* along the royal highway. This allowed the army to move without having to carry all of its supplies and provided spares and replacements as necessary. Large quantities of weapons, tunics, helmets, sandals, tents, and foodstuffs were stored. Most important, this system allowed the army to be fed without placing any burden on the provinces through which it moved. Unlike contemporary European armies that lived off the land and often despoiled even their own territory, Inca armies did no damage to the landscape, towns, or facilities that they passed.

Once the army left the borders of the empire and began a war of expansion, it was supplied by llama trains and large groups of human porters as well as any food that it might capture. The peoople drafted to this duty were required to carry for only a fixed distance and were rotated frequently so as to spread the burden evenly. Inca armies also moved with many camp followers. Individual soldiers had wives or relatives accompany them to look after them and, more important, to care for them if they should be wounded or become ill (Cobo 1990: 217–219; Murra 1980: 46–48, 76, 102).

## Diplomacy, Strategy, and Tactics

This primary strategic aim of the Incas in using their army was to avoid battle by intimidating their foe into surrender. Considering that what the empire gained from conquest was access to labor to work new lands, it was ultimately inefficient and impractical to kill large numbers of those who would otherwise be paying labor tax and to have the empire's own soldiers killed as well. Moreover, it would be expensive in the long run to have to coerce cooperation at the point of a spear. In view of this, the imperial policy was to first attempt a diplo-matic approach to incorporating new areas into the empire. The preferred method was to march a large and formidable army to the enemy's doorstep. Once there, the Incas sent emissaries to present rich gifts and explain how the empire worked and what its benefits were and to invite voluntary submission. At the same time, an assessment would be made of the enemy's strength and what allies they might have. Emissaries could also be sent to any potential al-lies of the targeted group with bribes to keep them from coming to their aid. This technique very often worked, and when it did, the native rulers of the new province were confirmed in place, given more great gifts, and treated with respect by the Incas. Food, flocks of camelids, clothing, or anything else needed would be immediately provided to the province in great quantity. The populace was ordered to worship the sun god Inti but allowed to keep its own native religion. The native rulers were ordered to follow Inca laws and cus-toms and to learn to speak Quechua (Cieza de León 1959: 158–161).

An alternative approach was to make an example of a strong local group to demonstrate Inca power to others. In the territory around Lake Titicaca to the south of Cuzco, there were two large and powerful kingdoms called the Collas and the Lupacas. The emperor Pachacuti took his army to confront the Collas and defeated them in a pitched battle that resulted in many Colla casualties. As a consequence, the Lupacas voluntarily joined the Inca Empire, and the In-cas did not have to fight them (Cobo 1979: 140).

When diplomacy failed, the Incas resorted to force. In planning a campaign, the most successful generals would be consulted for advice. Sacrifices would be made and omens read. If the emperor was to accompany the army an Itu ceremony of human sacrifice would be held, with its associated fasting and sacrifices. The basic military doctrine seems to have been to hit the enemy with an overwhelming force of numbers in bold assaults. Pitched battles involved wholesale assaults on massed enemy formations or assaults on fixed fortified positions. Tactics included false retreats to lure the enemy onto favorable ground, use of grass fires or deliberate flooding to move opposing troops into a killing zone, ambushes, and dawn assaults. Siege tactics were also employed against fortified positions. Battles normally began with the armies drawn up opposing each other. Insults were exchanged with much boasting in an at-tempt to demoralize the enemy. Long-range weapons would be first em-ployed, opening the way for the massed troops to advance. Inca troops ad-vanced together with their sacred *huaca* named Huanacauri, the patron of the Inca army, as well as with images of the sun and other major deities. Once bat-tle was joined, the Inca formations lost all cohesion, and the battle became a contest of individual combats with clubs and spears. Because of the noise and confusion of the battle, it became impossible to maneuver troops as a unit once they became engaged. It is likely that the deciding factor was mostly a matter of weight of numbers. Whichever side could inflict the greatest number of ca-sualties in the shortest time and shock the enemy into retreating won. Losses on both sides could be extremely heavy (Cobo 1990: 74, 215–219; Heath 1999: 89–90; Hemming 1970: 94; Rowe 1946: 274–282).

## Victory Celebrations

Upon the successful conclusion of a military campaign, formal triumphal ceremonies were held at Cuzco. Captured enemy generals and other prisoners were brought to the capital along with the most impressive spoils of war and paraded through the streets. The emperor formally received these in a public ceremony at the temple of the sun in which both the prisoners and the loot were placed on the ground, where he symbolically walked over them, treading on the necks of the defeated enemy leaders. This gesture sealed the victory. The prisoners were then executed, except for the common soldiers, who were sent back home to their native villages. The bodies of the defeated enemy generals and other important men killed in battle or afterward were made into grisly official war trophies. Some were skinned and made into drums, while others had their skulls lined with gold and fashioned into drinking cups. The collecting of heads of dead enemy warriors was a long-standing practice in almost all Andean cultures.

Rewards were given out to those who had performed with exceptional valor, and this provided one of the only means by which a common soldier could improve his status in life. The emperor gave rich gifts of cloth and decorative plates of gold and silver to be worn as battle decorations. Soldiers were also allowed to keep any women that they had captured during the campaign. Individuals worthy of special recognition might even be promoted to some official position in the government structure and be permitted to hand this position down to their descendants. Nobles who were singled out for outstanding performance were rewarded with gifts of cloth and precious metal ornaments, *acllas* given to them as wives, promotions, and privileges, including the right to be carried in a litter or hammock, use a parasol, or sit upon a stool (Rowe 1946: 279–280).

## SOCIAL ENGINEERING AND THE DISPOSITION OF CONQUERED TERRITORIES

Once diplomacy or, failing that, the army had done its work of conquest, the new territory was grafted onto the empire. The first step in this process involved taking a census of the population and making a survey of the new lands. The survey information was recorded on clay relief maps showing features such as the topography, locations of arable land, water sources, and human settlements. This information was sent back to Cuzco together with the report of the local commander.

In Cuzco the emperor and his advisors studied this information and decided how to organize the new territory. A site was selected for the new provincial capital, and the population was concentrated in towns near their fields, where it would be easier to supervise and control them. An Inca governor was appointed and positions in the administrative hierarchy were filled with both talented local people and specialists brought in from other areas of the empire. Local chiefs were confirmed in office and admitted to the *curaca* class at the level corresponding to their preconquest authority. All government officers were required to learn to speak the Inca language, Quechua. The entire population was divided into the standard system of dual divisions called *sayas* employed throughout the empire.

Two kinds of hostages were taken to Cuzco from the new province. One consisted of the sons of the native *curacas*, who were held to ensure the good behavior of their kin. These young men were taken to Cuzco to be schooled at the *yachaywasi* and indoctrinated with Inca ideology and customs. They would later in life inherit their fathers' positions as imperial officers. The other type of hostages consisted of the most important portable *huacas* of the conquered province. These were taken to Cuzco together with their priests and set up in appropriate temples. Whenever people visited Cuzco from the province, they could worship their *huacas* and feel a psychological connection with the capital. The *huacas* also were held with the threat that any disobedience or revolt by their people would result in reprisals against the *huacas* or even their destruction.

Special attention was paid to integrating the newly conquered population into the Inca system. Inca dress was mandated for the population, but the original native headdress and distinctive hairstyle was retained and required to be worn as a badge of ethnic identity. Social-engineering techniques were applied to secure the new territories' loyalty. The most resistant groups in the population were made into *mitimas* and removed physically to far-distant parts of the empire. Six to seven thousand families comprising entire communities or even ethnicities were moved and embedded in small groups in locations where the climatic conditions were similar to what they had known before, but the native population surrounding them was foreign and loyal to the empire. *Mitima* groups of loyal peoples were also moved into the areas vacated by those previously moved out. These served to provide a loyal population core for the new province and provided a military garrison that could also keep an eye on the rest of the population of the new province. As a result of these policies, large portions of the population of the Andes were relocated during the reign of the Incas, and old alliances and affiliations were broken down (Cobo 1979: 189–202; Rowe 1946: 272–273).

Inca policy on land use was designed to provide self-sufficiency for the common people and to generate wealth for the state. The people were allowed to use the products of the land, but ownership remained with the Inca emperor. All of the lands of the new province were reorganized by the imperial government, and boundary markers were set. The lands were divided into three parts: one part belonged to the Inca state, a second part was set aside to support religion, and a third part was set aside to support the native inhabitants. This division into three parts was not necessarily equal but depended on the density of the population and the needs of the state. The people of the province were to be self-sufficient through use of their part of the lands. Although ownership of this portion of the land was still retained by the government, the people had rights to what could be produced on it. These rights were held collectively and were redistributed annually based on the needs of individual *ayllus* and families. The people were also expected to work the lands of the church and state as part of their payment of labor tax, but all of the products of these lands belonged to the government.

The herds of llamas and alpacas and pasturage for these animals were also divided into three parts. The largest of these were the parts given to the state and to the church. The part reserved for the people was smaller and provided just enough wool and meat to satisfy their needs (Cobo 1979: 211–218; Rowe 1946: 265–267).

## POLITICAL RELATIONS BETWEEN THE INCAS AND THEIR SUBJECTS

In their relations with conquered peoples, the Inca policy was paternalistic and relied on a carrot-and-stick approach. The psychological underpinning of the state structure was the concept of reciprocal kin-based obligations. The emperor pretended to practice on a large scale the same sets of obligations experienced and recognized by the local *ayllus*. Therefore, the relationship between the ruler and his officials and the ruled was essentially that of a parent and child. Although the Inca ruler had the absolute power to take what he wanted, it was always politely asked for in the guise of kin-based reciprocity. *Curacas* had no power to say no to any request but were well rewarded for their cooperation. In this way, the transactions were veiled in a cloak of family ties and obligations. While a provincial *curaca* might not like his subordinate status in the empire, it was made palatable by the generosity of those he was forced to serve. Failure to obey and cooperate could have devastating consequences not only for the *curaca* but also for his people.

Despite the welfare cocoon provided by the Inca state and the fearful sanctions applied against those who rejected it, the Inca Empire was plagued with revolts. Having expanded so rapidly, the empire had had little time to consolidate its rule and to develop a real sense of integration of the people of the provinces. Their loyalty lay with their own *ayllus* and ethnic lords and not with the Inca state. Rebellions were frequent, bloody, and sometimes long-lived. This instability was the greatest weakness of the Inca Empire and probably accounts for the rapid success of the Spanish conquerors when the Europeans finally made contact.

From the earliest days of the empire, when Pachacuti was defending Cuzco against the Chanca invasion, ethnic groups allied with the Incas revolted at every opportunity. Especially troublesome were the peoples of Collasuyu to the south of Cuzco. Pachacuti had to conquer this region three separate times. His successor Topa Inca also had to deal with a revolt there but finally succeeded in integrating the region firmly into the empire. Another dangerous revolt broke out during the reign of Huayna Capac among the Chimu on the north coast, who had previously had an empire large enough to rival the early Inca expansion. The Incas finally overcame this rebellion, but ever after the Chimu were forbidden to carry weapons and were not used as soldiers in the Inca army. Huayna Capac also suffered a series of revolts and very stiff resistance during his campaigns in northern Peru and Ecuador.

One serious consequence of the vast size of the Inca Empire was that when the emperor and army were away on the frontier fighting to expand the state, as was Huayna Capac during most of his reign, the peoples at the opposite ends of the empire saw an opportunity to rebel. After all, their chances of success would seem much greater if the Inca army was thousands of kilometers away. As the Inca moved their army to put down the rebellion, it simply opened another apparent opportunity in the region that they had just left (Rostworowski de Diez Canseco 1999: 86–91).

## INTERNAL POLITICS AMONG THE INCAS

Another source of instability for the Inca Empire was the internal politics of the Inca caste itself. Constant plots, intrigues, and internal revolts plagued the Capac Incas. This was largely engendered by the ancient tension between Hanan and Hurin Cuzco and by the poorly defined rules of succession to the state's highest office.

Although the Capac Incas were essentially one extended kindred, there were numerous factions among them organized along the lines of the *ayllus* and *panacas* of Cuzco. Each of these groups was self-sustaining in terms of wealth and had members occupying important and powerful posts in the government and army. Although the Sapa Inca, the emperor, had absolute power in theory, he was in reality dependant upon support from a majority of these factions.

The greatest cause of infighting was the confused system of succession to the imperial crown. Unlike the European tradition of passing the crown to the oldest son of the reigning monarch, in Inca tradition the crown passed to the male of the royal bloodline who was judged by his peers to be the most able leader. The new ruler was in effect elected by his fellow Capac Incas. Because of the policy of the Incas that allowed them to take multiple wives, there was a numerous supply of men at any one time who were eligible by blood to ascend to the throne. A serious problem was that there were no clear legally encoded criteria for judging ability, and election to the highest office depended as much on political intrigues among the various Inca factions as on any other factor. Numerous disputes arose over election results, with some even leading to revolts and coups. Civil wars over the succession, such as that between Huascar and Atahuallpa just before the Spanish Conquest, were a frequent feature of the succession struggles. Emperors Capac Yupanki and Yahuar Huacac seem to have been assassinated while in office. Rulers Tarco Huaman and Inca Urcon were overthrown by their successors and written out of official Inca history. In an effort to prevent strife over the succession, some emperors appointed their heirs while still alive. These designated heirs were in some cases given coregency, the most notable being Topa Inca serving with his father, Pachacuti. This served as on-the-job training and allowed them to build up their own factions before the time came to ascend the throne. These efforts were not always successful, however. Designated heirs such as Quispe Yupanki, the son of Capac Yupanki, and Pahuac Gualpa, the heir of Yahuar

Huacac, were both assassinated by opposing factions (Rostworowski de Diez Canseco 1999: 97–110).

## REFERENCES

Adams, Robert McCormack. 1966. *The Evolution of Urban Society*. Chicago: Aldine.

Browman, David L. 1970. "Early Peruvian Peasants: The Culture History of a Central Highlands Valley." Ph.D. dissertation, Harvard University.

Cieza de León, Pedro de. 1959. *The Incas of Pedro de Cieza de León*. Translated by Harriet de Onis and edited by Victor W. von Hagen. Norman: University of Oklahoma Press.

Cobo, Bernabé. 1979. *History of the Inca Empire: An Account of the Indians' Customs and their Origin Together with a Treatise on Inca Legends, History, and Social Institutions*. Translated and edited by Roland Hamilton. Austin: University of Texas Press.

———. 1990. *Inca Religion and Customs*. Translated and edited by Roland Hamilton. Austin: University of Texas Press.

Conrad, Geoffrey W. 1981. "Cultural Materialism, Split Inheritance, and the Expansion of Ancient Peruvian Empires." *American Antiquity* 46: 3–26.

D'Altroy, Terrence. 1992. *Provincial Power in the Inka Empire*. Washington, DC: Smithsonian Institution.

———. 2002. *The Incas*. Oxford: Blackwell.

Espinosa Soriano, Waldemar. 1980. "Acerca de la historia militar Inca." *Allpanchis Phuturinqa* 14(16): 171–186.

Fried, Morton H. 1967. *The Evolution of Political Society: An Essay in Political Anthropology*. New York: Random House.

Heath, Ian. 1999. *The Armies of the Aztec and Inca Empires, Other Native Peoples of the Americas, and the Conquistadores 1450–1608*. Vol. 2, *Armies of the Sixteenth Century*. Guernsey, England: Foundry.

Hemming, John. 1970. *The Conquest of the Incas*. London: Macmillan.

Hyslop, John. 1984. *The Inca Road System*. New York: Academic.

Isbell, William H. 1978. "Environmental Perturbations and the Origin of the Andean State." In *Social Archaeology: Beyond Subsistence and Dating*, edited by C. Redman et al., 303–313. New York: Academic.

Kendall, Ann. 1985. *Aspects of Inca Architecture—Description, Function, and Chronology*. Oxford: British Archaeological Reports, International Series, no. 242.

McEwan, Gordon F. 1987. *The Middle Horizon in the Valley of Cuzco, Peru: The Impact of the Wari Occupation of Pikillacta in the Lucre Basin*. Oxford: British Archaeological Reports, International Series, S-372.

Morris, Craig. 1967. "Storage in Tawantinsuyu." Ph.D. dissertation, University of Chicago. Ann Arbor: University Microfilms.

Morris, Craig, and Donald E. Thompson. 1985. *Huanuco Pampa: An Inca City and Its Hinterland*. London: Thames and Hudson.

Murra, John V. 1980. *The Economic Organization of the Inca State*. Greenwich, CT: JAI.

Niles, Susan A. 1999. *The Shape of Inca History: Narrative and Architecture in an Andean Empire*. Iowa City: University of Iowa Press.

Protzen, Jean-Pierre. 1993. *Inca Architecture and Construction at Ollantaytambo*. Oxford: Oxford University Press.

Rostworowski de Diez Canseco, Maria. 1999. *History of the Inca Realm*. Translated by Harry B. Iceland. Cambridge: Cambridge University Press.

Rowe, John H. 1946. "Inca Culture at the Time of the Spanish Conquest." In *Handbook of*

*South American Indians,* edited by Julian Steward, Bureau of American Ethnology, bulletin 143, vol. 2, 183–330. Washington, DC: Smithsonian Institution.

Schaedel, Richard P. 1978. "Early State of the Incas." In *The Early State,* edited by Henri Claessen and Peter Skalnik, 289–320. The Hague: Mouton.

Schreiber, Katharina J. 1992. *Wari Imperialism in Middle Horizon Peru.* Anthropological Papers No. 87, University of Michigan. Ann Arbor: Museum of Anthropology.

Service, Elman. 1962. *Primitive Social Organization: An Evolutionary Perspective.* New York: Random House.

Wright, H. T. 1977. "Recent Research on the Origin of the State." *Annual Review of Anthropology* 6: 379–397.

Wright, H. T., and G. Johnson. 1975. "Population Exchange and Early State Formation in Southwestern Iran." *American Anthropologist* 77(2): 267–289.

Wright, Kenneth R., and Alfredo Valencia Z. 2000. *Machu Picchu: A Civil Engineering Marvel.* Reston VA: ASCE.

## CHAPTER 8
# Religion and Ideology

Inca religion was unusual in that it was inclusive rather than exclusive. Unlike the Catholic state religion of the Spanish Empire, which demanded wholesale conversion to Christianity and destruction of competing religions among its New World conquests, the Inca religion took a much more tolerant view. Peoples incorporated into the Inca Empire were allowed to keep their native religions as long as they were willing to also revere and honor the Inca gods. Sometimes the Incas would actually take the god or its idol and priests to reside in Cuzco, where it could serve as a hostage for the good behavior of its worshippers. In many cases the conquered peoples worshipped similar gods, if not the same ones with a different name. Thus the thunder god Thunupa from northern Bolivia was essentially the same being as the Inca thunder god Illapa. The greatest differences involved regional deities, who were not part of the official pantheon and held sway only in certain localities. There existed two basic categories of supernaturals: one was the official pantheon of the state religion that served to legitimize Inca rule and the other consisted of innumerable animistic spirits called *huacas,* which served as guardians of people, places, or things.

## ANDEAN COSMOLOGY

The Andean worldview in which the Incas participated was based on the principles of duality and reciprocity. The world was viewed as being balanced between a series of dual opposing forces. Contrasting forces encompassing such concepts as upper versus lower, light versus dark, wet versus dry, heat versus cold, male versus female, and so on, complemented each other, providing an equilibrium in which life could exist. This equilibrium was animated by reciprocal exchange between the active elements. Changes in state in the real world were the direct result of asymmetry in reciprocal relationships, an imbalance between the forces. Positive changes could be brought about by reciprocal exchange with the supernatural, such as offerings made by humans to a deity in exchange for that deity exercising its particular power for the benefits of those making the offering. Negative change could also be counteracted and the disequilibrium repaired through reciprocal exchange with the appropriate deities or supernaturals. The purpose of Andean religion was to delineate the basic divisions of the cosmos and maintain them in harmony through reciprocal exchange (Classen 1993: 11–12).

These principles were said to have been expressed in a cosmological model kept in the principal temple of the sun, the Coricancha, in Cuzco. In 1615 a native Andean author, Joan de Santacruz Pachacuti Yamqui, published a drawing representing what this model looked like. It depicts a series of oppositions: sky versus earth, sun versus moon, morning star versus evening star, summer versus winter, mother earth versus mother sea, man versus woman. Symbols of unification are also present, binding the whole together: a stellar cross, the human pair, and a great oval representing the creator Viracocha. The oval signifies Viracocha's power to transcend duality (Classen 1993: 21–22).

Inca cosmology also conceived of a cosmos divided into three parts: *hanaq pacha* (the world above), *kay pacha* (this world), and *ukhu pacha* (the world below). The Spanish compared these regions to the Christian concepts of heaven, earth, and hell, but apparently that was not their meaning to the Incas. The Incas expressed the belief that ordinary people went to *ukhu pacha* when they died regardless of their virtue unless they were sinful enough to be condemned to wander the earth as spirits. Members of the nobility were said to go to *hanaq pacha* after death regardless of their merits when alive. In both cases life seemed to continue much as it had on earth. There is also some evidence that there was a belief that the land of the dead was periodically bridged to the living world and that during these times communication was possible between the living and the dead (Sullivan 1996: 56–64). Our understanding of these concepts is greatly confused by the reporting of the Spanish chroniclers, whose understanding was so colored by their Christian beliefs.

As part of their cosmology, the Incas followed the practice of dividing time into ages. Each age ends with an event called a *pachacuti*, which can be translated as "cataclysm" or "world reversal." This concept had such an important place in Andean thought that the greatest of the Inca emperors adopted it as his name in order to signal his remaking the world anew. Scholars are divided about what constituted an "age" and whether or not the concept of several ages was introduced by the Spaniards, who had encountered it previously in Mexico, or if it was wholly a native Andean idea. The native chronicler Felipe Huamán Poma de Ayala (1978: 24–31) discusses four ages of man prior to the European Conquest. Other writers such as Cobo (1990: 11–18) report that Andean man was destroyed in the universal flood of the Bible, or as Betanzos (1996: 7–11) recounts, they were destroyed by the creator Viracocha as he made several false starts at creating men.

## INCA STATE IDEOLOGY

The religious beliefs and practices of the Incas and their ancestors, with their societies based primarily on farming and herding, were principally concerned with issues of land ownership and rights to its use, water-use rights, fertility of soils and animals, and abundance of water, crops, and herds. Archaeological evidence indicates that many elements of Inca ideology were the products of millennia of cultural experience stretching back to the founding of civilization in the Andes. Inca state ideology was simply the most recent interpretation and expression of widely held beliefs. The imperial ideology of the Inca was erected on this ancient foundation.

Although this underlying foundation was very conservative and ancient, the Inca expression of state ideology that rested on it could and did change at the whim of individual emperors, who also served as the head of the religious apparatus. Early rulers seemed especially concerned with establishing the predominance of the cult of Inti, the sun god. The Incas portrayed themselves as *Intip churin,* or "children of the sun," with a divine mission of conquest and subjugation. They were a special creation of Inti the sun and Viracocha the creator. The ruler was considered literally to be the son of the sun and therefore semidivine. His words and deeds were thus divinely inspired. So important was the state religion to the justification of Inca rule that the Inca Pachacuti is said to have completely reorganized its structure and to have placed himself at its head. Other Incas placed special importance on the cult of Viracocha. Viracocha Inca even adopted his name and constructed an enormous temple to him at the site of Raqchi in San Pedro de Cacha southeast of Cuzco. A certain tension resulted between adherents of these cults regarding the preeminence of their deities (Cobo 1990: 23).

## LOCAL-LEVEL IDEOLOGY

Two ancient and related religious themes dominated local-level Andean ideology at the time of the Incas: the cult of ancestor worship and the cult of water. These were the domains of animistic spirits, or *huacas,* rather than the formal pantheon of gods. As a matter of policy, the Incas manipulated and attempted to control both the worship of major deities and the worship of local-level spirits.

### Mummies, Ancestor Worship, and Kinship

One of the most unusual and perhaps most difficult features of Inca society to comprehend is the relationship of continuity between the living and the dead. In the Andean worldview, the dead exerted enormous influence and control over the actions of the living, and a reciprocal obligation existed between them to take care of each other. The living guarded, fed, and cared for the mummies of important dead ancestors. In return, the ancestors provided for the living in all essential ways but most especially in maintaining the access of the living to the land and water necessary to sustain life. As Gose (1993: 480) explains,

> The political structure of the Pre-Columbian Andes took form primarily around a system of sacred ancestral relics and origin points known generically as *huacas*. Each huaca defined a level of political organization that might nest into units of a higher order or subdivide into smaller groupings. Collectively they formed a segmentary hierarchy that transcended the boundaries of local ethnic polities and provided the basis for empire like that of the Incas. . . . these *huacas* were also the focus of local kinship relations and agrarian fertility rituals. The political structure that they articu-

lated therefore had a built-in concern for the metaphysical reproduction of human, animal, and plant life. Political power in the Pre-Columbian Andes was particularly bound up with attempts to control the flow of water across the frontier of life and death, resulting in no clear distinction between ritual and administration.

A *huaca* could take many different forms, but one of the most important was the form of ancestral mummies, called *mallqui* in the language of the Incas. These mummies were responsible for food, clothing, land tenure rights, health, fertility, and, most important, the water supply. Oracular advice was also provided by the mummies. Since the mummies in life had usually been political authorities, their influence on the people was understood in terms of rule (Gose 1993: 497).

The practice of mummification is ancient, was widespread in the Andes, and was not peculiar to the Incas. Inca mummies differ from those found in other parts of the world in that the intent was not to embalm the body and preserve it in a grave for some future resurrection but rather to preserve it so that the deceased could continue to function in society. Preparation of mummies varied considerably, but all were treated with reverence and respect. Not everyone was mummified; only those ancestors of special importance to the lineage were so preserved. The majority of the people, those without rank, were simply buried with a few grave goods.

Lower-ranking individuals might simply have their bodies dried and were then placed in a cave or a small, specially constructed house (*chullpa*) with an open door and free access that permitted visits by living relatives. It was also common to build walls with doors or windows across the front of shallow caves or cracks in a stone cliff as residences for the dead. The living members of the lineage would periodically visit the dead ancestor, bringing gifts of food, drink, clothing, or anything else the deceased might need for their comfort. Mummified ancestors were believed to bridge the gap between the natural and supernatural worlds and to have the ability to communicate between the realms. They were therefore consulted on all matters of importance to the family and could offer advice concerning marriages, illnesses and their causes, and how to deal with the present and the future. The mummy's most important function was to intervene in the spirit world in order to maintain the flow and abundance of water. In keeping with the Incas' notion of duality, opposition, and the natural balance of forces, mummies by virtue of being very dry were thought to attract water. If mummies were not kept comfortable and regularly fed, they might retaliate by ceasing to intercede with the supernatural and catastrophe could result.

At the highest levels of Inca society, the mummies of dead emperors were treated magnificently. Great efforts were made to preserve the body of the deceased. Internal organs were removed and placed in a special container and the body was dried until desiccated (Rowe 1946: 259). Once prepared, the mummy was dressed in fine clothing and installed in the palace it had occupied in life. It was in fact treated as if still alive. Mummies of dead Inca rulers continued to own all of the property and estates that they possessed in life.

A *chullpa* or burial tower in the Valley of Cuzco. (Gordon F. McEwan)

They were fed each day as if alive and provided with drink and entertainment. Mummies attended all important state ceremonies, visited and entertained relatives and friends, and were believed to enjoy all the best things as in life. A priest spoke for each of the mummies who were consulted on all important matters. Rites were conducted to "wine, dine, praise, and reassure the ancestors" (Salomon 1995: 323).

The place of each *ayllu* and each individual member of society in the larger social system was determined by descent from their founding ancestor. As a consequence, loss or destruction of the ancestral *huaca* was a very grave matter. Legitimacy of land and water rights could be lost and survival itself imperiled. Political power in society could be severely curtailed or extinguished by loss of the ancestors. Through conquest and holding hostage the *huacas*, including mummies, belonging to conquered peoples, the Incas maintained control. Physical control of the ancestors allowed the wielding of enormous social power.

Prestige and power could also be accrued through alliances with important and prestigious lineages. This could be accomplished through marriages, adoptions, or discovery of more ancient links to common ancestors or *huacas*. The establishment of kinship bonds engendered a set of reciprocal obligations and legitimized power relationships in a way that mere force of arms could not.

By manipulating this system at the state level, the Incas were able in many cases to achieve, through social coercion, the power to govern. By inserting themselves into the existing web of social relationships at the highest level, they would legitimize their rule as a natural consequence of divine order. Furthermore, the rulers would take upon themselves the responsibility for maintenance of the cycle of life in the Andes, including the all-important continuity of water supply.

Ultimately the pervasive power of the mummified Incas would contribute to the downfall of the empire. Dead Inca emperors owned vast amounts of land and wealth that were not passed on to the succeeding ruler but were in fact controlled by the *panaca*, or descent group, of each ruler. A newly crowned emperor inherited power and titles but not the wealth of his predecessors. As a result, he had to immediately set about new conquests as a means of generating his own wealth. As the empire expanded, this became an increasingly difficult problem. With all of the best land and resources near Cuzco already owned by former rulers, the emperor had to spend large amounts of time on campaigns far away from the Inca heartland.

### Water Ideology

The Inca reverence for water was strongly expressed in a water cult. Springs and rivers were regarded as sacred and animated by living spirits. The city of Cuzco itself was located between two rivers: the Saphi and the Tullu. These joined at the eastern limit of the city to form the Huatanay River. The places where rivers and streams joined were considered to be especially sacred places. An annual festival called Purapucyo was held at the point of confluence. Offerings of *chicha* (beer) were poured into the river so that its spirit might drink. Fine cloth and llamas were also given to the waters by burning them. The climax of the ceremony came with the release of a flood of water into the rivers from the reservoirs above the city. These torrents washed the ashes and remains of the sacrifices into the rivers and carried them away downstream.

It was also believed that the waters at the joining of two streams or rivers, called a *tincuy*, had special properties. People came to wash away sin and illness by bathing their faces in the water. Water was carried through the city by an elaborate canal and piping system with numerous fountains, where it could be accessed. Each fountain had a name and a guardian *huaca*, to whom prayers and supplications could be directed (Brundage 1967: 86–92).

## INCA STATE RELIGION

The state religion of the Incas was hierarchically organized in a fashion that roughly paralleled state political organization. The head of the religious apparatus was the ruler himself. Second to the Inca at the top of the hierarchy was the high priest or Villac Umu. This official oversaw the administration of the state religious apparatus and was usually a close relative and confidant of the Inca ruler. Below this official was an enormous hierarchy of priests, priestesses, and temples both in the capital of Cuzco and out in the provinces. The highest-ranking members of the clergy who presided over the most prestigious temples would have been of the highest nobility (Rowe 1946: 299).

Religious institutions were frequently endowed by the emperor with their own lands and wealth. As the empire expanded, land for support of the state religion was also taken from conquered provinces. Labor to work these fields was provided by local communities as part of their taxation. The income from these lands supported the priests and priestesses and provided for the goods, such as cloth, food, and llamas, needed for sacrifice during religious ceremonies. Some temples, such as the Coricancha, the principal temple of the sun in Cuzco, were enormously wealthy, and the buildings were partially sheathed in gold.

## Religious Practitioners

**Priests and *Mamacona*.** Priestly duties included taking care of the temples, serving the idols, and conducting the appropriate sacrifices and offering prayers. Priests also heard confession of sins and prescribed purification rituals. Certain priests spoke for the deities that they served, providing oracles and divinations. There were also considerable numbers of virgin women called *mamaconas* that lived a cloistered existence in houses called *aclla wasi*. These women were assigned to the temples of the major deities and spent their lives helping to take care of the temples while producing fine cloth, *chicha*, and other necessities for consumption by ritual. Some *mamaconas* as well as certain noble ladies became priestesses (Cobo 1990: 158–159, 172–174).

**Healers.**  Medicine was practiced in Inca culture by both men and women who were called either *camasca* or *soncoyoc* in Quechua. As with shamanistic practice throughout the Americas, healing required both practical and spiritual intervention. Knowledge of medicines and herbal remedies was combined with advice from the supernatural in order to effect a cure. Healers were well paid with food, cloth, and silver. Healers could also be involved in sorcery to the extent of having extensive knowledge of poisons and spells. Killing by means of witchcraft was a criminal offense and had to be practiced secretly (Cobo 1990: 165–167).

**Sorcerers.**  In Inca culture the signs were read before undertaking any activity, ranging from the mundane, such as building a house or planting a field, to the most important decisions, such as marriage or warfare. Men or women who were weak or elderly and could not support themselves by working could make a living as sorcerers. They required a sacrifice for their performance, which provided income for their sustenance. Their principal function was to read fortunes by casting lots. Most commonly this was done with grains of maize, beans, or pebbles of various colors. Another method used large spiders that were kept in jars for this purpose. When the jar was uncovered, the position of the spider's legs was observed. If all eight were visible, it was a good omen. If any one of its legs was pulled in to the body, it was considered a bad

A Peruvian shaman making a *pago*, or payment, to Pachamama in a manner similar to what the Incas would have done. (Mariana Bazo/Reuters/Corbis)

omen. Coca juice from chewed leaves would be spit into one's palm and two fingers dipped in it. The fingers were held up and if the juice ran equally down both it was a good omen. Still another method was to kill an animal, most commonly a llama, and remove the lungs. The lungs would be inflated by blowing into them and the marks of the veins visible would provide information for making a prediction (Cobo 1990: 160–163).

## The Inca Pantheon

Inca formal state religion emphasized ritual and hierarchical organization rather than mysticism and spirituality. As with many agriculturally based societies, the chief concern was food production and the health and well-being of people, animals, and plants (Rowe 1946: 293). A highly organized ritual calendar was observed, and the proper rites for the season and conditions were conducted. Fertility and water were of particular concern in the variable climate of the Andes. The Sapa Inca himself as a divine being could mediate with the gods of the state pantheon and ask for their aid. Principal gods and goddesses of the Inca pantheon included the following:

**Viracocha.** Viracocha (sometimes spelled Wiracocha) created all of the other gods, as well as men and animals, and so ruled them all. This greatest of the gods had no name but only a series of titles. These are most commonly given as Ilya-Tiqsi Viracocha Pachayacachiq, which in Quechua means "ancient foundation, lord, instructor of the world." The Spanish most commonly referred to him as Viracocha, using one of his titles as a name. The most important image of this god was in the Quishuarcancha temple in the city of Cuzco. There the Spanish conquistadores reported seeing a solid gold statue of a man about the size of a ten-year-old boy. The statue was of a standing figure with his right arm raised as if in command and the hand clenched except for the thumb and forefinger.

Viracocha was believed to have created humanity at the ancient site of Tiwanaku in Bolivia or on an island in Lake Titicaca near the border between modern Peru and Bolivia. After the creation he traveled through the Andes performing miracles and teaching people how to live. He is said to have appeared as an old man with a long beard wearing plain clothes and carrying a staff. People often didn't recognize him as a deity. Those who showed kindness to him were rewarded and those who did not he punished. When he arrived at Raqchi, in the district of San Pedro de Cacha, about 110 kilometers southeast of Cuzco, legends say that the people did not recognize him and treated him badly. In a demonstration of his identity and power, he called down fire from the heavens and burned the earth, causing the people to recognize him and to beg forgiveness of their creator. The Incas later erected the largest and greatest of his temples on the site of this miracle. Every place where Viracocha rested on his journey to the north became a shrine. A prominent shrine near Cuzco is Cerro Wiracochan, a mountain above the modern towns of Huaro and Urcos about 50 kilometers east of Cuzco. After journeying the length of the Andes, Viracocha finally set off across the Pacific Ocean, walking on the water, from a place near Manta on the coast of Ecuador. It was believed that he turned over the administration of his creations to the deities of the Inca pantheon and to the *huacas* or natural spirits. After the creation he was no longer seen as taking an active role in the affairs of men (Cobo 1990: 22–24; 1979: 134–135; Rowe 1946: 315–316; Sarmiento de Gamboa 1999: 27–36). The term Viracocha also came to be applied to Europeans by the natives of the Andes. It is still used today as the common Quechua name for foreigners and people of the upper classes (Cobo 1979: 8).

**Inti.** The Incas' special patron deity, Inti the sun god was the most important servant of the creator and was believed to be the divine ancestor of the Inca dynasty. The Incas referred to themselves as *Intip churin,* which means "children of the sun." The sun was conceptualized as male and was represented by an idol in the form of a golden disk with a human face with rays emanating from it. The sun idol was kept in the temples of the sun throughout the empire,

Bolivian Aymara Indians give an offering to "Pachamama." (Reuters/David Mercado/Corbis)

the most important being the Coricancha temple at Cuzco. The sun was believed to protect and mature the agricultural crops vitally important to a farming-based economy. Priests of the sun were chosen exclusively from the *ayllu* of Tarpuntay, and the name of this lineage became synonymous with the priesthood (Cobo 1990: 25–28, 158–159).

**Illapa.** The Inca thunder god was believed to control the weather. The Incas prayed to Illapa for rain and protection from drought. He was envisioned as a warrior in the sky who held a sling and was dressed in shining garments. The lightning was believed to be the flashing of his clothing and the thunder was the crack of his sling. His sling stone was the lightning bolt that broke his sister's water jug, causing the rain to fall (Cobo 1990: 32–33). In a land of frequent drought, where all depended on agriculture to sustain them, the god of rain was of paramount importance.

**Pachamama.** Pachamama was the earth-mother goddess of the Incas. *Pacha* means "earth" (as well as time and space) and *mama* was a title or honorific meaning, more or less, "lady." An agricultural deity, she was worshipped with regard to fertility and the protection of the crops (Cobo 1990: 34). Little is known of the specifics of her cult as practiced by the Incas, but it seemed to have much in common with earth-mother cults around the world. The cult of the Virgin Mary introduced by the Catholic Spaniards had, in the minds of the Incas, a close affinity to that of Pachamama. Today the earth mother is still revered often in the guise of the cult of the Virgin. It is still customary in the Andes when drinking *chicha* to pour a small portion on the ground as an offering to Pachamama.

**Pachacamac.** A creator deity in the ancient Andean pantheon, Pachacamac translates from Quechua as "creator of the earth." *Pacha* means "earth, time, and space" and *camac* is "one who makes or creates." Pachacamac was a pre-Inca deity of enormous prestige dating back at least as early as the Middle Horizon (circa A.D. 540–900). The principal shrine to Pachacamac was a large complex of adobe buildings and pyramids located on a hill above the shore of the Pacific Ocean at the mouth of the Lurin Valley, just to the south of the modern city of Lima. This shrine was one of the most sacred places in all of the Andes. Pilgrims came from everywhere to visit the shrine and to receive prophecies from its oracle. Some important people were also brought there for burial. The Spanish described the shrine as a small, dark chamber on top of a pyramid that contained a wooden idol smeared with the blood of offerings. In order to approach the idol, the supplicant had to be purified through fasts and rituals, which were reputed to last a whole year. Admittance had to be gained through three successive precincts of the temple before one could approach the inner sanctum. Even there the idol was addressed through the priestly intermediary, and the Spanish report that even the priests were very much afraid of the idol. The cult of Pachacamac was administered by a large and highly organized priesthood that established branch oracles in other parts of the country. Even though Pachacamac was not an Inca god and seemed to have been redundant to Viracocha, the Incas nevertheless co-opted this cult into the imperial religion and enlarged and embellished the shrine, eager to share in the prestige of the cult. The temple of Pachacamac was visited by Hernando Pizarro, brother of Francisco and one of the first conquerors, in January 1533. He and his companions observed the cult, questioned the priests, and finally overthrew the idol in front of the shocked natives (Cobo 1990: 85–90; Hemming 1970: 62–63).

**Mamaquilla.** The Inca name for the moon, Mamaquilla in the Quechua language means "Lady Moon," and she was believed to be a goddess and wife of the sun. The moon was used to measure time and to regulate the timing of certain festivals. Her idol, a large silver disk, was kept in the temples of the sun throughout the empire along with the other members of the Inca pantheon (Cobo 1990: 29–31; Rowe 1946: 295).

**Mamacocha.** Mamacocha translates from Quechua as "Lady Sea." The Incas revered the Pacific Ocean as a goddess. Streams and springs throughout the land were considered to be daughters of the sea and were venerated and given offerings of shells, which were thought to be pleasing to them (Cobo 1990: 33–34).

**Stellar Deities.** Stellar deities were common in Inca belief, and stars and constellations were considered to be the special patrons of certain animals or activities. Chuquichinchay was a star thought to be the patron of mountain lions or pumas and could be appealed to for protection from these beasts. Llamas and alpacas were thought to be protected by the constellation Urcuchillay, which is known to Western astronomers as Lira. The constellation known today as the Pleiades was called Qolqa, or "granary," by the Incas. It was believed to influence success in agriculture. The chroniclers allude to a great many more stars of importance but give few details (Cobo 1990: 30–31; Rowe 1946: 295).

### Acts of Worship and Devotion

The Spanish sources expressed amazement at how religious and devoted the Incas were to their native deities. To Spanish eyes, the Incas and their subjects were the most religious people they had ever encountered.

**Gestures.** When addressing the gods or an emperor, a gesture called the *mocha* was performed. In this gesture, the arms were held parallel outward from the body with the palms of the hands facing outward and the head and torso lowered in a solemn bow while making a kissing or smacking noise with the lips. The hands were then brought to the mouth and the fingertips were kissed. When passing a shrine or *huaca*, a quid of chewed coca or maize was tossed at the sacred object as an offering. When drinking *chicha*, one would dip a finger into the liquid and flick the drops toward the sun or earth. Sometimes a small portion of the drink would be poured on the ground for Pachamama (Cobo 1990: 118–119; Rowe 1946: 301). It was customary when approaching an idol or *huaca* or entering a temple to remove one's shoes; noble Incas would remove their earplugs. Coca was chewed to purify the worshipper and a large quid of leaves was held in the cheek. Inca figurines also seem to show a position assumed for prayer in which the hands are laid on the chest with elbows tightly flexed, perhaps analogous to the Christian practice of holding or folding the hands together in front of the body.

**Prayer.** Incas prayed both silently and aloud, and prayers could be quite elaborate. Some prayers were formalized and preserved by tradition, being passed from parents to children. Other prayers were made up to suit the occasion. Prayers could be directed at both the formal pantheon of major gods and the innumerable *huacas*.

**Rites.** Inca ritual behavior also included rites of fasting, confession of sins, and doing penance. Various fasts could be observed depending on the occasion. Light fasting meant giving up salt, chili pepper, or other minor dietary changes. A more serious fast would involve abstention from *chicha*, meat, and

A group of Quechua women at the market in Urcos, Peru, enjoy a glass of *chicha*. *Chicha* is a popular regional drink made from fermented corn. (Robert van der Hilst/Corbis)

sexual relations for a period of time. Confessions were made aloud to priests and priestesses of the *huacas,* except by the Inca caste, who confessed silently and privately to the sun. After confession, ritual bathing cleansed the person from their sins. Sins were understood to be misbehavior such as lawbreaking, failure in religious observances, or disobeying the Inca. If a man had many or great sins, he would bring tribulations and calamities to himself and his family. If the ruler became ill, it was thought to be the fault of his subjects' sins. All the provinces would make confessions to restore his health. Penance could be assigned by the confessor if the sins were grave. Penance could also involve fasts or spending the night in prayer at some shrine. In severe cases, it might involve being flagellated by a dwarf or hunchback who specialized in this service (Cobo 1990: 118–125).

**Sacrifice.** Many different types of sacrifices were made for a variety of purposes. The objects to be sacrificed were produced by the property—that is, the fields and flocks—of the various gods and *huacas* and were selected by a process of divination conducted by the priest of the particular supernatural involved. Individuals could also provide for sacrifices for their own particular purposes. In these cases, the sacrifice provided was divided between the god or *huaca* and the priests, who treated it as income.

The most common sacrifices were llamas, guinea pigs, food, and *chicha*. Llamas in particular were chosen as being appropriate for the god or occasion based on their color, markings, or wool. The animal was led around the idol by a priest, who then cut its throat. Except for birds, only domesticated animals were sacrificed. Food and drink were frequently offered to the dead and to *huacas*. The food was dispatched by burning it and the *chicha* was poured on the ground. When offered to the major deities, the *chicha* was poured into a golden vessel and later emptied into a gold-lined stone basin in the main plaza. Coca leaves were also frequently offered by burning, as were fine textiles, grain, wool, and llama fat. Gold and silver were offered to deities in the form of figurines of humans and animals. These objects were commonly buried in the ground around the shrine. Offerings to ensure the water supply were made using seashells. The most important of these shells was the *Spondylus princeps,* a type of oyster with spines on its shell that is found in the ocean off Ecuador and further north. This shell was prized for its color, which ranges from light pink to red to deep orange. The shells were buried after being cut into pieces or carved into figurines of humans or animals. Even the poorest people, if they had nothing else, could sacrifice by plucking out hairs from their eyebrows or eyelashes and blowing them toward the sacred object.

The most important and solemn sacrifices were those of human beings. These were offered only on very special occasions. In times of great national distress brought on by natural disasters, a ceremony called the Itu was performed. A ceremony called the Capac Ucha was conducted at the accession of a new ruler, the death or illness of a ruler, and when the ruler personally led the army to war.

The sacrificial victims were normally children who were considered physically perfect. Boys of the age of ten years and younger and girls of the age of sixteen years and younger were most commonly selected for sacrifice as part of the regular annual taxation by the state. Even infants could be included in the sacrifice. The girls often came from the ranks of the *acllas,* and children of both sexes could be volunteered by their families. The victims were feasted and made drunk before the sacrifice. They were then walked around the cult object several times before being killed by strangulation or having their throats cut or their hearts cut out. They were also sometimes buried alive. Blood from the victims was smeared on the cult object, and if it were a mummy or a statue, a line of blood was drawn across the face from ear to ear. The bodies of the victims were then buried near the shrine together with gold or silver objects in a grave dug only with wooden tools, since metal tools were forbidden. In some cases, when the Capac Ucha ceremony was to be celebrated in the whole of the empire, the victims would be required to walk to distant shrines or sometimes sacred mountain peaks throughout the realm. They were to travel as nearly as possible in perfectly straight lines from Cuzco to their place of sacrifice.

One other type of human sacrifice involved war captives. Defeated rulers or generals were brought to Cuzco for ceremonies of triumph and then killed. A selection of the most perfect men and women from a newly conquered province would also be sacrificed to the sun as thanksgiving for a victory (Cieza de León 1959: 190–193; Cobo 1990: 109–117; Rowe 1946: 305–306).

**Feasting.** All rituals, ceremonies, or religious events of a public nature were accompanied by feasting and drinking bouts. Large quantities of food, including stews, soups, roasts, fresh fruits and boiled vegetables, baked potatoes, and roasted, toasted, and boiled maize were consumed. Huge quantities of *chicha* were also provided to intoxicate the celebrants. This was accompanied by dancing, singing, and the playing of games (Cobo 1990: 121).

## PRINCIPAL RITUALS AND CEREMONIES OF THE STATE RELIGION

The Incas possessed a very complex ceremonial calendar, with a series of rituals that were tied to the agricultural year. In addition, there were numerous ceremonials held only on special occasions (Cobo 1990: 126–150). Public ceremonies were very elaborate and often theatrical, taking place before large audiences in open public spaces, since Inca temples were designed to accommodate only the images of the gods and their priest attendants. Most Inca cities or administrative centers included large plazas to accommodate the masses that contained platforms called *ushnu* on which the emperor and officiating priests could perform in full view of everyone.

### The Ritual Calendar

The Inca calendar was divided into twelve lunar months, and the year began in December (Rowe 1946: 308). Each month had specific public rituals and ceremonies related to its position in the annual agricultural cycle. These ceremonies were attended and participated in by the emperor and his court and the nobles of the empire, including the images of the principal deities and the mummies of the dead emperors. They were also carried out in each of the provinces by their respective governors.

**The First Month: Capac Raymi.** The first month coincided with the onset of the rainy season in December and was marked by the summer solstice. According to Cobo (1990: 126), the name of this month meant "principal festival," and it was the most important event of the year. During this festival, there was held a ceremony called *huarachicoy,* during which the boys of noble birth were initiated into manhood by receiving their earplugs and breechclouts. This maturity ceremony was viewed by the Spaniards as the equivalent to the knighting ceremonies carried out in Europe. Festivities included singing, dancing, presenting weapons to the boys, a footrace down the hill of Huanacauri, many offerings to the deities, and the sacrifice of many llamas. An equivalent ceremony called *quicuchicoy* was held at the same time for young women coming of age to be married. The girls ritually bathed in the Saphi River to purify themselves. They received a new name from their kinsmen and a new headdress to mark the transition. During these rites, all provincial people resident in Cuzco were required to leave the city. They were lodged in places specially prepared for this purpose that were located on the highways running to each *suyu* or quarter of the empire (Brundage 1967: 91; Cobo 1990: 126–134).

**The Second Month: Camay.** In January a series of ceremonies were held that included a mock battle among the boys newly elevated to adult status. This event was held at the new moon and followed by two days of dancing. Other festivities held at the new moon included sacrifices, the drinking of *chicha*, and more dancing, ending with a special dance in which a large wool cable of four colors was paraded around the main plaza of Cuzco (Cobo 1990: 135–138).

**The Third Month: Hatun Puquy.** This month, the height of the rainy season, corresponded to February. On the first day, a sacrifice of 100 chestnut-colored llamas was consecrated. Three or four of the animals were killed each day, until all had been sacrificed by the end of the month. A ground-breaking ceremony was held in the agricultural fields by the people who would plow them. Twenty large *cuy* (guinea pigs) were sacrificed and burned on twenty loads of firewood. Prayers were offered to the sun asking for help in the tilling of the fields (Cobo 1990: 139).

**The Fourth Month: Paucar Huaray.** No information is recorded for this month, which corresponds to March (Cobo 1990: 139).

**The Fifth Month: Ariguaquiz.** This month corresponds approximately to the month of April. One hundred spotted llamas of different colors were sacrificed, and symbols of royal authority were honored during ceremonies in the main plaza. One such symbol was called *sunturpaucar* and consisted of an elaborate tassel on a staff. Another was a pure white llama called the *napa*. This llama had been trained to eat coca leaves and to drink *chicha* and was itself never sacrificed. Other animals were sacrificed in its name. The *napa* was also trained to sacrifice *chicha* by kicking over jars placed before it. The purpose of these ceremonies was to ensure that the maize seeds that had been planted would sprout (Cobo 1990: 139; Rowe 1946: 309).

**The Sixth Month: Hatun Cuzqui (Great Cultivation).** This month corresponded approximately to May. During this month, 100 llamas of all colors were sacrificed for the maintenance of order in the Inca world. There was a festival called Amoray that celebrated the maize harvest. The young men initiated that year ritually harvested the maize crop of a special field called Sausero and carried the maize back to Cuzco. Following this, all of the leading lords returned to this field and ritually plowed it. Another maize ritual called Mamazara was also carried out in individual households during this month. People would save the ears of maize that were unusual or strange in shape and

A reenactment of the Inca ruler presiding over the Inti Raymi festival in Cuzco. (Nevada Wier/Corbis)

wrap them in fine textiles. These were considered *huacas* of the corn mother. Shamans would ask these *huacas* to predict a good harvest in the next year (Cobo 1990: 140–141).

**The Seventh Month: Aucay Cuzqui (Warriors Cultivation).** During this month, which corresponds to June in the modern calendar, the winter solstice festival called Inti Raymi was celebrated. One hundred brown llamas were sacrificed to the sun on a hill near Cuzco. Only male Incas of royal blood could attend this festival, which involved much drinking, dancing, and elaborate sacrifices (Cobo 1990: 142–143; Rowe 1946: 310).

**The Eighth Month: Chahua Huarquis.** During this month that corresponds to July, another 100 brown llamas were sacrificed. Additional sacrifices were made to the *huaca* named Tocori. This *huaca* presided over the irrigation systems of Cuzco and was asked to provide abundant water. During this time, irrigation canals were also cleaned and repaired (Cobo 1990: 143).

**The Ninth Month: Yapaquis.** This month corresponds to August on the modern calendar. During this month, 100 chestnut-colored llamas were sacrificed. There was a festival called Guayara during which all of the *huacas* of Cuzco were asked for an abundant year. A thousand *cuy* were sacrificed to ensure protection from frost and the abundance of water and sun. The sacred corn-field of Sausero, dedicated to the sun, was also ritually planted at this time (Cobo 1990: 143–144; Rowe 1946: 310).

**The Tenth Month: Coya Raymi (Queen's Festival).** During September, 100 white llamas were sacrificed and the Inca celebrated the solemn and important festival of Citua. This festival's purpose was to prevent illness, and it was cele-brated at the beginning of the rainy season, when many people were likely to get sick. All people from the provinces and anyone who had a physical defect were required to leave the city of Cuzco for the duration of the festival. Dogs were also removed from the city so that they would not howl during the cere-monies. At the appointed time, the people shook out their clothes from their doorways, symbolically throwing out disease and evil. They went through the streets with torches in their hands playfully hitting at one another. As they passed they shouted for sickness, disaster, and misfortune to leave the land. Four groups of armed warriors ran out along the four main highways that con-verged in Cuzco, passing along the cry of "Go away, evil" in relay fashion. The last of the runners ritually bathed in rivers so that the evil would be carried away by the water. The people remaining in Cuzco also ritually bathed and smeared maize porridge on their faces and the lintels of their doors to symbol-ize purification. Following this were days of dancing and feasting, after which the provincials were finally allowed back in. All of the peoples of the empire then brought their *huacas* that were residing in Cuzco to the main square to show allegiance to the Inca emperor.

**The Eleventh Month: Homa Raymi Puchayquiz (also called K'antaray).** This month corresponds to October of our modern calendar. The principal concern at this time was for there to be sufficient water for the maturing crops. During this time, the usual sacrifice of 100 llamas took place. If there were drought, ad-ditional sacrifices were made to induce the gods to provide rain (Cobo 1990: 149).

**The Twelfth Month: Ayamarca.** The activities of this month, which corre-sponds to November on our modern calendar, concerned the readying of the young men who would be initiated as adults in the following month. The usual 100 llamas were sacrificed and offerings made. The boys made pilgrim-ages to the sacred *huaca* of Huanacauri and spent a night there asking permis-sion to become initiates or knights (Cobo 1990: 149–150).

## Special State Rituals

Some rituals were held only on special occasions that were not tied to the cere-monial calendar. The most important of these was called Itu Raymi and was used to get the attention of the gods when help was needed. Generally, these ceremonies were reserved for severe crises, such as plagues, droughts, natural disasters, or war. All people from the provinces and dogs were sent out of the city of Cuzco. Those remaining then fasted for two days, avoiding salt, chili pepper, *chicha,* and sexual intercourse. The images of the gods were then brought into the main plaza and sacrifices were made. Depending on the seriousness of the occasion, llamas or even children could be sacrificed. There followed a solemn procession of boys under twenty years of age who circled the plaza wearing special costumes and beating drums. After circling the plaza once, they sat down in silence. A noble followed their path scattering coca leaves on the ground. The boys then circled the plaza again and more coca was scattered. After repeating the ritual eight times, the participants remained in the square all night praying to Viracocha and Inti. The following two days a joyous feast was held with dancing and drinking (Cobo 1990: 151–153; Rowe 1946: 311–312).

Funerals, especially those of an Inca ruler, could require very elaborate rituals. Family members of the deceased dressed in black for up to one year. Faces were smeared with black pigment. Women cut their hair and wore their cloaks over their heads. Food and drink were served to those who attended. Some of the personal effects of the deceased were burned, and the remainder kept with the body. For the funeral of the Inca Pachacuti, it is said that elaborate rituals were carried out in a month-long ceremony that he himself had designed. His possessions such as weapons, clothing, and jewelry were carried in processions to all the places around Cuzco that he had usually visited during his lifetime. The mourners would call out to him and recount his deeds. Other events included a mock battle between the moieties in Cuzco as well as dancing and feasting. Five thousand llamas were sacrificed and 1,000 children (Betanzos 1996: 134–137; Rowe 1946: 286).

Another infrequent state ritual was the coronation of a new emperor. All of the greatest lords and deities came to Cuzco for the ceremony. After a three-day fast in a house specially built for that purpose, the new emperor was crowned with the royal fringe called the *mascapaycha.* The lords of the realm then swore allegiance using a light-colored feather to make obeisance and also swore loyalty in the name of the sun and the earth. Lavish sacrifices were made of fine cloth, gold and silver vessels, gold and silver statues of animals, a large amount of seashells of all types, and large quantities of colored feathers. A thousand llamas were sacrificed and burned and 200 children aged from four to ten years were strangled as sacrifices.

## PRINCIPAL TEMPLES OF THE STATE RELIGION

Inca temples were meant to be houses for the deities and were not designed to accommodate large gatherings of people. For worship and public ceremonies, the images of the deities were brought out to the principal plazas of the city. The only people who were allowed to enter the temples were the ruler, designated high nobles, and the priests and virgins serving the gods.

### Coricancha

In his study of Inca religion Bernabé Cobo (1990: 48) remarks on the great number of temples throughout the Inca realm. The most important of all of these was the temple of the sun in the city of Cuzco, the religious heart of the empire. This temple was called the Coricancha, which means "golden enclosure." This name derives from the enormous quantity of gold used to decorate the temple's chapels, walls, ceilings, and altars. The Coricancha was heavily looted during the Conquest and the gold carried off to be part of Atahuallpa's ransom. Only three Spaniards actually saw it before major destruction began; eyewitness European accounts of its splendor are thus very few.

The temple was sited on a flat piece of land between the Saphi and Tullu rivers and above their conjunction or *tincuy* in the Pumap Chupan (tail of the puma) sector of the city. It was built of extraordinary fine masonry, with blocks so carefully fitted that no mortar was needed to hold them together. There is some evidence that thin silver sheets were placed between the stones where mortar might normally be expected. The plan of the temple was typically Inca, consisting of a great irregular enclosure encompassing about 2,000 square feet. Within this enclosure were four large buildings forming the sides of a square. In these were chapels to the principal deities, including Viracocha, Inti, Illapa, Mamaquilla, and the other principal gods. One building served to house the *mamaconas*, or sacred virgins who served the temple. There was also said to be an additional large building that housed the priests of the temple and served as residence for the high priest Villac Umu (Cobo 1990: 48–50).

The riches of this temple were legendary. The chapel housing the sun and other principal deities was said to have walls and a ceiling completely covered with gold sheets. Running along the upper part of the enclosure wall surrounding the complex was a band of gold 30 centimeters wide that was said to have been three fingers thick. Within the temple complex was a ceremonial garden with the earth made of small lumps of gold. Planted in this golden soil were golden corn stalks complete with ears modeled of the same metal. More than twenty statues of life-sized golden llamas were present, along with life-sized statues of shepherds to guard them, complete with golden slings and staffs. The roofs of the buildings were said to be thatched with strands of gold wire woven into the grass thatch. In addition the temple contained numerous images and statues of gold and silver, large quantities of gold and silver serving vessels, ornaments and jewels, and quantities of fine cloth (Cieza de León 1959: 146–147; Cobo 1990: 49–50).

## Temple of Apurimac

Where the royal highway running northwest of Cuzco crossed the Apurimac River gorge there was a temple to the spirit of the river. Apurimac means "Great Speaker" in the language of the Incas, who regarded the idol associated with the river as an oracle of paramount importance. A colorfully painted enclosure there contained a wooden post about the size of a human being. A golden band about the width of one hand was wrapped around the post, and two golden female breasts were attached to it. This post was dressed as a woman in fine garments, some made of gold, that were fastened with *tupu* pins of gold. Surrounding the idol in its enclosure were other posts also dressed as women and smeared with the blood of sacrifices. The spirit of the great river was regarded as a woman and was attended by a female priest called Sarpay, who spoke for the idol. The oracle was of such importance that the priestess was a sister or close relative of the emperor, and its advice was sought on the most important matters of state.

## Temple of Viracocha

This temple is located at Raqchi on the bank of the Vilcanota River 110 kilometers south of the Inca capital of Cuzco and is one of the most famous in the Inca Empire. The sacred complex is very large, consisting of approximately 80 hectares enclosed by a wall of more than 3,500 meters in length. Within this enclosure are a row of six carefully aligned courtyards with houses opening onto them in the classic Inca *cancha* pattern. Adjacent to these on the south side were more than forty circular structures arranged in orderly rows. Their exact numbers and function are not known, since only limited archaeology has been carried out here. Unlike other Inca temples, the temple of Viracocha itself is the largest roofed building that the Incas constructed. The temple consisted of a large hall measuring 92 meters by 25.25 meters with a roofed area of 2,323 square meters. Exactly how this temple and its associated structures functioned is not known, since it was not recorded by the Spaniards (Gasparini and Margolies 1980: 234–255).

## Temple of Copa Cabana Complex

This religious complex, named for the nearby town of Copa Cabana, consisted of two islands in Lake Titicaca to the south of Cuzco. The islands were called Titicaca, or "Island of the Sun," and Coati, or "Island of the Moon." On the basis of its reputation and authority, this was considered to be the third most important religious establishment in the Inca Empire. Temples, lodgings for the Inca as well as priests and *mamaconas,* and storehouses were built here under the patronage of Topa Inca. Great wealth is said to have been in these island temples, but it was never found by the Spaniards (Cobo 1990: 91–99).

## Temple of Pachacamac

The famous temple of Pachacamac, located in the Lurin Valley just south of the modern city of Lima, may have been the most sacred shrine in all of Peru. For the Incas it was second in importance only to the Coricancha sun temple in Cuzco. Pachacamac was much older than the Incas and had been a major temple and religious center since at least A.D. 600. Although conquered and incorporated into both the Inca and the much earlier Wari Empire, its prestige was such that it was allowed and even encouraged to flourish. The Incas lavishly renovated the existing temple and made their own additions, including an *aclla wasi,* or house for sacred virgins. Like the Coricancha, the inner chambers were said to be covered with sheets of gold, and there were many golden vessels and ornaments associated with the temple furnishings. The principal idol was made of wood and was not very impressive according to the Spaniards who saw it. Offerings were made to it on a regular basis and it was smeared with the blood of sacrifices. The idol itself functioned as an oracle with a priest who spoke for it. People came from all over the ancient Andes on pilgrimages to bring offerings and hear the words of the idol (Cobo 1990: 85–90; Hemming 1970: 62–63).

## HUACAS: THE ANIMISTIC FOLK RELIGION

A *huaca* was any person, place, or thing that was considered sacred to Andean peoples. The idea behind the notion of *huaca* was the belief that there were supernatural spirits that animated everything in nature. Therefore, anything could be a *huaca,* ranging from mountain peaks, to rivers, to lakes, to mummies, to oddly shaped rocks or even strangely shaped potatoes or ears of corn. Anything at all unusual in nature was immediately classified as a *huaca*. *Huacas* could also be such things as bridges, caves, buildings, quarries, battlefields, and archaeological sites such as the ruined city of Tiwanaku in Bolivia. The spirits that animated the *huacas* had certain specific powers and responsibilities, effective mostly in a specific locale. Thus a field guardian *huaca* protected a specific field, a spring that was a *huaca* was responsible for its own flow, and an ancestral *huaca* was responsible for its lineage. *Huacas* varied in their power and were hierarchically ranked. The larger the *huaca* was, the more power it had. Thus mountain peaks, especially high snow-covered peaks, were the most powerful *huacas* (Rowe 1946: 295–297).

The Incas firmly believed in the power of the *huacas* and saw no contradiction in worshipping them alongside the formal pantheon of gods. Cuzco itself was an important *huaca,* and royal Inca estates and architecture often incorporated stone *huacas*. Many estates featured special platforms for mountain worship with spectacular views of mountain peaks (Reinhard 1991). Associated with royal sites were carved stone *huacas* called *inti huatana,* or the "hitching post of the sun." The most famous examples are at the royal estates of Machu Picchu and Pisac. These were believed by the Spanish to be associated with the cult of Inti the sun, but there is very little information about how they functioned. Unfortunately, most were destroyed by the Spanish conquerors. Other *huacas* of special importance to the Incas were places connected with the events of their lineage history. The hill of Huanacauri where Ayar Ucho was believed to have turned to stone was a major *huaca*. So were the places associated with emperors such as Pachacuti or Topa Inca. The numerous stones, called *puruauca,* that Pachacuti claimed had turned to warriors to help him defeat the Chanca army during the siege of Cuzco were all worshiped as *huacas.* Travelers over mountain passes commonly carried a small stone to be deposited as an offering at the top with a prayer for strength and protection. These *huacas* were called *apachita* and were marked by piles of stones contributed over the years (Cobo 1990: 35–36; Rowe 1946: 296).

### Huaoque

A very important type of *huaca* was a guardian spirit called the *huaoque.* It consisted of a statue made to represent an Inca ruler or high-ranking lord. The size, form, and material used to make the statue varied according to the whim of the person being represented. They could be made of many different materials, including stone, wood, or precious metals. The image was formally adopted as a *huaoque,* which means "brother" in the Inca language, in a special ceremony. Family members were required to treat the *huaoque* in the same way that they treated the living person it represented or his mummy. Like mummies, these statues were dressed and fed and participated in daily activities. *Huaoques* were even taken into battle during wartime, since they were believed to lend a degree of luck and success to the army (Cobo 1990: 37–38).

## Huacas as Oracles

Some, but not all, *huacas* had oracular powers. Some of the most famous, such as Pachacamac and Apurimac have already been mentioned. In Inca culture all decisions were made only after consulting the supernatural. Questions put to oracles usually had to do with seeing the future and result of certain actions. People wanted oracles to tell them the most auspicious time for a particular undertaking, advise what course of action should be taken, predict outcomes, diagnose diseases, find lost objects, and determine truth or falsehood. The questions would be put to the *huaca,* and the priest who spoke for it would usually provide the answer after entering a trance through using drugs or alcohol (Cobo 1990: 169).

## The *Ceque* System for Organizing the *Huacas* of Cuzco

In Cuzco and its vicinity were over 350 *huacas* recorded by the Spanish. These were carefully organized into groupings, and certain Inca kin groups were responsible for their upkeep and making the proper sacrifices on the proper days. The basic concept in the organization of these *huacas* was that they all were located along forty-one distinct straight lines called *ceques* that radiated outward from the Coricancha sun temple to distances up to 12 kilometers from Cuzco. Each line connected between four and fifteen *huacas* that were unevenly distributed along the lines. The lines were grouped by the quarter or *suyu* of the empire within which they fell. Chinchaysuyu, Antisuyu, and Collasuyu each contained nine lines, while Contisuyu contained fourteen lines. In the three quarters with nine lines, the lines were further divided into groups of three. As John Rowe has observed, the whole system is very reminiscent of the method used by the Inca for recording information on knotted cords, or *quipu* (Rowe 1946: 300). Bernabé Cobo (1990) recorded the names and descriptions of the *huacas* and *ceques* that he based on a now-lost diagram made by Juan Polo de Ondegardo around 1561. In recent years there have been a number of attempts by scholars to understand the *ceque* system but these have resulted in little agreement on the nature and functioning of the system. Many of the *huacas* mentioned by Cobo have since disappeared, making the decipherment of the system problematic (see Bauer 1998; Kirchoff 1949; Rowe 1979; Zuidema 1964, 1983). It is possible that a similar system was common in all Inca towns and administrative centers but not enough information survives to indicate with certainty.

## REFERENCES

Bauer, Brian S. 1998. *The Sacred Landscape of the Incas: The Cuzco Ceque System.* Austin: University of Texas Press.

Betanzos, Juan de. 1996. *Narrative of the Incas*. Translated and edited by Roland Hamilton and Dana Buchanan. Austin: University of Texas Press.

Brundage, Burr C. 1967. *Lords of Cuzco: A History and Description of the Inca People in Their Final Days*. Norman: University of Oklahoma Press.

Cieza de León, Pedro de. 1959. *The Incas of Pedro de Cieza de León*. Translated by Harriet de Onis and edited by Victor W. von Hagen. Norman: University of Oklahoma Press.

Classen, Constance. 1993. *Inca Cosmology and the Human Body*. Salt Lake City: University of Utah Press.

Cobo, Bernabé. 1979. *History of the Inca Empire: An Account of the Indians' Customs and their Origin Together with a Treatise on Inca Legends, History, and Social Institutions*. Translated and edited by Roland Hamilton. Austin: University of Texas Press.

———. 1990. *Inca Religion and Customs*. Translated and edited by Roland Hamilton. Austin: University of Texas Press.

Gasparini, Graziano, and Luise Margolies. 1980. *Inca Architecture*. Translated by Patricia J. Lyon. Bloomington: University of Indiana Press.

Gose, Peter. 1993. "Segmentary State Formation and the Ritual Control of Water Under the Incas." *Comparative Study of Society and History* 35: 480–514.

Hemming, John. 1970. *The Conquest of the Incas*. London: Macmillan.

Huamán Poma de Ayala, Don Felipe. 1978. *Letter to a King: A Peruvian Chief's Account of Life under the Incas and under Spanish Rule*. Translated by Christopher Dilke. New York: E. P. Dutton.

Kirchoff, Paul. 1949. "The Social and Political Organization of the Andean Peoples." In *Handbook of South American Indians: The Comparative Ethnology of South American Indians*, edited by Julian Steward, Bulletin 143, vo. 5, 293–311. Washington, DC: Bureau of American Ethnology.

Pachacuti Yamqui Salcamaygua, Joan de. 1968. *Relación de antigüedades deste Reyno del Perú*. Biblioteca de Autores Españoles, 209, 279–319. Madrid: Ediciones Atlas.

Reinhard, Johan. 1991. *Machu Picchu: The Sacred Center*. Lima: Nuevas Imagines S.A.

Rowe, John H. 1946. "Inca Culture at the Time of the Spanish Conquest." In *Handbook of South American Indians*, edited by Julian Steward, Bulletin 143, vol. 2, 183–330. Washington, DC: Bureau of American Ethnology.

———. 1979. "An Account of the Shrines of Ancient Cuzco." *Ñawpa Pacha* 17: 2–80.

Saloman, Frank. 1995. "'The Beautiful Grandparents': Ancestor Shrines and Mortuary Ritual as Seen through Colonial Records." In *Tombs for the Living: Andean Mortuary Practices*, edited by Tom D. Dillehay, 315–353. Washington, DC: Dumbarton Oaks.

Sarmiento de Gamboa, Pedro. 1999. *History of the Incas*. Translated and edited by Sir Clements Markham. Mineola, NY: Dover. Originally published 1907. Cambridge: Hakluyt Society.

Sullivan, William. 1996. *The Secret of the Incas: Myth, Astronomy, and the War Against Time*. New York: Crown.

Zuidema, R. Tom. 1964. *The Ceque System of Cuzco*. Translated by Eva M. Hooykaas. International Archives of Ethnography, supplement to vol. 50. Leiden, The Netherlands: E. J. Brill.

———. 1983. Hierarchy and Space in Incaic Social Organization. *Ethnohistory* 30: 49–75.

———. 1995. *El sistema de los ceques*. Lima: Pontificia Universidad Católica del Perú, Fondo Editorial.

CHAPTER 9

# Material Culture

Inca material culture was extensive, with distinctive objects produced in a variety of media. Portable objects were most commonly produced out of readily available raw materials, including stone, wood, metal, leather, bone, clay, and fibers. Individual households produced objects for their own needs. For needs of the state, the labor tax provided a means of mass production of objects. The state supplied the raw materials, and the taxpayer provided the labor to produce large volumes of goods. Nonportable material culture included architecture, public works, and monuments.

Individuals living in the Inca Empire had few possessions, and these were mostly functional or ritual items. Household furniture was extremely simple, consisting primarily of raised stone platforms on which bedding could be placed. Beds were made of skins, furs, and blankets. Chairs, tables, and other articles of furniture were unknown. Items were stored in ceramic vessels, baskets, and woven bags suspended from stone pegs that protruded from the walls of the house. Small stoves were modeled out of clay and consisted of a framework enclosing the fire with several holes on top into which pots could be set. A small opening in the front of the stove allowed fuel for the fire to be introduced. Inca stoves were said to be extremely fuel efficient, which conserved scarce firewood. Rich and poor alike had similar goods and furnishings, only the quality and material would have differed. A very few of the highest-ranking individuals, including the emperor, were allowed to sit on low, carved wooden stools called *tiana*. Everyone else sat on the ground or stood (Cobo 1990: 194–197).

## POTTERY

Inca pottery is the most widely surviving element of portable material culture, but it has not yet been extensively studied by scholars. Inca pottery of the Imperial Period is of very high technical quality and is very durable. Vessels have thick walls made of fine-grained paste and were highly polished. The pottery was fired at high temperatures in an oxidizing atmosphere, achieving a hardness surpassing most other pre-Columbian pottery of ancient Peru. The resulting colors of the vessels fired in this way ranged from brick red to buff. According to John Rowe (1946: 243–244), the most famous center for the manufacture of Inca pottery was at Sañu (modern San Sebastián) located about

5 kilometers east of Cuzco. The name of this town became synonymous with pottery and was a generic term for it, similar to the way that the word "china" is used in English.

Inca pottery of the Imperial Period was of two basic types: the mass-produced standardized imperial ware and the much rarer individual pieces that are unique works of art. The standardized imperial ware was distributed throughout the whole of the empire and represents what most people regard as Inca-style pottery. It can be seen in museums throughout Peru and the Western world.

### Standardized Pottery

Inca imperial ceramics were highly standardized. Scholars have identified fourteen common shapes of vessels and a limited and recurring set of decorative motives (Bray 2003: 11–14; Meyers 1975). These shapes consist of bottles, brewing vessels, storage containers, cooking vessels with a pedestal foot, and serving vessels such as plates and cups. The single most widely distributed vessel type is the long-necked bottle with a pointed base that is commonly called an *aryballo* (*aríbalo* in Spanish) because it was thought by some to resemble the classical Greek vessels called *aryballos*. In recent years, scholars have tried to avoid using this term for the Inca bottle because of a desire to avoid confusion with Greek pottery forms, but the name has endured in the litera-

Large Inca ceramic vessels for making and storing corn beer. (Gordon F. McEwan)

ture and popular use. These bottles are so distinctive and ubiquitous throughout Inca territory that they are considered by some as a signature of Inca influence, much like the Coke bottle is of modern America.

Handles on Inca pottery vessels are usually straps. One exception is the handle found on some plates that projects outward like a pan handle. Rims and lips of Inca vessels are usually made with a flat or everted lip and are not thickened. Bases tend to be flat or pointed, and ring bases are unknown.

Decoration of Inca pottery was both plastic and painted. Plastic decoration consisted of handles modeled in the form of animals (birds, snakes, felines); human faces modeled on bottle necks; nubs on the shoulders of some large jars and bottles that are often modeled as feline or animal heads; plate handles modeled as animals such as felines, birds, or occasionally humans; and protruding bumps or "ears" on the rims of plates and body of pedestal vessels.

Painted decoration consists usually of geometric designs executed in only a limited palette of purple, red, black, white, and orange. Design elements consist of triangles, rectangles, diamonds, zigzag lines, and a branching design called the "fern pattern" by scholars. Some vessels are painted all one color, such as red or white, or painted half red and half white. Vessels are rarely decorated with stylized painted figures of humans or animals; geometric designs tend to predominate.

## Unique or Singular Pottery Objects

In addition to the standard imperial Inca pottery, there were unique pieces produced that must have reflected the artistic taste of a particular Inca or noble. Some of these pieces are simply fancier versions of the standard vessels, either more finely executed or decorated with unusual motifs. Other examples are truly unique. In the Museo Inka in Cuzco, for example, there is a ceramic box with a lid that is fashioned to resemble an architectural tower. There are also unique offering pieces called *paqcha* used in making liquid libations during religious performances. A famous example is a ceramic vessel in the Museo Inka that is modeled to represent the Inca architectural enclosure called a *cancha*, in which several small modeled houses are grouped within an enclosing wall. Other *paqcha* vessels resemble concentric stacked bowls or a variety of other shapes. Much of this unique material would never have been recognized as Inca had it not been found in Cuzco in Inca contexts. Another class of unique vessels is that produced by conquered peoples of the Inca Empire. These are generally examples of a particular regional style that incorporate certain Inca elements or vessel shapes, especially the *aryballo*.

## Functions of Inca Pottery

Inca ceramic vessels served a variety of practical functions as well as important social functions. Tamara Bray catalogues the practical uses of Inca ceramic vessels as follows: cooking, processing, fermentation, serving, eating, wet and dry storage, transportation of liquids, and washing (2003: 11). According to the Spanish chronicler Bernabé Cobo (1990: 194), the greatest number of vessels in any household were those devoted to brewing and serving the corn beer called *a'qa* (*chicha* in modern usage). Standardized vessels for use in brewing and serving *chicha* are also the most widely distributed Inca pottery types throughout the empire.

The social functions of Inca pottery were as important as or more so than the practical functions. The distinctive standardized Inca pottery served as a social status marker. In the provinces, high-ranking local lords received Inca vessels as a token of esteem and symbol of power. In the ideology of the Andes, power relationships were mediated through feasting and drinking. Reciprocal obligations were established and maintained through the generosity of the feast. Higher-ranking individuals provided *chicha* in great quantity to lower ranks served out of Inca-style vessels. As noted in Chapter 7, administration of the empire was largely carried out through means of feasting rituals.

## WOODEN OBJECTS

The Incas used wood as an architectural element (for example, upper-story floors and roofing) and for the manufacture of portable utilitarian objects. Spoons for eating, flutes, drums, agricultural tools such as the *chaquitaqlla* foot plow or digging stick, and a variety of hoes and clod breakers were made of wood. Spear shafts and club handles as well as a swordlike weapon called the *macana* were also produced out of wood. Some prestige items were also made of wood and included elaborately carved and decorated staffs of office carried by officials, the litter in which the emperor was carried, and the stool or *tiana* used by the highest ranks. Most important was the wooden cup called *kero* used in ritual drinking and ceremonies. These cups, with capacities ranging from one cup to two quarts, were produced in pairs and were usually in the form of a large tumbler, but some were carved in the shape of a feline head or a human head. The decoration on these cups was very elaborate, and a variety of techniques were used. Geometric patterns of lines were incised in the outside surface. Patterns were also inlaid with metal strips or wire. Sometimes patterns were picked into the surface with a series of small holes that were filled with lead. Many were decorated with a lacquerlike technique, producing colorful patterns and scenes with people and animals. The tradition of painted cups persisted into the colonial period and many fine specimens still exist (Rowe 1946: 244–245).

## METAL

Curiously, the Incas never developed the techniques for working hard metals and thus produced no iron or steel. They were highly skilled metallurgists, however, and worked extensively with many metals, including bronze, copper, gold, and silver. Metals and their ores were theoretically a state monopoly and owned by the emperor. Mining was carried out using the labor tax, but under much more humane conditions than those employed by the Spaniards in colonial times. Workers had limited shifts in the mines of short duration because of the hardships of the job. Metals were extracted from the natural environment by relatively simple methods. Andean peoples obtained gold mostly by panning river gravel, although they also worked some surface outcrops and shallow mines. It was more difficult to refine the ore produced from mines than to use the relatively pure gold found by panning. Copper ore was mined in open pits or shallow shafts. These produced a blue-green sandy material called atacamite, which is easily refined into copper. Silver ore is difficult to work with, and the metal rarely occurs in pure form. It was, nevertheless, widely used in the ancient Andes. Gold, copper, and silver were the metals most commonly used, but mercury, lead, and platinum were also known and used in small quantities. Metals were smelted in clay furnaces in which a high temperature was achieved through the use of blowing tubes. Several men blowing simultaneously on the fire through metal tubes or reeds could create a draft sufficient to raise the temperature of the fire to the level required to smelt metal. Alloys of gold and silver, gold, silver and copper, and gold and copper were commonly used. Alloys of tin and copper, and arsenic and copper, were used to make bronze. The precious metals, gold and silver, were used exclusively for making ornaments, serving vessels, and plates for the royalty and for ceremonial objects. Bronze, being much harder, was a more utilitarian metal. Although some ornaments were made of bronze, it was largely used for making tools and weapons.

Metals were worked using several methods. Cold hammering was one of the most common. Hammered pieces had to be annealed in order to prevent them from becoming brittle and cracking. This process involved heating the metal to a temperature just below the melting point and then rapidly cooling it in water. Hammered sheet metal was decorated in various ways. Embossed designs were pressed into it with a bone or wood tool worked against a soft anvil of leather. Sheet metal could also be hammered over a mold to produce a repoussé design, or decorations could be engraved or cut out. Individual pieces were built of parts fastened together by clinching, welding, and soldering.

Casting was another very common metallurgical technique, and both open and closed molds were used. Fine objects were produced by the lost wax casting method. In this technique, the object was originally modeled in wax, and the wax model was then covered with clay. Once the clay had formed a mold around the wax object, the wax was melted out and molten metal poured in to replace it. The metal object that emerged would be an exact replica of the wax model.

Gold and silver work produced cult images and decorations for shrines and temples and ornaments for the elite. The cult images are rather uniform in execution and frequently took the shape of small human figurines that were sometimes dressed in miniature garments. Other figurines were fashioned in the form of animals such as llamas, alpacas, birds, reptiles, and felines. These figurines seem to have functioned as offerings and were often buried at religious shrines. The Spanish conquistadores reported seeing such sights as a garden at the temple of the sun that was planted with carefully crafted golden plants, including flowers and ears of corn. They also saw life-size replicas of animals and even human statues (Cobo 1990: 48–50).

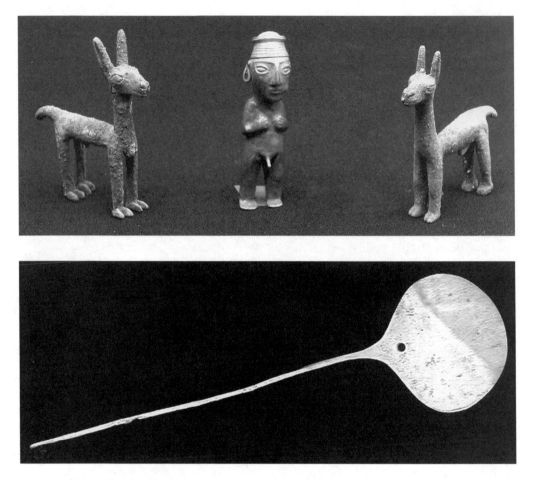

*Above:* A gold figurine of an Inca with two silver llama figurines.
*Below:* A *tupu* pin of gold.
(Gordon F. McEwan)

Personal ornaments included bangles and sequins sewn on clothing, elaborate earplugs worn only by male nobles, bracelets, shawl pins, and plates worn suspended around the neck. The most common ornament was the *tupu*, or shawl pin, worn as a fastener for women's clothing. The *tupu* was a straight pin with a broad spatulate head often pierced by a small hole, which allowed it to be attached to clothing by a thread to prevent its loss. The *tupu* was made of both gold and silver but most commonly of bronze. Another common women's ornament was a metal disk worn in pairs suspended around the neck and dangling over the chest.

Utilitarian objects were commonly made of cast or hammered bronze. These included sharp-edged tools and weapons such as axes, knives, chisels, and lance points. After casting, the edges of these tools were hammered to achieve sharpness. Other bronze objects included bola weights, plumb bobs, mace heads, mirrors, bells, needles, and tweezers.

## CLOTH

Cloth, above all else, was especially prized by the Incas and represents their greatest artistic achievement. Textiles were extremely important to nearly all the Andean peoples, and the Incas had inherited a textile tradition that was thousands of years old. The importance of cloth to Andean peoples resulted from the vast amount and varied types of labor involved in its production. The Spanish chronicles report that nearly everyone in the empire was involved in some aspect of cloth production in order to produce the vast quantities required by the society and the needs of the empire. Cotton was raised, harvested, washed, combed, dyed, and spun. Alpacas were herded and sheared; the wool had to be washed, carded, dyed, and spun. All of this had to be accomplished before the weaving could begin. Then the design of the cloth had to be planned, the loom set up, and skilled artists began to weave. Weaving was a painstaking, time-consuming, labor-intensive skill. Even plain utility cloths a yard square, such as might be used for sacking and storage, consumed more than 650 meters of yarn. A small village might have 65 kilometers of yarn invested in utility cloth alone. Cloth for clothing, with its tighter weave and higher thread count, would consume even more yarn. The needs of the empire must have consumed thousands of kilometers of yarn annually. The labor involved in producing the fibers, spinning the yarn, and weaving the cloth is staggering to contemplate.

The most common type of loom used in weaving was the backstrap loom. This was a simple device composed of two sticks with the warp threads stretched between them. One end was tied to a support such as a post or tree, and the other end was fastened to a belt passing around the back of the weaver. By leaning backward the weaver could control the tension on the warps. This type of loom limited the maximum width of the cloth to the arm span of the weaver. Cloth was never cut to form garments; instead, all garments were formed from whole rectangular pieces of cloth. If a larger piece of cloth was required, two or more pieces could be sewn together. Thus there was little variety in clothing styles since all garments were based on a rectangular unit of cloth. Larger pieces of cloth, such as tapestry woven tunics, could also be woven on the less commonly used vertical frame looms (Gayton 1961).

The Incas produced three basic types of cloth that differed in terms of their quality. The coarsest type was called *chusi* and was used only for making sacking, rugs, or blankets. Individual threads used in this type of cloth were said to sometimes be as thick as a finger. A somewhat better grade of cloth was known as *ahuasca*. This was relatively coarse cloth made of wool from alpacas and llamas and was worn as clothing by the lower classes.

The finest quality of cloth, reserved for the emperor and nobility, was called *cumpi*. Made of alpaca or vicuña wool and cotton, or sometimes more exotic materials such as bat hair or hummingbird down, it was a tapestry weave decorated with complex multicolored designs. *Cumpi* cloth was produced in state-run institutions called *aclla wasi* where cloistered chosen women, selected for their beauty and skill, devoted their lives to weaving cloth for clothing the emperor, cult images, and for sacrifices. Another source of *cumpi* was the requirement for the wives of provincial nobility to weave garments made of it for use by the emperor. There were also male full-time specialists called *cumpi camayoc* who did nothing but weave *cumpi* for the state. Garments of *cumpi* could be worn by persons other than the royal family only if they had received them as gifts from the emperor. The emperor commonly awarded these garments in recognition for services rendered to the state; thus they were considered a mark of great prestige (Cobo 1990: 223–226; Rowe 1946: 242–243).

Tunics woven of *cumpi* cloth and decorated with diamonds, checkerboard squares, and other abstract geometric designs were characteristic of Inca-style

An Inca tunic decorated with *tocapu* designs. (Dumbarton Oaks, Pre-Columbian Collection, Washington, DC)

male garments and highly prized as status symbols. The surviving examples of these tunics are few in number but provide an idea of what standard Inca fine cloth garments were like. These were woven using interlocking tapestry technique. A finished *cumpi* tunic might contain sixteen kilometers of fine yarn that produced a cloth as fine as silk. The warps are of cotton and the wefts of wool. The tunic was woven as a single strip of cloth that was doubled over in the middle and sewn up the sides leaving space for the armholes. The neck opening was usually woven in but in some cases a slit was cut into the finished cloth to accommodate the wearer's head. The garment was designed to fit loosely, falling to about the knees and covering the shoulder and part of the upper arm. Tunics with rows of small rectangular designs called *tocapu* were made as special garments for the emperor. Some of these tunics had three or four rows of *tocapu* across the middle at waist level or down the front, while others were completely covered in these designs.

The similarities of this type of tunic to the tapestry tunics of the earlier Tiwanaku and Huari empires suggest that the imperial Inca tunic tradition may be descended from the high-status garments of the Middle Horizon. Fine *cumpi* tunics represent thousands of hours of labor and the highest degree of weaving skill ever achieved in the Americas and perhaps the world. They were thus a fitting artistic expression to adorn the paramount ruler of the great Inca Empire (Rowe 1979; Niles 1992).

## STONE

Stone working was an art form in which the Inca particularly excelled. In addition to architectural stonework, which occasionally included figures of snakes or pumas in low relief, many other beautiful objects were made of stone. Some objects such as mace heads, axes, grinding stones, and bola stones were purely practical in nature, while others were elaborations of everyday objects for ceremonial purposes. These included highly decorated mortars and pestles, as well as round and rectangular stone plates and bowls used for catching the blood of sacrificed animals. Sculptured figurines called *conopas* that represented llamas and alpacas were finely made of specially selected stone and used as offerings. Large-scale realistic sculpture was extremely rare. Surviving examples depict pumas or other felines and one or two examples depicting humans. What is most remarkable about Inca sculpture is that it was achieved without the use of steel chisels. Cutting was done using hammers of harder stone and also by using saws of bronze or sinew together with a sand abrasive to shape the stone.

Inca sculptors delighted in finding naturally occurring stones, boulders, or out-

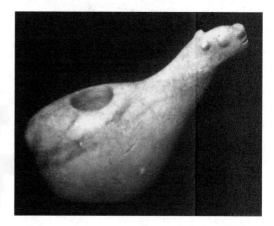

A stone *conopa* in the form of a llama. (Gordon F. McEwan)

crops that suggested the shape of something in nature. There are several examples at Machu Picchu and other royal estates near Cuzco where naturally occurring outcrops seem to mirror a mountain peak or other feature on the horizon. Sometimes these stones would be modified, but many were left just as they were found and framed by low walls, while others were placed on pedestals. *Huaca* stones were accorded the same treatment and were sometimes elaborately carved. For example, the outcrop at the site of Kenko above Cuzco and many other stone outcrops nearby are elaborately carved with platforms, low relief figures, and what appear to be altars.

Throughout Machu Picchu there are numerous natural outcrops that seem to mimic the mountain peaks surrounding the site. These are carefully framed and some have been polished or carved. The most famous of the sculpted outcrops are the *huaca* stones known as *inti huatana*, the so-called hitching posts of the sun. It is not understood exactly what these monuments represented or if they even had anything to do with solar worship, but the care lavished on them indicates their importance in Inca ideology. The *inti huatana* at Machu Picchu is a highly polished monolithic sculpture rising out of the bedrock below the site. Arms of different lengths project at various angles, creating a

The *inti huatana* stone at Machu Picchu. (Gordon F. McEwan)

pleasing abstract form. The sculpture is surrounded by and framed by small terraces and niched walls.

## SHELL AND BONE

Ornaments, jewelry, and offering pieces as well as some utilitarian objects were made of shell and bone. The thorny oyster *Spondylus princeps* was highly valued for religious reasons as an offering given to the supernatural in honor of water. Fine figurines of humans and llamas were made of the bright red and white shells for use in a variety of offering contexts, including human sacrifice. *Spondylus princeps* was also fashioned into beads and pendants and was sometimes used as an inlay in objects made of wood. Another shell commonly used was the spiral-shaped *Strombus* shell. These were used to make trumpets called *pututu*. They were used by postal runners (*chasqui*) and in warfare for signaling, and also in ceremonial and religious performances. Objects made of bone included musical instruments such as bone flutes, utensils such as spoons, weaving tools and picks, blanket pins, and items of jewelry.

## ARCHITECTURE

Inca architecture, like their pottery, was highly standardized, and its very recognizable style found throughout the empire is a hallmark of Inca conquest. As with the pottery, there are unique examples of architecture commissioned by individual Incas, but these are normally found on royal estates or in the royal palaces of the Inca capital at Cuzco. The architecture of administrative sites throughout the empire was relatively uniform. Specific elements that mark a building as Inca are constantly repeated in all Inca architecture. Inca buildings, both large and small and of all functions, seem to have niches built into the interior face of their walls. These niches are generally trapezoidal in shape with the shortest side across the top. Unlike earlier Andean cultures, which often used niches only in temples, the Incas placed niches in all of their buildings. Some of these niches are quite large and could accommodate a standing man, but most are smaller and located in the upper half of a wall. Niches are usually distributed symmetrically within a building and sizes are not mixed at random. The function of these niches is not clear, and the Spanish sources give little information about what was in them. Depending on the building's function, they may have contained idols or simply been used for storage.

Like the wall niches, Inca doorways were also trapezoidal in form, narrower at the top than at the bottom. Lintels were usually monolithic stones or made of logs. Important buildings such as temples or those belonging to or housing the nobility would have what are referred to as double-jamb doorways. In these doorways, the jamb was inset or stepped to form a frame around the doorway. This technique is thought to have been copied from the masonry of the ruins at Tiwanaku in Bolivia. Inca doorways were also sometimes fitted with what is termed a bar hold. This consists of a stone cylinder set within a

Inca-style niches in a wall at the royal estate of Pisac. (Gordon F. McEwan)

small niche. They were located on either side of the doorway on the inside wall of a building and are believed to have been used to fasten a door of some kind. No Inca doors have survived, so we can only speculate on how the bar holds worked. Inca houses had few windows, although doorways are quite common, and larger buildings had multiple doorways that would have served to allow both access and light into the building.

Another distinctive characteristic of Inca architecture was the use of battered walls. This refers to the fact that the walls of Inca buildings were built so that they lean inward at a pronounced angle. Scholars have speculated about the function or purpose of battered walls. It has been argued that by inclining the walls, the thrust of the roof beams holding up thick thatch roofs could be more easily absorbed (Gasparini and Margolies 1980: 310).

One other striking feature of Inca architecture is the presence of stone knobs and grooves in some of the large blocks of important buildings. Some scholars think these functioned by giving purchase to pry bars and levers when workmen needed to move or lift a stone (Rowe 1946: 227). However, not all stones have these knobs or grooves. In some cases, they may have been polished off

Double-jamb doorway in a wall at Ollantaytambo. (Gordon F. McEwan)

after the stone was laid, but then we must ask why all of them were not re-moved.

A great deal of Inca architecture, including the houses of most commoners, was apparently constructed of adobe. Inca adobe bricks were made of mud and straw and then dried in the sun. They had a distinctive shape, with a rec-tangular cross section, and were about 20 centimeters wide and as much as 80 centimeters long. Stone walls were frequently combined with adobe bricks; the lower portion of the wall was stone and the upper portion made of adobe. Purely adobe buildings have not survived in any great quantity in the highlands, and as a result the Incas are best known for their stone buildings. On the Pacific coast, the Incas built state installations largely of adobe, since rainfall was not an issue.

## Masonry

Inca architects and stonemasons were professionals exempt from labor tax. They worked full time on building projects and were supported by the state. Since there was no system of writing, nor pens and paper, planning was done by means of clay or stone models of sites, projects, and buildings. Building and site plans may also have been recorded on the knotted cords of the *quipu*. There is little information about measuring instruments and tools used in construction, but the system of measures would have had to be accurate and uniform. Tools used in construction projects included plumb bobs, bronze pry bars and chisels, and digging sticks of wood (Lee 1996; Rowe 1946).

Inca stonework consisted of two basic types. Fieldstone laid in mud mortar was referred to as *pirca*. Walls made in this way were usually plastered over with mud or clay so that the stonework was not visible. The other basic type of Inca stonework was the famous dry-fitted masonry without mortar. Inca fitted-stone masonry was either laid in courses of rectangular blocks or con-

The stone of twelve angles in Cuzco. (Gordon F. McEwan)

structed of polygonal blocks that fit together like the pieces of a jigsaw puzzle. The joints on the front faces of stone walls were so precise that even today a knife blade and sometimes even a pin cannot be inserted into the joint. The edges of the blocks were usually slightly beveled so that the joints where two blocks abutted were slightly recessed. The result was a pillowing effect that provided a pleasing play of light and shadow over the surface of the wall.

In recent years there has been a great deal of study of Inca masonry techniques, and scholars have learned how the stone blocks were dressed and fitted. Stone blocks were rough cut at the quarry and hauled by workers to the work site, sometimes over great distances and steep inclines. There is some archaeological evidence that rollers were used to move the stones or that they were slid on gravel or sand, but there is no direct testimony of how this was done. Once there, the blocks were finished with a variety of sizes of stone hammers. The blocks were individually carved to fit the next stone after being placed in the wall. In many cases only the front and visible face of the stone was finely fitted; it was unnecessary to dress the surfaces that did not show. It still remains a mystery, however, as to how the truly enormous stones of such sites as Sacsayhuaman and Ollantaytambo, some of which weigh 60 to 100 tons each, were moved into position (Lee 1987; Protzen 1985, 1986, 1993, 2004).

## Building Types

The majority of Inca architecture is rectangular and is made up of two basic building types called the *cancha* and the *kallanka*. Most Inca settlements are made up of variations of these two forms, although there exist some round and uniquely shaped buildings as well. Gasparini and Margolies (1980: 134–137), in their analysis of Inca architecture, remark upon the ubiquity of rectangular floor plans that lack internal communication between rooms. Groups of separate and unconnected chambers were characteristic of Inca architecture. No matter the size of a building or number of entrances, there was usually only one chamber inside.

The *cancha*, probably residential architecture, consisted of a grouping of small, one-room houses sharing a common patio. Often, but not always, there was a wall with a single entrance enclosing the whole group. The houses were built against the inside perimeter of the enclosure wall with their doorways opening to the patio. *Canchas* were generally one story high; the houses were gabled and roofed with thatch. In long gabled houses where the roof beams could not span the width of the gables, wooden posts were used to help support the roof. Houses without gables also occurred and are covered with hip roofs resting directly on the tops of the walls. Multistoried buildings were occasionally built but tended to lack internal communication such as staircases between stories. Instead, two-story houses were built on steep slopes so that the upper floor could be entered at ground level on one side and the lower level entered at ground level on the other side. Roofs were steeply pitched to shed rainwater, made of wooden armatures covered with woven mats, and capped by grass thatch up to 1 meter thick. Special stone fasteners resembling pegs and circular stone eye-bonders were built into the tops of walls and pro-

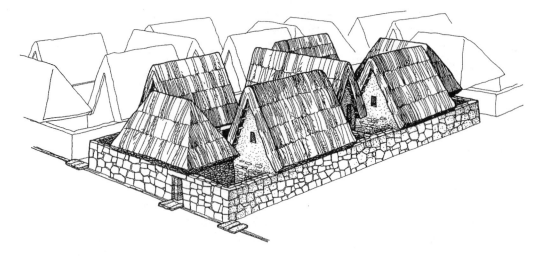

A reconstruction drawing of an Inca *cancha* architectural form, from *Inca Architecture and Construction at Ollantaytambo* by Jean Pierre Protzen with drawings by Robert Batson, copyright 1993 by Oxford University Press, Inc. Used by permission of Oxford University Press, Inc.

vided a means to tie the roof onto the top of the building. No chimneys were provided; smoke from cooking fires escaped through the roof thatch or windows built into the walls (Rowe 1946: 227).

The *kallanka* was a very large hall with gabled end walls that together with a number of wooden pillars running the length of the building supported an extensive thatched roof. Multiple doorways affording both light and access were located on only one of the long sides of the building and opened onto a plaza. The interior faces of the walls of this structure contained long rows of niches. The *kallanka* was the largest type of building that the Incas constructed and served a variety of functions. It served as a place to hold large public ceremonies during bad weather and a place for feasting and celebration. It could also be used as temporary lodgings for large groups of people like a military unit. Some surviving *kallanka* are truly enormous. The *kallanka* at Inkallaqta in Bolivia measures 78 meters long by 26 meters wide. It has twelve doorways and contains a row of 44 niches in its walls.

Although the standardized *cancha* and *kallanka* forms were repeatedly used in imperial settlements and administrative centers, other classes of architecture with more freedom of expression did exist within the empire. Each of the major temples of the Inca Empire described in Chapter 8 had its own unique form. Some, like the Coricancha sun temple in Cuzco, seem to have been derived from the *cancha* form, and others, like the temple of Viracocha, were derived from the *kallanka,* but in each case, certain unique elements were introduced that individualized these structures. Round, elliptical, and sinuous ground plans occur in the religious architecture of a number of sites, including Ingapirca in Ecuador, Machu Picchu, and Pisac, among others.

Royal estates by far show the greatest variety of architecture. Individual Inca rulers seem to have employed architects that reflected their own personal taste. Sites associated with Inca Pachacuti, such as Machu Picchu, Runtu Raccay, Sayacmarca, Phuyupatamarca, and Wiñay Wayna, exhibit a stylistic unity suggesting a single architect and employ a variety of both rectangular and irregular building forms. Many of the buildings of these sites are dramatically perched on bedrock prominences and seem to grow organically out of the mountainside. It was also common to incorporate a stone outcrop into the wall or interior of a building. Aesthetic considerations obviously came into play when these sites were selected; their environments and views are spectacular. Huayna Capac's estate at Quispihuanca near Yucay in the Sacred Valley of the Incas is dramatically different from Pachacuti's architectural style. Huayna Capac's architect made use of adobe in large quantity, as well as stone, and incorporated such landscape elements as reflecting pools. Far from the cool, rigid uniformity seen in the imperial state-sponsored architecture of the provinces, the royal estates were vivid expressions of the personalities of their owners.

Royal estates served many functions that are comprehensible only in terms of Inca culture and belief systems. As a divine ruler, the emperor could express his power and divine will by physically altering the sacred landscape. He had his estate not built on a mountain but incorporated within it and its sacred environment. This was meant not only to impress his mortal subjects but also to demonstrate his power among the other gods and to tie himself closely to their supernatural power. Several key aspects of the location of royal estates stand out. What is important in a location is that it is related to the Urubamba River valley. This river is a major *huaca* embracing these sites. Sight lines at these locations also provide views of several major mountain peaks, another category of powerful *huacas*, and this renders them an appropriate place to worship mountain spirits. Within the sites are numerous sacred *huaca* stone outcrops. These *huacas* are generally tied into the architecture of a site, and some are actually enclosed in buildings specially constructed for this purpose. Many of these are also aligned with the sacred mountain peaks and in some cases are carved to echo the contours of the mountain in the distance on which they are focused.

Water was provided to the sites by means of canal systems that carried it through a series of elaborate fountains and then allowed it to drain into the Urubamba River. These hydraulic systems, although on one level a practical water supply for the inhabitants of the site, also recreate the sacred water cycle regulated by the ancestors. Water falls from the sky and is collected into the canal system from which it nourishes human life before flowing into the river and ultimately the sea. There it evaporates back into the atmosphere to begin the cycle again. Ultimately royal estates served as places where the divine emperor could commune with his fellow deities and participate in the great cycle of life, land, and water. Balance and harmony between the real world and supernatural world were expressed and maintained (Niles 1999, 2004).

## REFERENCES

Bray, Tamara L. 2003. "Inca Pottery as Culinary Equipment: Food, Feasting, and Gender in Imperial State Design." *Latin American Antiquity* 14(1): 1–22.

Cobo, Bernabé. 1990. *Inca Religion and Customs.* Translated and edited by Roland Hamilton. Austin: University of Texas Press.

Gasparini, Graziano, and Luise Margolies. 1980. *Inca Architecture.* Translated by Patricia J. Lyon. Bloomington: University of Indiana Press.

Gayton, Anna H. 1961. "The Cultural Significance of Peruvian Textiles: Production, Function, Aesthetics." *Kroeber Anthropological Society Papers,* no. 25, 111–128.

Lee, Vincent R. 1987. *The Building of Sacsayhuaman and Other Papers.* Wilson, WY: Sixpack Manco.

———. 1996. *Design by the Numbers: Architectural Order among the Incas.* Wilson, WY: Sixpack Manco.

Meyers, Albert. 1975. "Algunas problemas en la Clasificación del estilo incaico." *Pumapunku* 8: 7–25.

Niles, Susan A. 1992. "Inca Architecture and the Sacred Landscape." In *The Ancient Americas: Art from Sacred Landscapes,* edited by Richard F. Townsend, 347–358. Munich: Prestel Verlag.

———. 1999. *The Shape of Inca History: Narrative and Architecture in an Andean Empire.* Iowa City: University of Iowa Press.

———. 2004. "The Nature of Inca Royal Estates." In *Machu Picchu: Unveiling the Mystery of the Incas,* edited by Richard L. Burger and Lucy Salazar, 49–68. New Haven, CT: Yale University Press.

Protzen, Jean Pierre. 1985. "Inca Quarrying and Stone Cutting." *Ñawpa Pacha* 21: 183–214.

———. 1986. "Inca Stonemasonry." *Scientific American* 254(2): 94–105.

———. 1993. *Inca Architecture and Construction at Ollantaytambo.* Oxford: Oxford University Press.

———. 2004. "The Fortress of Saqsa Waman: Was It Ever Finished?" *Ñawpa Pacha* 25–27: 155–175. Institute of Andean Studies, Berkeley, California.

Rowe, John H. 1946. "Inca Culture at the Time of the Spanish Conquest." In *Handbook of South American Indians,* edited by Julian Steward, Bureau of American Ethnology, bulletin 143, vol. 2, 183–330. Washington, DC: Smithsonian Institution.

———. 1979. "Standardization in Inca Tapestry Tunics." In *The Junius B. Bird Pre-Columbian Textile Conference,* edited by Ann Pollard Rowe, Elizabeth P. Benson, and Anne-Louise Schaffer, 239–264. Washington, DC: Dumbarton Oaks.

CHAPTER 10

# Intellectual Accomplishments

## FINE ARTS

Unlike other pre-Columbian Peruvian cultures that perfected portraiture, mural painting, and sculpture, the Incas seemed uninterested in developing their own traditions in these areas, or, perhaps, they did not have time to do so given the short life of the empire. The arts in which they were most accomplished were architecture and weaving, especially tapestry. Nevertheless, the Incas were appreciative of fine artisans and would occasionally uproot artists from their native communities and move them to Cuzco to produce art for the imperial elite. A notable example occurred with the Inca conquest of the Chimu Empire. Master metalworkers and their families were removed to Cuzco to produce jewelry and other fine objects for their new masters. Likewise, master stonemasons were moved from the province of Collasuyu to work on building projects including temples, palaces, and royal estates in Cuzco and its environs.

## SYSTEM OF MEASURES

In his classic work on Inca culture, John Rowe (1946: 323–325) provides a useful synthesis of the abundant but scattered information on Inca systems of measurement that had been reported in the Spanish chronicles. Human body parts formed the basis for Inca measures of length. These included the following:

*Rok'ana:* a finger
*Yuku:* the distance between the thumb and forefinger of an outstretched hand, about 12–14 centimeters
*K'apa:* a palm or 20 centimeters
*Khococ:* the distance from the elbow to tip of hand, about 45 centimeters
*Rikra:* the distance of an average man's outstretched arms, about 162 centimeters
*Sikya:* half the length of a *rikra*, about 81 centimeters

Measures of distance were the pace, or *thatkiy,* of about 130 centimeters, the *topo* of 6,000 paces or 7.8 kilometers, and the *wamani* of 30 *topos* or 234 kilometers. Area was measured in *topos* of 25 *rikra* by 50 *rikra* or about 3,280 square meters. Bernabé Cobo (1990: 240) reports that the Incas had no system of liquid measurement, but this seems unlikely given their keen interest in water, heavy use of ceramic containers for liquids, and the importance of brewing corn beer for almost every occasion. A unit of dry measure for grains was the *collo* or about 3.8 liters. There was no standard system of weights recorded by the Spanish, but the use of the balance scale called *aysana* was known, thus implying that things were measured by weight comparison.

## LANGUAGE AND LITERACY

The language of the Incas was called *runasimi* or man's speech. Modern dialects of this language are still spoken by millions of people and are referred to today as the Quechua language. The name Quechua more properly refers to a geographic area and may have been used by the Spanish to name the language spoken by the inhabitants of the Quechua zone. John Rowe preferred to refer to the Inca language as Classic Inca (2004).

### The Quechua Language

Quechua appears to be far older than the Incas themselves and possibly originated more than a thousand years before their time. Linguistic studies are difficult and confusing because of the lack of written records. A very complicated geographic distribution adds to the confusion, but the language appears to have originated in central Peru. It is known, however, that Quechua, or *runasimi*, served as the lingua franca of the Inca Empire and was spread by the Incas into non-Quechua-speaking areas. Elites in newly conquered provinces were required both to learn Quechua and to send their sons to Cuzco to be educated in the language as well. Because Quechua was in widespread use at the time of the Spanish Conquest, it was further spread by Spanish missionaries who used it as the language of proselytization.

According to linguist Paul Heggarty the structure of Quechua is agglutinating, whereby meaning is changed by the addition of suffixes rather than modifying words. Large compounded words allow for very subtle variance and shades of meaning. Quechua is also notable for being extremely regular; no irregular verbs exist. Quechua is an unwritten language, and there is no standardized method of representing its words in writing. Nevertheless, scholars have attempted to convert spoken Quechua into a written form by using a variety of alphabetic systems. However, there is considerable controversy concerning the vowel system that should be used to write Quechua using other alphabets. At present there are two competing approaches using either three vowels ("a," "i," and "u") or five vowels ("a," "e," "i," "o," and "u"). Usage of these two approaches is hotly disputed (Heggarty 2004).

### The Secret Language of the Incas

Some of the Spanish sources refer to a secret or private language spoken and understood only by the Inca nobility. Garcilaso de la Vega (1966: 59, 103, 374, 403, and 626) refers to this private language and laments that it died out after the Spanish Conquest. Scholars, however, are unsure whether this secret language ever existed. Various possibilities for which language may have been used as the secret language have been proposed. These include Aymara, Puquina, and Callahuaya (Heggarty 2004). Peruvian linguist Alfredo Torero (2002: 135–146) argues that if such a private language was used it was likely a variant of Aymara.

## Inca Literature

The Incas seem to have had a well developed oral literature tradition that has largely been lost since it typically was not recorded. Only a few fragments survive that provide an idea of the rich tradition that has been lost. John Rowe (1946: 320) divided the surviving texts into four types: prayers and hymns, narrative poems, drama, and songs.

Examples of prayers are preserved by Bernabé Cobo (1990: 119–120) in his famous work on Inca religion. A prayer to Viracocha, the creator:

O most happy, fortunate Creator, you have compassion on men and take pity on them! Behold your people here, your children, poor, unfortunate, whom you have made and given life; take pity on them and let them live safe and sound with their children and descendants; guide them in the ways of good health and let them not perceive or think about bad and harmful things; let them live for a long time and not die in their youth; let them eat and drink in peace.

A prayer to Inti, the sun:

O Sun, my father, who said "let there be Cuzco!" and by your will it was founded and it is preserved with such grandeur! Let these sons of yours, the Incas, be conquerors and despoilers of all mankind. We adore you and offer this sacrifice to you so that you will grant us what we beg of you. Let them be prosperous and make them happy, and do not allow them to be conquered by anyone, but let them always be conquerors since you made them for that purpose.

A prayer to the *huacas* and mummies:

O fathers, guacas, and vilcas, our grandfathers and ancestors! Protect these little children of yours so that they will be happy and very fortunate as you are yourself; intercede with Viracocha on their behalf; bring them closer to him so he will give them the protection that he gives to you.

The most popular literary form was the oral narrative poem used to relate history and literature. Unfortunately none of these have survived. The Spanish chroniclers Sarmiento de Gamboa (1999: 38–42) and Cieza de León (1959: 173–174, 187–188) indicate that these oral poems related history, mythology, and legends that were passed down word for word by memory through the generations. These works were frequently recited by professional performers on public occasions or during ceremonies. Eventually, with frequent recitation everyone would be familiar with the stories.

There is some indication of dramatic performances but whether these were plays in the European sense, that is staged by professional actors for the entertainment of the audience, is doubtful. Rowe (1946: 321) comments that the only surviving example, called the drama of Ollanta, is suspiciously European in character and cannot be proven to predate the Conquest. He feels that Inca drama probably consisted of narrative or dialogue between two actors accompanied by a chorus.

Like the narrative poems, songs were performed on similar occasions and also conveyed history and narrative. A song believed to be pre-Conquest is one sung by the emperor Pachacuti on his deathbed as reported by Sarmiento de Gamboa (1999: 139):

> I was born as a flower of the field,
> As a flower I was cherished in my youth,
> I came to my full age, I grew old,
> Now I am withered and die.

## INCA LITERACY, MATHEMATICS, AND METHODS OF RECORDING

One of the most remarkable aspects of Inca intellectual life was the apparent lack of a writing system. Scholars have long puzzled over this fact with many straining to understand how the Incas could have developed and administered such a complex imperial society without a means of transmitting written information. While it seems impossible that the Inca civilization could exist without some form of writing, no written records or examples of writing have ever been found. There were several memory aid devices mentioned by the Spanish sources that seem to have permitted the storage and transmission of information. These include painted wooden boards showing scenes from Inca history, the knotted string device called the *quipu*, and an abacus-like counting device. These last two devices also shed some light on Inca mathematical knowledge.

### Painted History

The painted wooden boards are lost to history as none are known to have survived. Evidence of their existence is compelling and has been summarized by Catherine Julien in her important work on Inca history (Julien 2000: 52–61). The Spanish chronicler Sarmiento de Gamboa (1999: 41–42) in explaining how the Incas knew their history explicitly states:

> . . . they had and still have, special historians in these nations, a hereditary office descending from father to son. The collection of these annals is due to the great diligence of Pachacuti Inca Yupanqui, the ninth Inca, who sent out a general summons to all the old historians in all the provinces he has subjugated, and even to many others throughout those kingdoms. He had them in Cuzco for a long time, examining them concerning their antiquities, origins, and the most notable events in their his-

tory. These were painted on great boards, and deposited in the temple of the Sun, in a great hall. There such boards, adorned with gold, were kept as in our libraries, and learned persons were appointed, who were well versed in the art of understanding and declaring their contents. No one was allowed to enter where these boards were kept, except the Inca and the historians, without a special order of the Inca. (Translation by Clements Markham)

Another reliable Spanish account by Cristóbal de Molina ([1576]; 1989: 49–50) states:

They kept in a house of the Sun called Poquen Cancha, which is near Cuzco, the life of each one of the Incas and the lands he conquered, painted in their figures on some tablets and [also] what their origins were. (Translation by Catherine Julien)

## The *Quipu*

Records in the Inca Empire were kept on a device called the *quipu,* whose name derives from the Quechua word for knot. This apparatus consisted of a length of cord from which a number of strings were suspended. These pendant strings were marked at regular intervals with different types of knots which served to encode the information being recorded. Variations in the number of turns in a knot as well as the color and direction of twist or spin of the string and whether it was attached to the top or bottom of the main cord also seem to have served to encode information. The Spanish chroniclers observed and commented on the *quipu,* but none seem to have learned how to make or read the device. Because of their construction from perishable fiber materials most *quipus* have not survived into modern times. Nevertheless there remains a substantial sample preserved in museums and private collections worldwide. In his work on *quipus,* Gary Urton (2003: 2) has estimated that there are as many as 600 surviving examples.

*Quipus* were made and read by a professional class of officials called *quipocamayoc.* The Spanish sources (e.g., Acosta 2002: 342–344; Betanzos 1996: 51, 90–91; Cieza de León 1959: 172–175; Cobo 1979: 253–254; Molina 1913: 125–126, among others. See also Rowe 1946: 325–327) discuss the construction and use of the *quipu* commenting on the extremely accurate accounts that were kept on them. Inventories, harvests, census data, and all manner of statistical data were encoded using a decimal system indicated by the size and position of the knots. It is also claimed that histories, stories, and other literature were remembered by use of this device. The principal flaw with this system, according to the Spaniards, was that a *quipu* could only be read by its maker or someone familiar with the subject being recorded. It was generally believed that the device acted only as an aid to memory in the same way that a rosary is used by worshippers to remember their prayers.

Because of the belief that *quipus* could not be read and the general lack of context for surviving examples, they did not attract serious scholarly studies until quite recently. In the early part of the twentieth century science historian

A *quipocamayoc*. (Felipe Huamán Poma de Ayala)

Leland Locke (1923, 1928) began studying *quipus* and was able to demonstrate that numbers were being recorded on some of them based on the decimal system of notation. John Rowe (1946: 326) observed that the *quipus* with recorded numbers also demonstrated that the Incas were familiar with the concept of zero and were able to record it. Study of *quipus* was continued by Marcia and Robert Ascher (1981) who intensively studied how they were made and the types of information that might be encoded on them. Robert Ascher (2002) has argued that *quipus* were not just a mnemonic device or memory aids but instead represent a true system of writing. Because it is effectively a three dimensional writing system completely alien to western experience, he feels that *quipus* were misunderstood and ignored. As a true system of writing, it should be possible to decipher and read *quipus* as a text. A recent scholarly roundtable on the topic of approaches to reading narratives in *quipus* (Quilter and Urton 2002) has sparked new interest in their study. An intriguing hypothesis has also been offered by Gary Urton (2003) that suggests that *quipus* were based on a binary coding system analogous to binary computer code. He calculates that the possible variations of color, cord twist or spin, and knot types could yield as many as 1,500 possible combinations, each of which could be used as a unit of information in the same way that signs in cuneiform or Egyptian hieroglyphs convey units of information. Despite the renewed interest, no one has yet succeeded in reading a *quipu*.

## COUNTING AND CALCULATING DEVICES

*Quipus* were used for recording numbers and other information but were ill suited for use as a calculator. John Rowe (1946: 326) points out that the chroniclers make clear that calculations were done using seeds or pebbles moved into piles. There is also some evidence of an abacuslike tray with compartments arranged to indicate values and markers or tokens that could be moved through the device.

### Inca Knowledge of Mathematics

Given their emphasis on recording and manipulating statistics, the decimal organization of their society, their calculating devices, and their superb knowledge of civil engineering it is obvious that the Incas had considerable mathematical expertise. Little direct knowledge of their mathematical abilities exists but studies of *quipus* by Marcia and Robert Ascher have provided some clues (Ascher and Ascher 1981: 133–156). In addition to a base ten number system, ". . . the body of arithmetic ideas used by the Incas must have included, at a minimum, addition, division into equal parts, division into simple unequal fractional parts, division into proportional parts, multiplication of integers by integers, and multiplication of integers by fractions" (Ascher and Ascher 1981: 152).

## ASTRONOMICAL KNOWLEDGE

Because of their lack of a writing system, our knowledge of what the Incas knew about astronomy and how they conceived of the universe is indirect. What is known is based on Spanish accounts written after the European Conquest and on insights provided by modern ethnographic studies of Andean communities that may have preserved some of the Incas' knowledge in their contemporary traditions. Serious attempts at reconstructing Inca astronomical knowledge date only from the mid-nineteenth century. Scholars initially tended to take an approach to interpreting Inca astronomy based on European models of constellations and calendars (Bollaert 1860, 1861). Later, in the first half of the twentieth century, attempts were made to recover knowledge from the Inca point of view. This encompassed reviewing the early Spanish accounts and examining the remains of Inca material culture such as *quipus* and masonry observation markers that have survived into modern times (Urteaga 1913; Müller 1972; Nordenskiöld 1925; Lehman-Nitsche 1928; Rowe 1946; Valcárcel 1946). By the second half of the twentieth century, especially in the 1970s and 1980s, there was a considerable increase in interest in the topic of Inca astronomy with a number of scholars making major contributions. Models of Inca astronomy were devised and tested on various Inca sites and monuments (Aveni 1981, 1987; Bauer and Dearborn 1995; Dearborn and Schreiber 1986; Dearborn, Schreiber, and White 1987; Dearborn and White 1983; Hyslop 1990; Williams-León 1992; Ziólkowski and Sadowski 1989, 1992; Zuidema 1977a, 1977b, 1981a, 1981b, 1982a, 1982b, 1988). Studies of native Quechua astronomy were also undertaken to provide an understanding of the native point of view (Urton 1980, 1981, 1982). Celestial observations of the sun, moon, various planets, stars, and constellations were made by the Incas and used for both religious and secular purposes.

## Solar and Lunar Observations

The sun not only was a principal deity for the Incas but also provided the basis for their agricultural calendar. Likewise the moon was also a deity but additionally served to mark the months of the year (see Chapter 8). The phases of the moon were carefully observed to mark a lunar calendar. The sun was observed for purposes of establishing the agricultural cycle, but months were based on lunar observations. Solar and lunar years are not of the same length. The solar year is about 365 and one quarter days long, whereas the twelve-month lunar year is only about 354 days in length. As Rowe (1946: 327) observed, this discrepancy causes the solar and lunar year to differ quite dramatically over relatively short periods of time. It is not known how the Incas reconciled the years of different lengths.

Solar observations were made against the horizon. Rising and setting phenomena of the sun were marked by means of stone pillars, called *sucanca*, erected on the hillsides above Cuzco to the east and west. Sources disagree on how many pillars there were with accounts ranging from four to sixteen. These pillars could be seen from some central point in Cuzco, perhaps the *ushnu* platform in the main plaza, from which observations were made (Cobo 1990: 27; Rowe 1946: 327). Solstices and equinoxes were important ritually but it is not known whether they could be determined with precision. The Spanish chronicler Garcilaso de la Vega (1966: 116–118) made claims that solstices and equinoxes were observed but no other chronicler before him did so, causing Rowe to express doubt about this claim (Rowe 1946: 327).

Another possible means for solar observations involved the use of shadow casting or light casting. An upright stone or gnomon would cast a shadow rather like a sundial. The position of the shadow would be indicative of a certain day. Likewise certain openings or windows in buildings or even caves were believed to catch the rays of the sun on only a particular day (Dearborn and Schreiber 1986; Dearborn, Schreiber, and White 1987; Dearborn and White 1983). Exactly how these systems of observation functioned is unclear since the Spanish sources are vague and contradictory.

In measuring time the Incas had terms for the year (*huata*), month (*quilla* or moon), and day (*punchao*). According to the chronicler Bernabé Cobo (1979: 251–253) there were no names for the individual days of the week and whether or not the concept of a week was used is debated. Neither was there any grouping of months into seasons such as spring, summer, fall, and winter. Time during a day was not recorded in hours but by the movement of the sun with someone pointing to the position of the sun at the start and finish of some activity to express how much time had elapsed. Another method was to divide time into the intervals necessary for accomplishing common tasks. Thus a person might express an amount of time as the time it takes to boil potatoes.

## Observations of Stars and Planets

The Incas, in common with all Andean peoples, had a complex mythology regarding the stars and planets and keenly observed the heavens. In the cold clear night of the highlands, the stars and Milky Way are especially brilliant. Stars were believed to correspond to particular animals and were viewed as guardians of well-being and fertility of that animal. Stars could be grouped into constellations which were also worshipped for specific purposes. The Pleiades constellation was called *qolqa* or granary, and the planet Venus was called *chaska cuyllor*. Both the Pleiades and Venus were observed closely since their periodic movements helped to fix the agricultural cycle. Rising and setting phenomena were observed against the horizon, as with the sun, and it is possible that some of the ceremonial lines called *ceques* that radiated outward from the Coricancha temple may have marked these events for calendrical purposes (Cobo 1990: 29–30; Zuidema 1982: 451).

One of the more curious aspects of Inca sky watching is their lore regarding the Milky Way. The Milky Way is especially vivid in the night sky of the Andes and was known as *mayo*, or river, because it appeared as a broad band of stars flowing across the sky. Within this brilliant flow were dark areas where interstellar clouds blocked the light. Each of these dark clouds was viewed in the same way as constellations were in western lore. These dark entities were thought of as animals and were named accordingly: llama and her baby, condor, partridge, toad, serpent, and fox.

While some scholars have believed that Inca astronomical knowledge was limited in its accuracy (Rowe 1946: 327), William Sullivan (1996) has argued that Incas observed the planets and Milky Way with extreme precision and viewed their apparent oscillation across the sky as marking long periods of time. The mythological animals viewed in the heavens and tales about them were metaphors used to mark or date actual historical events. The apparent movement of stars and planets relative to the Milky Way was believed to

Gorge of the Urubamba. (Corel)

predict the beginnings and endings of great ages. The past and the future were written in the stars. Sullivan believes that in order to secure and control the future the Incas conceived a replica of the Milky Way on earth in the heart of their territory. The Urubamba River was believed to be the physical analog of the river of stars in the sky, and along its banks in the Sacred Valley of the Inca were located prominent landmarks that were physical manifestations of the animals represented in the dark clouds of the Milky Way. Believing that the heavens influenced what happened on earth, the Incas attempted to turn the tables and to have their earthly efforts influence the heavens.

## REFERENCES

Acosta, José de. 2002 [1590]. *Natural and Moral History of the Indies.* Edited by Jane E. Mangan. Translated by Frances López-Morillas. Durham, NC: Duke University Press.

Ascher, Marcia, and Robert Ascher. 1981. *Code of the Quipu.* Ann Arbor: University of Michigan Press.

Ascher, Robert. 2002. "Inka Writing." In *Narrative Threads,* edited by Jeffrey Quilter and Gary Urton, 103–115. Austin: University of Texas Press.

Aveni, Anthony F. 1981. "Horizon Astronomy in Incaic Cuzco." In *Archaeoastronomy in the Americas,* edited by Ray A. Williamson, 305–318. Los Altos, CA: Ballena Press.

———. 1987. "On Seeing the Light" (a reply to "Here Comes the Sun" by D. Dearborn and K. Schreiber). In *Archaeoastronomy* 10: 22–24.

Bauer, Brian S., and David S. P. Dearborn. 1995. *Astronomy and Empire in the Ancient Andes.* Austin: University of Texas Press.

Betanzos, Juan de. 1996 [1551]. *Narrative of the Incas.* Translated and edited by Roland Hamilton and Dana Buchanan. Austin: University of Texas Press.

Bollaert, William. 1860. *Antiquarian, Ethnological, and other Researches in New Granada, Equador, Peru, and Chile, with Observations on the PreIncarial, Incarial, and Other Monuments of Peruvian Nations.* London: Trübner and Company.

———. 1861. "An Account of the Zodiac of the Incas, and Also of Some Antiquities Recently Found at Cuzco, Now in the Possession of General Echanique, Late President of Peru." In *Proceedings of the Society of Antiquarians of London,* 2nd ser., 1: 78–81.

Cieza de León, Pedro de. 1959 [1553]. *The Incas of Pedro de Cieza de León.* Translated by Harriet de Onis and edited by Victor W. von Hagen. Norman: University of Oklahoma Press.

Cobo, Bernabé. 1979 [1653]. *History of the Inca Empire: An Account of the Indians' Customs and their Origin Together with a Treatise on Inca Legends, History, and Social Institutions.* Translated and edited by Roland Hamilton. Austin: University of Texas Press.

———. 1990. *Inca Religion and Customs.* Translated and edited by Roland Hamilton. Austin: University of Texas Press.

Dearborn, David S. P., and Katharina J. Schreiber. 1989. "Houses of the Rising Sun." In *Time and Calendars in the Inca Empire,* edited by Mariusz S. Ziòlkowski and Robert M. Sadowski, 49–74. Oxford: British Archaeological Reports, International Series, no. 479.

Dearborn, David S. P., Katharina J. Schreiber, and Raymond E. White. 1987. "Intimachay, A December Solstice Observatory." *American Antiquity* 52: 346–352.

Dearborn, David S. P., and Raymond E. White. 1983. "The 'Torreón' at Machu Picchu as an Observatory. *Archaeoastronomy* 5:37–49.

Garcilaso de la Vega, El Inca. 1966 [1609]. *Royal Commentaries of the Incas and General History of Peru, Parts One and Two.* Translated by Harold Livermore. Austin: University of Texas Press.

Heggarty, Paul. http://www.shef.ac.uk/q/quechua/i_HOME.HTM.

Hyslop, John. 1990. *Inka Settlement Planning.* Austin: University of Texas Press.

Julien, Catherine. 2000. *Reading Inca History.* Iowa City: University of Iowa Press.

Lehman-Nitsche, Robert. 1928. "Coricancha: El Templo del Sol en el Cuzco y las imagines de su altar mayor." *Revista del Museo de La Plata* 31–1–256.

Locke, L. Leland. 1923. *The Ancient Quipu or Peruvian Knot Record.* New York: American Museum of Natural History.

————. 1928. "Supplementary Notes on the Quipus in the American Museum of Natural History." *Anthropological Papers of the American Museum of Natural History,* Vol. 30, Part 2: 37–71. New York: American Museum of Natural History.

Molina, Cristóbal. 1943 [1573] "Fábulas y ritos de los Incas." In *Las crónicas de los Molinas,* 1–84. Los pequeños grandes libros de historia americana. vol. Serie I, Tomo IV, Lima: Müller 1972.

Nordenskiöld, Erland. 1925. "Calculations with Years and Months in the Peruvian Quipus." *Comparative Ethnographical Studies,* vol. 6, pt. 2. Göteborg: Elanders Boktryckeri Akjebolag.

Quilter, Jeffrey, and Gary Urton, eds. 2002. *Narrative Threads: Accounting and Recounting in Andean Khipu.* Austin: The University of Texas Press.

Rowe, John H. 1946. "Inca Culture at the Time of the Spanish Conquest." In *Handbook of South American Indians.* Bureau of American Ethnology, bulletin 143, vol. 2. Julian Steward, 183–330. Washington DC: Smithsonian Institution.

————. 2004. "How did the Incas say 'Sacsahuaman' in the Sixteenth Century?" *Ñawpa Pacha* 25–27: 151–153. Institute of Andean Studies, Berkeley.

Sarmiento de Gamboa, Pedro. 1999. *History of the Incas.* Translated and edited by Sir Clements Markham. Mineola: Dover Publications. Originally published 1907: Hakluyt Society.

Sullivan, William. 1996. *The Secret of the Incas: Myth, Astronomy, and the War Against Time.* New York: Crown Publishers, Inc.

Torero, Alfredo. 2002. *Idiomas de los Andes - Lingüística e Historia.* Lima: Editorial Horizonte/IFEA.

Urteaga, Horacio H. 1913. "Informe sobre los observatories astronómicos o piedras del sol de los Incas." *Boletín de la Sociedad Geográfica de Lima* 29: 40–46.

Urton, Gary. 1980. "Celestial Crosses: The Cruciform in Quechua Astronomy." *Journal of Latin American Lore* 6 (1): 87–110.

————. 1981. *At the Crossroads of the Earth and the Sky: An Andean Cosmology.* Austin: University of Texas Press.

————. 1982. "Astronomy and Calendrics on the Coast of Peru." In *Ethnoastronomy and Archaeoastronomy in the American Tropics,* edited by A. F. Aveni and G. Urton, 231–259. New York: Annals of the New York Academy of Sciences, vol. 385.

————. 2003. *Signs of the Inka Khipu.* Austin: University of Texas Press.

Valcárcel, Luis E. 1946. "Cuzco Archaeology." In *Handbook of South American Indians,* Bureau of American Ethnology, bulletin 143, vol. 2, edited by Julian Steward, 177–182. Washington, DC: Smithsonian Institution.

Williams-León, Carlos. 1992. "Sukankas y ceques: La medición del tiempo en el Tahuantinsuyu." *Pachacamac* (Revista del Museo de la Nación, Lima). 1 (1): 101–113.

Ziólkowski, Marius S., and Robert M. Sadowski. 1989. *Time and Calendars in the Inca Empire.* BAR International Series 479. Oxford: British Archaeological Reports.

———. 1992. *La arqueoastronomía en la investigación de las culturas Andinas.* Quito: Instituto Otavaleño de Antropología, Banco Central de Ecuador.

Zuidema, R. Tom. 1977a. "The Inca Calendar." In *Native American Astronomy,* edited by Anthony Aveni, 219–259. Austin: University of Texas Press.

———. 1977b. "La imagen del sol y la huaca de Susurpuquio en el sistema astronómico de los Incas en Cuzco." *Journal de la Société des Américanistes* 63: 199–230.

———. 1981a. "Anthropology and Archaeoastronomy." In *Archaeoastronomy in the Americas,* edited by Ray A. Williamson, 29–31. Los Altos, CA.: Ballena Press.

———. 1981b. "Inca Observations of the Solar and Lunar Passages through Zenith and Anti-Zenith at Cuzco." In *Archaeoastronomy in the New World,* edited by Ray A. Williamson, 319–342. Los Altos, CA.: Ballena Press.

———. 1982a. "Bureaucracy and Systematic Knowledge in Andean Civilization." In *The Inca and the Aztec States, 1400–1800: Anthropology and History,* edited by G.A. Collier, R. A. Rosaldo, and J. D. Wirth, 419–458. New York: Academic Press.

———. 1982b. "The Sidereal Lunar Calendar of the Incas." In *Archaeoastronomy in the New World,* edited by A. Aveni, 59–107. Cambridge: Cambridge University Press.

———. 1988. "The Pillars of Cuzco: Which Two Dates of Sunset Did They Define?" In *New Directions in American Archaeoastronomy,* edited by A. Aveni, 143–169. BAR International Series 454. Oxford: British Archaeological Reports.

# PART 3
## Current Assessments

# CHAPTER 11

# Major Controversies and Future Directions in Inca Studies

Despite intense scholarly attention, Inca history remains controversial because of the nature of the sources of information. Spanish accounts of Inca oral history are biased, as are the accounts given to them by the Incas themselves, by misunderstandings arising from cultural differences and by the various agendas of those telling the stories and those recording them. In the end, Inca history is now studied, nearly five centuries after the fact, through the lens of sixteenth-century Spanish culture, which in turn is studied through the lens of modern interpretation. As a result, there are many contradictions between both original accounts and scholarly interpretations. Today the fundamental issue revolves around just how different the Inca perception of reality was from both the sixteenth-century Spanish reality and our modern perceptions. How can scholars approach such a complicated problem and penetrate to the core truths of Inca history? Close study of the Spanish texts has produced remarkably divergent interpretations of Inca history. These interpretations, as well as the basic Inca accounts, it would seem, could best be tested through archaeological work, in much the same way that scholars have attempted to use biblical archaeology to confirm Old Testament history. Unfortunately, nothing in this complicated enterprise of understanding the Incas is simple or completely straightforward. Yes, archaeology can give and has given us insights, but it is still in its infancy in the Andes and conducted with interpretive tools that lack the precision necessary for resolving such a complex problem. Nevertheless, strides are being made toward at least a better understanding of the Incas.

## HISTORICISTS VS. STRUCTURALISTS: THE GREAT INCA DEBATE

Throughout the latter half of the twentieth century, the field of Inca studies has been dominated by a lengthy, sometimes bitter debate over the structure of both the Inca dynasty and its history. Two perspectives, the historicist approach and the structuralist interpretation, have generally been identified with two great Andean scholars, John H. Rowe and R. Tom Zuidema, respectively, and their various students. While other perspectives have occasionally surfaced, such the Marxist approach advocated by Patterson (1991) and others, the field has been largely divided by these two basic points of view.

## The Historicist Perspective

Fundamental to the historicist perspective is the proposition that the Incas did in fact have a linear, sequential concept of history. While recognizing the biases and distortions that may be in the historical record, historicist scholars believe that the information that the Incas gave the Spanish conquerors, at least with respect to the latter reigns of the Inca dynasty from Pachacuti onward, are basically historical in character. The earlier reigns may be more or less mythical but likely still have a core of historical content (Julien 2000). As outlined in Chapter 3, John Rowe (1944 and 1946) was able to suggest dates of rule for the last four reigns with reasoning based on reports of various eyewitnesses' memories, providing a chronology and sequence of events for the latter part of Inca history.

Within this framework there are still problems to be considered. The historicists recognize that individual rulers had history composed and sometimes reworked to cast themselves in a flattering light and to obscure the deeds of their rivals. Therefore it is still necessary to verify the events and their sequence and to consider which should be assigned to what ruler. Taking this approach, scholars can gradually fill in the gaps and resolve errors, working toward a coherent, event-based history in which Inca government was a monarchy characterized by dynastic succession.

## The Structuralist Perspective

As a point of departure, the structuralist perspective argues that there was no history, in the Western sense, recorded by the Spaniards when they wrote down the stories of the Inca dynasty. The gulf between the two cultures, Inca and Spanish, was so great that the chroniclers simply did not understand what they were told. They tried to make it coherent by forcing the information into European categories of interpretation, describing a European-style monarchy where there was in fact something quite different. Their stories of the deeds of Inca emperors are thus considered to be not history but myths that encoded and legitimized a model of Inca social organization. Zuidema argues that the various rulers mentioned in the Spanish accounts can be viewed as representing contemporary social groupings or lineages (*ayllus* or *panacas*) among the ruling Incas, reflecting the Spanish chroniclers' conceptualization of how the different lineages fit together into a coherent whole (Zuidema 1964, 1990, 1995; Rostworowski de Diez Canseco 1999; Urton 1990).

Zuidema's ideas were further developed by Pierre Duviols (1979), who interpreted the traditional king list in quite a different manner. He proposed that the Incas were ruled by a diarchy with a limited time depth of only five or six generations. In this scheme, the two moiety halves of Cuzco, Hanansaya and Hurinsaya, would have each provided a king and these two individuals would have ruled simultaneously, representing their respective moiety, with the king from the upper moiety, Hanansaya, being the senior and ultimate power. Thus the second king, Sinchi Roca of Hurinsaya, would have coruled with the sixth king, Inca Roca of Hanansaya. This model is not without critics, however, and has remained a minority view. Peter Gose (1996) has argued that while there is much precedent for this model at the lower levels of administration in the provinces of the Inca Empire, the evidence for use of this rulership pattern by the Incas at the apex of imperial power is doubtful and problematic. Spanish references supporting this structure are few and not specific enough. The vast majority of the sources seem to be in agreement regarding a monarchy.

## ISSUES IN INCA ARCHAEOLOGY

Given these conflicting ideas about Inca government and history, archaeological investigations should provide help in clarifying which of the models of Inca history and governance is more likely. However, as indicated in Chapter 4, the archaeological record has its own problems that scholars must contend with. As in the case of the historicist-structuralist debate outlined above, archaeological methodology in Inca studies has also oscillated between two primary theoretical approaches: a cultural-materialist processual approach and a historicist approach.

### Processual, Post Processualist, and Historicist Approaches

The processual approach to the archaeological record enjoyed great popularity in the Americas during the last several decades of the twentieth century. It grew out of a reaction to the purely historicist methodology used by earlier generations of archaeologists, which was criticized as being inadequate to explain social process and change (Johnson 1999). The processualist archaeologists viewed environmental adaptation as the key to understanding a society's behavior, motivations, and history. Moreover, this adaptive process could be interpreted relatively easily based on the types of material remains—plant, animal, and human, as well as ceramics, stone tools, metal objects, and architecture—that were best preserved in the archaeological record. It would be relatively easy to understand how a society made its living in terms of what resources were exploited, its distribution over the landscape, and how these things changed through time. This information could then be used to understand and decipher a society's history. Even if all of the information on the Inca was purely mythical, that is, nonhistorical, it should still be possible to observe the broad trends in their social history, although the specifics would remain obscure.

Processual studies such as this were conducted by Timothy Earle and his students (Earle et al. 1987; Earle and D'Altroy 1989; D'Altroy 1992) in the upper Mantaro drainage, which included the major Inca provincial center of Hatun Xauxa. While these studies yielded a large amount of information on material culture and economic practices of the Incas and the local Huanca ethnicity, they could provide only a very narrow picture of the Inca occupation. The advantage of this methodology is that it provides concrete, science-based answers to certain questions regardless of one's stance on the issue of the authenticity of Inca historical accounts. The disadvantage is that it cannot address questions of ideology and individual agency and therefore does not contribute much to clarifying the debate over Inca history. As reported through the Spanish chronicles, the Inca accounts of their history were very much event based and dependent on the specific personalities, abilities, and actions of a series of "great men." Unfortunately, the processual approach to archaeology is not able to account for these individual actors or their thoughts and motivations.

Processualist methodology has in turn provoked its own counterreaction called Post Processualist methodology. Advocates of this approach such as William Isbell (1997) have explicitly rejected a purely scientific approach in favor of an empathetic, humanistic one. To achieve this it is deemed necessary to take ethnographic knowledge of modern Andean native culture, social organization, and belief systems and project it backward in time to interpret the archaeological record. A primary weakness, however, is the acknowledged fact that people change over time, raising questions about how accurate a picture modern culture can provide of things that happened more than five centuries ago. Mitigation of this problem requires a careful selection of which cultural traits to use in interpreting the past, with an eye toward selecting those that are most conservative and least prone to change. Ultimately these choices become subjective and the results little more than opinion and conjecture.

An alternative methodology is the historicist approach, which starts from the premise that there is true history embedded in the accounts of the Inca dynasty and then seeks corroborative evidence in the archaeological record. Judicious use of Spanish documents and chronicles as well as the archaeological record, such as in the work of Catherine Julien (1983) at the major Inca administrative center of Hatun Qolla, can produce fruitful results. Nevertheless, this approach is vulnerable to the criticism that it requires a fundamental (and possibly somewhat subjective) belief that there is a true history to work with. Great care must be employed to avoid circular logic in interpreting archaeological data in light of the Inca history in the chronicles.

## Limitations of Dating Methodology

These different strategies for looking at the archaeological record of the Incas can produce divergent results that may obscure rather than clarify certain issues. Consider a basic question for students of the Incas: the chronology of their imperial expansion. When did the empire form and start its conquests? Finding the answer to this fairly straightforward question is clouded by a number of issues. The best existing means for establishing absolute dates (i.e., calendar dates) for events in the Andes that are earlier than the European Conquest is the radiocarbon method. As discussed in Chapter 3, this method is accurate within about a century, yet this is a major handicap for archaeologists because the Inca Empire only lasted for perhaps 80 years. Therefore the radiocarbon method can only tell us whether something falls within the Inca period but can't tell us if it pertains to the early or later parts of Inca history. Radiocarbon samples are also prone to contamination and the method is restricted to dating organic remains.

These limitations can lead to anomalous results when trying to date the arrival of the Incas in a particular location. Inca presence is typically recognized by the presence of Inca ceramics or architecture, which cannot be dated directly by the radiocarbon method but only by associations with organic material. The validity of associations is often a judgment call on the part of the excavator, resulting in claims that are utterly inconsistent with what little we do know about the Inca chronology (e.g., Pärssinen and Siiriäinen 1997). When this occurs the inevitable debate rages over whether the Incas could really have built their empire and all of its monuments in the short time allowed by the traditional accounts. Is it possible that the anomalous information indicates that time depth of the empire was much greater than previously believed, with the Inca expansion occurring much earlier? Only more fieldwork and better dating methods will resolve this question.

Attempts to determine the timing of the Inca imperial expansion are also clouded by the methodology chosen to detect the formation and rise of the Inca state. The processual method discussed above has been applied to this question (Bauer and Covey 2002; Covey 2003), with the results indeed suggesting that the Inca state formed much earlier than previously believed. The specific criteria used to observe the political formation of the Inca polity was the distribution over the landscape of a particular ceramic style called K'illke. This approach assumes that ceramic style can be equated with a particular ethnicity or allegiance and that its presence or absence reveals the distribution of people over the landscape and their political relationships. To achieve this analysis it is necessary to have firm chronological control of (i.e., be able to date accurately) the ceramic material and to be able to precisely associate the ceramic style with a particular ethnic group such as the Incas. This is very difficult to achieve because of the limitations of the radiocarbon dating method discussed above. Furthermore, deciphering the relationship between polities and ceramic styles is essentially subjective. There may be many reasons for the distribution of a particular style in an area, not all of which are related to political activity. Ultimately, no matter how rigorously the methodology is applied, it is in the final analysis based on a subjective assumption about the meaning of the artifacts.

Historicist methodologies are also limited by the necessity to make subjective judgments and prone to the same deficiencies of the radiocarbon dating method. The historicist approach also has to assume that there is a knowable and a real Inca history within which archaeological results can be interpreted. More difficult is trying to match the material objects in the archaeological record with the peoples mentioned in the Inca histories. For example, a great turning point in Inca history, according to the traditional accounts, was the war against the Chanca. The Incas' struggle with them was prolonged and monumental, yet scholars have no idea of what Chanca material culture looked like, where to find it, or how to recognize it if it is found. The same is true for the various ethnic groups mentioned by the Inca histories as occupying the Cuzco Valley when the Incas arrived on the scene.

## Further Methodological Inquiry

Given the limitations of these methods, scholars are constantly on the lookout for other methodologies that might grant access to knowing the Inca past. Is there an information database that is being overlooked? Did the Incas record their history in ways that we haven't thought of? The discussion of the *quipu* in the last chapter shows one avenue for potentially recovering written Inca history through the binary code suggested by Gary Urton (2003). Another area in the search for an Inca writing system is the study of the *tocapu* designs found woven into royal garments. William Burns (1981) has the idea that *tocapu* are more than just a royal insignia and may in fact have been a forerunner to the development of a glyphic writing system. He has developed a syllabary to decipher the designs but has not yet succeeded in convincing many scholars with his claims.

Inca studies have shed light on many aspects of this fascinating culture, but there is still much to be learned and many questions to be resolved. Despite years of intensive research, many fundamental issues remain unresolved. Who were the Incas in terms of their ethnic origins? Were they a local tribe that somehow gained ascendancy over their neighbors, becoming a first among equals in the Late Intermediate Period? Did they come from somewhere else, either in the neighborhood of Cuzco or perhaps from farther away to the south near Lake Titicaca, as some of their legends seem to suggest? How did the Incas construct their huge empire so rapidly? If the short timeline suggested by the Spanish sources is correct, there would have been little time for trial and error in the invention and construction of the institutions and techniques of statecraft. How did the Incas know how to put together an empire and successfully operate it? Did they inherit the knowledge? If so, how much and from whom?

Finally, the question that seems to intrigue the public most: have all of the Inca cities been found? Not a year goes by without some claim in the press of a new lost Inca city being discovered in the jungles and *montañas* of Peru. These claims never seem to hold up to reveal the next Machu Picchu. Yet given the amount of still unexplored terrain, there always exists the possibility that new Inca sites will come to light. Even should one be discovered, however, it would be unlikely to fundamentally alter what we know about the Incas. Still there is much yet to be learned about the Incas, and current and future studies will be directed at resolving these issues.

## REFERENCES

Bauer, Brian S., and R. Alan Covey. 2002. "Processes of State Formation in the Inca Heartland (Cuzco, Peru)." *American Anthropologist* 104(3): 846–864.

Burns, William Glynn. 1981. "La Escritura de los Incas: Una Introducción a la clave de la Escriturea Secreta de los Incas." *Boletín de Lima* vols. 12–14: 1–32.

Covey, R. Alan. 2003. "A Processual Study of Inca State Formation." *Journal of Anthropological Archaeology* 22: 333–357.

D'Altroy, Terrence N. 1992. *Provincial Power in the Inka Empire*. Washington, DC: Smithsonian Insitution.

Duviols, Pierre. 1979. "La dinastía de los Incas: ¿monarquía o diarquía? Argumentos heurísticos a favor de una tesis estructuralista." *Journal de la Société des Americanistes* 64: 67–83.

Earle, Timothy K., and Terrence N. D'Altroy. 1989. "The Political Economy of the Inka Empire: The Archaeology of Power and Finance." In *Archaeological Thought in America*, edited by Carl C. Lamberg-Karlovsky, 183–204. Cambridge: Cambridge University Press.

Earle, Timothy K., Terrence N. D'Altroy, Christine Hastorf, Catherine J. Scott, Cathy L. Costin, Glenn S. Russell, and Elsie Sandefur. 1987. *Archaeological Field Research in the Upper Mantaro, Peru, 1982–1983: Investigations of Inka Expansion and Exchange.* Monograph 28. Los Angeles: University of California Institute of Archaeology.

Gose, Peter. 1996. "The Past is a Lower Moiety: Diarchy, History, and Divine Kingship in the Inca Empire." *History and Anthropology* 9(4): 383–414.

Isbell, William H. 1997. *Mummies and Mortuary Monuments: A Postprocessualist PreHistory of Central Andean Social Organization.* Austin: University of Texas Press.

Johnson, Matthew. 1999. *Archaeological Theory: An Introduction.* Oxford: Blackwell Publishing.

Julien, Catherine. 1983. *Hatunqolla: A View of Inca Rule from the Lake Titicaca Region.* Publications in Anthropology, vol. 15. Berkeley: University of California Press.

———. 2000. *Reading Inca History.* Iowa City: University of Iowa Press.

Pärssinen, Martti, and Ari Siiriäinen. 1997. "Inca-Style Ceramics and their Chronological Relationship to the Inca Expansion in the Southern Lake Titicaca Area (Bolivia)." *Latin American Antiquity* 8(3): 255–271.

Patterson, Thomas C. 1991. *The Inca Empire: The Formation and Disintegration of a Pre-Capitalist State.* New York: Berg Publishers.

Rostworowski de Diez Canseco, Maria. 1999. *History of the Inca Realm.* Translated by Harry B. Iceland. Cambridge: Cambridge University Press.

Rowe, John H. 1944. "An Introduction to the Archaeology of Cuzco." *Papers of the Peabody Museum of American Archaeology and Ethnology* 27, No.2. Cambridge, MA: Harvard University Press.

———. 1946. "Inca Culture at the Time of the Spanish Conquest." In *Handbook of South American Indians.* Bureau of American Ethnology, edited by Julian Steward, Bulletin 143, vol. 2, 183–330. Washington, DC: Smithsonian Institution.

Urton, Gary. 1990. *The History of a Myth: Pacariqtambo and the Origin of the Incas.* Austin: University of Texas Press.

———. 2003. *Signs of the Inka Khipu.* Austin: University of Texas Press.

Zuidema, R. Tom. 1964. *The Ceque System of Cuzco.* Translated by Eva M. Hooykaas. Supplement to vol. 50, International Archives of Ethnography. Leiden, The Netherlands: E. J. Brill.

———. 1990. *Inca Civilization in Cuzco.* Austin: University of Texas Press.

———. 1995. *El sistema de los ceques.* Lima: Pontificia Universidad Católica del Perú, Fondo Editorial.

# Chronology

| | |
|---|---|
| 12,500 B.C. | Earliest recorded date for human occupation of Andean South America. |
| 1800 | First appearance of ceramics in Andean South America. |
| 1500–1300 | Beginning of the Early Horizon. Chavín stylistic influence spreads widely throughout northern Peru. |
| 1000 | Chavín stylistic influence spreads down the Peruvian coast as far as modern Lima. |
| 500 | Chavín influence extends in the highlands from the modern cities of Cajamarca in the north to Ayacucho in the south. |
| 400–370 | Early Intermediate Period begins. Chavín cult disappears, and new regional traditions assert themselves. Nazca and Moche cultures flourish. The Cuzco Valley is occupied by the Chanapata culture. |
| A.D. 540 | Middle Horizon begins. The empires of Wari and Tiwanaku expand. |
| 600 | The Wari Empire conquers the Cuzco Valley. Local Cuzco culture at this time is called Q'otakalli. |
| 900 | Late Intermediate Period begins. Chimu Empire begins to rise on the north coast of Peru. |
| 1000–1100 | Final collapse of both Wari and Tiwanaku empires. Wari imperial center of Pikillacta in the Cuzco Valley is abandoned. Local regional center of Chokepukio is constructed. New ceramic styles called Lucre and K'illke appear in the Cuzco Valley. |
| 1200 | Traditional beginning of the Inca dynasty as calculated by John Rowe. |
| 1200–1438 | Reigns of the first eight rulers of the Inca dynasty. |
| 1438 | Chancas attack Cuzco; Viracocha Inca is overthrown by his son Pachacuti, who ascends to the throne. The Inca Empire is founded and the imperial expansion begins. |

| | |
|---|---|
| 1463 | Topa Inca becomes coregent with Pachacuti and assumes command of the army. |
| 1471 | Pachacuti retires and Topa Inca becomes sole ruler. |
| 1473 | Pachacuti dies. |
| 1492 | Columbus discovers America. |
| 1493 | Topa Inca dies. Huayna Capac becomes ruler. |
| 1511 | Huayna Capac leaves Cuzco to expand the frontier in Ecuador. |
| 1513 | An expedition led by Vasco Núñez de Balboa crosses the Isthmus of Panama and discovers the Pacific Ocean. Among Balboa's lieutenants is Francisco Pizarro. |
| 1519 | Discovery of the Aztec Empire in Mexico by Hernán Cortés. |
| 1522 | Explorer Pascual de Andagoya has pushed down the Pacific coast to the south and reports finding the province of "Birú." Cortés conquers Mexico. |
| 1524–1525 | Pizarro's first expedition goes as far as the San Juan River in Colombia. |
| 1525 | Huayna Capac dies and Huascar becomes ruler of the Inca Empire. |
| 1525–1527 | Epidemic diseases introduced by the Spaniards ravage the Peruvian populations. |
| 1526–1527 | Pizarro's second expedition makes it to Tumbes on Peru's north coast and then follows the coast south as far as modern Chimbote. |
| 1528 | Pizarro returns to Spain to seek royal backing for his expedition and to raise money and men. |
| 1529 | On July 26 Pizarro receives license from the Spanish crown to conquer Peru and titles of governor and captain general. |
| 1530 | Pizarro begins his third expedition to Peru on December 27. Civil war between Huascar and Atahuallpa begins over the question of succession to Huayna Capac. |
| 1531–1532 | Pizarro advances down the coast to Piura in northern Peru. |
| 1532 | Early in the year Atahuallpa defeats Huascar. On September 24 Pizarro and his army leave Piura and set out for Cajamarca. Atahuallpa is captured by the Spaniards at Cajamarca on November 16. Late in the year Atahuallpa has Huascar executed. |
| 1533 | Spaniards execute Atahuallpa on July 26. Topa Huallpa is crowned ruler of the Incas in August but dies in October of the same year. Manco Inca is crowned ruler of the Incas in December. |

| | |
|---|---|
| 1535–1536 | Manco Inca is abused by the Spaniards and escapes to lead first rebellion. His rebellion fails, and he retreats to the town of Vitcos in Vilcabamba. |
| 1537 | Spanish replace Manco Inca as ruler with his brother Paullu Inca. |
| 1538 | Manco Inca leads a second major revolt that fails, and he flees into the Vilcabamba region and establishes a rump state. |
| 1544 | Manco Inca is murdered by renegade Spaniards. |
| 1545 | Sayri Topa, the younger son of Manco Inca, inherits the Inca throne in the eyes of the Inca population. |
| 1549 | Paullu Inca dies and his oldest son, Carlos Inca, replaces him as ruler in the eyes of the Spanish. |
| 1550–1560 | Juan Polo de Ondegardo writes numerous reports of his investigations of the Inca government and religion. |
| 1551 | Pedro Cieza de León writes his account entitled "La crónica del Perú." |
| 1557 | Juan de Betanzos writes his account of the Incas entitled *Suma y narración de los Ingas*. |
| 1558 | Sayri Topa dies after moving from Vilcabamba to Cuzco. He is succeeded by his brother Titu Cusi, who becomes ruler of the Vilcabamba Incas. |
| 1570 | Last of the six eyewitness accounts of the Conquest is written by Pedro Pizarro. |
| 1571 | Titu Cusi dies and is succeeded by his brother Tupac Amaru. |
| 1572 | Carlos Inca dies. Tupac Amaru is captured by the Spanish and publicly executed at Cuzco. The Inca dynasty ends. Sarmiento de Gamboa finishes the history of the Incas commissioned by the Viceroy Toledo. |
| 1612 | Inca Garcilaso de la Vega finishes his book entitled *Royal Commentaries of the Incas*. |
| 1615 | Probable date of Felipe Huamán Poma de Ayala completing his work entitled *Nueva Corónica y Buen Gobierno*. |
| 1642 | Father Fernando de Montesinos completes his book *Ophir de España. Memorias Antiguas Historiales y Politicas del Perú*. |
| 1653 | Father Bernabé Cobo finishes his work entitled *Historia del Nuevo Mundo*. |
| 1847 | William Hickling Prescott publishes his classic *History of the Conquest of Peru*. |

1896   Max Uhle excavates at the site of Pachacamac. Systematic and scientific archaeology begins in Peru.

1911   Hiram Bingham brings the site of Machu Picchu to worldwide attention.

1946   John H. Rowe publishes his classic article "Inca Culture at the Time of the Spanish Conquest." The modern era of Inca studies begins.

# Glossary

**ACHIRA:** Quechua word for a tuber grown for food in the Andes.

**ACLLA:** Chosen women. On an annual basis the Incas collected as tribute the most beautiful and talented young girls from throughout the empire. These chosen women were used for state purposes or dedicated to the state religion.

**ACLLA WASI:** Quechua word for the house of the chosen women.

**AHUASCA:** (sometimes spelled *awasqa*) Quechua word for ordinary quality cloth.

**AKAPANA:** The largest of the platform mounds in the ancient city of Tiwanaku.

**ALMAGRO, DIEGO DE:** Francisco Pizarro's partner in the expedition to conquer the Incas.

**ALPACA:** Quechua word for a wool-bearing camelid, relative of the llama. Produces fine wool used for making cloth.

**ALTIPLANO:** Spanish word for a very high elevation plain in southern highland Peru, highland Bolivia, and northwestern Argentina.

**AMARANTH:** Plant with grainlike seeds grown as a food crop in the Andes.

**AMARU TUPAC INCA:** Original designated heir to Inca Pachacuti. He was removed in favor of another son Topa Inca because he was not viewed as being sufficiently gifted as a war leader.

**AMARUPATA:** Inca site in the Lucre Basin of the Valley of Cuzco that consists solely of terraces.

**AMAUTA:** Quechua word for a wise or learned person.

**AMAUTAS DYNASTY:** Powerful legendary dynasty of pre-Inca kings reported by the Spanish chronicler Montesinos.

**AMORAY:** Festival that celebrated the maize harvest.

**ANCASMAYO RIVER:** River forming the northern boundary of the Inca Empire near the modern border between Colombia and Ecuador.

**ANDAGOYA, PASCUAL DE:** Early Spanish explorer who in 1522 reached the coast of Peru.

**ANDES:** Mountain range running the length of the west coast of South America. Named for the Inca province of Antisuyu.

**ANGARA PROVINCE:** Inca province to the west of Cuzco.

**ANTISUYU:** Quechua word for the northeastern quarter of the Inca Empire, including the jungle lowlands.

**APACHITA:** *Huacas* in mountain passes that were marked by piles of stones, each stone contributed by passing travelers.

**APU:** Quechua honorific title used by the governors of the four *suyus* and by military officers of various ranks.

**APUPANACA:** Quechua term for the royal inspector who was charged with collecting the tribute paid in young girls who were to become *acllas*.

**APURATIN:** Quechua term for deputy military commander of a unit of 2,500 men.

**APURIMAC, RIVER OF:** Quechua name for one of the major tributary rivers of the Amazon that runs through the heart of the Inca Empire. The name means "great speaker."

**APURIMAC, TEMPLE OF:** A major shrine or *huaca* located above the river of the same name.

**APUSQUIPAY:** Quechua term for a general in command of a field army.

**APUSQUIPRATIN:** Quechua term for deputy commander of a field army.

**A'QA:** (also spelled aqha) Quechua word for maize beer; called *chicha* by the Spaniards.

**ARAHUAYA:** Quechua name for the site of an Inca prison located in the Cuzco Basin.

**ARIGUAQUIZ:** Quechua name for the fifth month of the year in the Inca calendar. It corresponds approximately to the month of April in the Western calendar.

**ARYBALLO:** (*aríbalo* in Spanish) Name given by early scholars to the Inca pointed-bottom bottle.

**ATAHUALLPA:** (also spelled Atahualpa, Atawallpa, Atabalipa) Name of the last independent Inca ruler, who was captured and executed by Francisco Pizarro.

**AUCA:** Quechua word that means warrior and enemy.

**AUCAY CUZQUI:** Quechua name for the seventh month of the year in the Inca calendar. It corresponds approximately to the month of June in the Western calendar.

**AVACUMBI ISLAND:** An island said to have been visited by Topa Inca and his army off the coast of Ecuador. Possibly one of the Galápagos Islands.

**AYACUCHO:** Modern city in the central highlands of Peru. It was previously known as Huamanga in the colonial period. The site of the capital of the pre-Inca Wari Empire lies nearby.

**AYAMARCA:** Quechua name for the twelfth month of the year in the Inca calendar. It corresponds approximately to the month of November in the Western calendar.

**AYAR:** Quechua word that was a title given to the founding male ancestors of the Incas.

**AYAR AUCA:** Quechua name of one of the four brothers who emerged from the cave at Pacariqtambo and founded the Inca line.

**AYAR CACHI:** Quechua name of one of the four brothers who emerged from the cave at Pacariqtambo and founded the Inca line.

**AYAR MANCO:** Quechua name of one of the four brothers who emerged from the cave at Pacariqtambo and founded the Inca line. Manco became known as

Manco Capac and was considered the most important founding male ancestor in the Inca lineage.

**AYAR UCHO:** Quechua name of one of the four brothers who emerged from the cave at Pacariqtambo and founded the Inca line.

**AYARMACA:** (also spelled Ayamarca) An ethnic group native to the Cuzco Valley and nearby areas that was a principal rival of the emerging Inca polity.

**AYAVIRI:** Ethnic group located in the Titicaca Basin that was conquered by Inca Pachacuti.

**AYLLU:** Quechua term for the basic Andean social unit. The term is a bit confusing, since the Spanish sources use it to describe a number of different-sized social units, ranging from a single lineage to a grouping of several extended families or even a half division of a community called a moiety.

**AYMARA:** One of the two principal surviving native languages in the Andes, it is spoken in southern highland Peru and in Bolivia. This term also is used to refer to the modern ethnic group defined by use of this language.

**AYMARAES PROVINCE:** Inca province just west of Cuzco.

**AYNI:** Quechua word referring to the obligation for reciprocal labor exchange.

**AYSANA:** Quechua term for the balance scale.

**AZANGARO:** Wari archaeological site located in the Ayacucho Basin of the central highlands of Peru.

**AZTECS:** Post-Conquest term that refers to the empire of the Mexica in central Mexico. They were contemporary with the Incas.

**BALBOA, VASCO NÚNEZ DE:** Spanish explorer who first crossed the Isthmus of Panama to find the Pacific Ocean.

**BETANZOS, JUAN DE:** One of the most important and reliable of the Spanish chroniclers. He married a former wife of Atahuallpa and spoke Quechua fluently, which gave him access to an Inca version of their history.

**BINGHAM, HIRAM:** North American explorer who is credited as the scientific discoverer of the Inca royal estate of Machu Picchu.

**BIRU:** The name of a province reportedly discovered by the Spanish explorer Pascual de Andagoya while exploring the Peruvian coast. The name Peru derives from this word.

**BOLA:** A weapon made of two or three cords joined at one end with weights tied to the other ends. The device is thrown at the legs to entangle the prey.

**CACHI:** Quechua word for salt.

**CAIMAN:** American crocodile.

**CAJAMARCA:** City in the north highlands of Peru where Atahuallpa was captured by Pizarro.

**CALCA:** A town near Cuzco in the Urubamba Valley.

**CALLEJON DE HUAYLAS:** A valley in the north highlands of Peru known for its spectacular views of surrounding snow peaks.

**CAMASCA:** Quechua word for healers.

**CAMAY:** Quechua name for the second month of the year in the Inca calendar. It corresponds approximately to the month of January in the Western calendar.

**CAMAYOS:** Quechua word for specialists in management or a particular trade, such as metalsmithing, weaving, or reading *quipu*.

**CANARI:** Ethnic group in highland Ecuador that fiercely resisted the Incas.

**CANAS:** Ethnic group located south of the Incas that were conquered by Viracocha Inca during his expedition to the altiplano.

**CANCHA:** Quechua word meaning enclosure or house grouping.

**CANCHAS:** Ethnic group located to the south of Cuzco next to the Canas who were conquered by Viracocha Inca.

**CANIPU:** Quechua name for military decorations consisting of metal disks worn by warriors who demonstrated valor in battle.

**CAPAC:** Quechua term for people of the highest status. The Spaniards translated it to mean "very much more than king."

**CAPAC ÑAN:** Quechua name for the Inca royal highway.

**CAPAC RAYMI:** Quechua name for the first month of the year in the Inca calendar. It corresponds approximately to the month of December in the Western calendar.

**CAPAC TOCCO:** Quechua name for the central and most important of the caves of Tambo Tocco from which the Incas' ancestors emerged at Pacariqtambo.

**CAPAC UCHA:** (also spelled capaccocha) Quechua term for human sacrifice involving children. It literally means royal obligation.

**CAPAC YUPANKI**: (also spelled Capac Yupanqui) Army general executed by Emperor Pachacuti for disobeying orders while successfully expanding the empire to the north.

**CARLOS INCA:** Fourth of the post-Conquest Inca rulers. Ruled from A.D. 1549 to 1572.

**CAYAMBI:** Highland Ecuadorean ethnic group conquered by Huayna Capac.

**CEJA DE SELVA:** Spanish term for the edge of the jungle on the eastern slope of the Andes.

**CEQUE SYSTEM:** (sometimes spelled zeqe or seque) System of imaginary lines, called *ceque* in Quechua, radiating outward from the Coricancha temple in Cuzco. Functioned to organize the *huacas* of Cuzco and their ritual calendar.

**CERRO BAUL:** Wari imperial center located in the Moquegua drainage of the south coast of Peru.

**CERRO WIRACOCHAN:** A mountain above the modern towns of Huaro and Urcos about 50 kilometers southeast of Cuzco. In legend it was a place where the creator god stopped to rest on his journey to the north.

**CHACHAPOYA:** Ethnic group located on the eastern watershed of the north highlands of Peru. They were conquered by the Inca Huayna Capac.

**CHAHUA HUARQUIS:** Quechua name for the eighth month of the year in the Inca calendar. It corresponds approximately to the month of July in the Western calendar.

**CHAMPI:** Quechua term for the preferred weapon of the Incas, a short club about 60 centimeters to 1 meter in length with a heavy weight on one end.

**CHANAPATA:** Archaeological culture of the Early Intermediate Period in Cuzco.

**CHANCA:** Ethnic group living to the north of Cuzco with whom the Incas fought at the beginning of their empire. Pachacuti Inca came to the throne after defeating the Chanca.

**CHAQUITAQLLA:** Quechua word for the Andean foot plow.

**CHARCAS:** Inca province located in eastern highland Bolivia.

**CHARQUI:** (also spelled *ch'arki*) Quechua word for freeze-dried meat. The English term for jerky or jerked meat derives from this term.

**CHASKA CUYLLOR:** Quechua name for the planet Venus.

**CHASQUI:** (also spelled *chaski*) Quechua name for runners in the Inca postal system.

**CHAVIN:** Archaeological culture named for the site of Chavín de Huantar in the north central highlands of Peru.

**CHICHA:** Arawak language term used by the Spanish to refer to alcoholic beers made from maize or other ingredients; called *a'qa* in Quechua.

**CHILQUE PROVINCE:** Inca province directly to the south of Cuzco.

**CHIMBOTE:** Town at the mouth of the Santa River on Peru's north coast.

**CHIMOR, KINGDOM OF:** Spanish name for the Chimu Empire, centered on the north coast of Peru.

**CHIMU:** Name of the ethnic group controlling the Kingdom of Chimor.

**CHINCHA PROVINCE:** Inca province on the south coast of Peru.

**CHINCHAYSUYU:** One of the four quarters of the Inca Empire; located to the northwest of Cuzco.

**CHINCHERO:** Royal estate of Topa Inca just to the north of Cuzco.

**CHIRIMOYAS:** A tropical fruit grown in the lowlands of Peru.

**CHONTA:** A species of palm tree with dense hardwood used to make weapons.

**CHRONICLE:** A chronological record of historical events.

**CHUCUITO:** Inca provincial center at Lake Titicaca south of Cuzco.

**CHULLPA:** Burial structures found in the highlands of Peru and Bolivia that often take the form of small towers.

**CHUMBIVILCA PROVINCE:** Inca province south of Cuzco.

**CHUNCA CAMAYOC:** Military officer in charge of a unit of ten men.

**CHUNO:** (also spelled Chuñu) Potatoes preserved by freeze drying.

**CHUQUIABO:** Inca administrative center at La Paz, Bolivia.

**CHUQUICHINCHAY:** A star thought to be the patron of mountain lions or pumas.

**CHUSI:** Quechua word for the coarsest grade of Inca cloth.

**CIEZA DE LEON, PEDRO:** Spanish soldier who wrote an important account of the Incas based on his visit to Peru shortly after the conquest of the Incas.

**CITUA:** (also spelled Situa) Inca festival that had as its purpose the prevention of illness.

**COATI:** The Island of the Moon in Lake Titicaca.

**COBO, BERNABE:** Jesuit priest who wrote a history of the Incas and an account of their customs and religion early in the seventeenth century. Considered to be one of the most comprehensive and accurate accounts of the Incas.

**COCA:** The narcotic plant *Erythroxylon coca,* whose leaves are chewed by

Andean peoples and used in fighting fatigue, in healing, and in most rituals and sacrifices.

**COLLASUYU:** One of the four quarters of the Inca Empire; located to the southeast of Cuzco.

**COLLO:** Quechua unit of dry measure; about 3.8 liters.

**CONOPAS:** Quechua word for small stone figurines usually of llamas or alpacas believed to protect the flocks and household.

**CONTISUYU:** One of the four quarters of the Inca Empire; located to the southwest of Cuzco.

**COPA CABANA, TEMPLE OF:** A major Inca religious shrine located at Lake Titicaca.

**CORA:** Quechua word that means weed.

**CORDILLERA BLANCA OR ORIENTAL:** Eastern chain of the Andes.

**CORDILLERA NEGRA OR OCCIDENTAL:** Western chain of the Andes.

**CORICANCHA:** Quechua for "Golden Enclosure"; the temple of the sun in Cuzco.

**CORTES, HERNAN:** Spanish conqueror of Mexico.

**COYA RAYMI:** Quechua name for the tenth month of the year in the Inca calendar. It corresponds approximately to the month of September in the Western calendar.

**CUMPI:** (also spelled qombi) Quechua term for the finest quality of Inca cloth.

**CURACA:** Quechua term for local hereditary nobility.

**CUY:** Quechua term for guinea pig.

**CUZCO:** The capital of the Inca Empire.

**EARLY HORIZON:** Time period extending from circa 1500 –370 B.C.

**EARLY INTERMEDIATE PERIOD:** Time period extending from 370 B.C. to A.D. 540.

**ECCLESIASTICAL:** Pertaining to a church.

**EL NINO PHENOMENON:** A temporary shift in the ocean currents causing unpredictable weather; a climatological phenomenon usually occurring in December and called El Niño after the Christ Child.

**ENDOGAMY:** Marriage only within a specific group.

**ESTETE, MIGUEL DE:** One of Pizarro's soldiers who wrote an eyewitness account soon after the conquest of Peru.

**ETHNOGRAPHY:** The anthropological description of primitive societies.

**GALLO, ISLAND OF:** Island off the coast of Ecuador where Pizarro drew his famous line in the sand with his sword.

**GARCILASO DE LA VEGA:** Most famous of the Spanish chroniclers, he was the son of a Spanish captain and an Inca princess.

**GUANACO:** Wild camelid; relative of the llama and alpaca.

**GUAVAS:** A tropical fruit.

**GUAYARA:** Quechua name of an Inca festival during which all the *huacas* of Cuzco were asked for an abundant year.

**GUAYLLACAN:** (also spelled Huayllacan) Ethnic group living in the Cuzco Valley with the early Incas.

**HAHUA INCAS:** Quechua term for outer Incas or Incas by adoption.

**HANANSAYA:** Quechua term for upper moiety.

**HANAQ PACHA:** Quechua for "the world above"; the uppermost layer in the three tiers of cosmology.

**HASTU HUARACA:** One of two Chanca generals leading an army that attacked Cuzco during the reign of Viracocha Inca.

**HATUN:** Quechua word for "big."

**HATUN APU:** Quechua term for military officer in charge of a unit of 5,000 men.

**HATUN APURATIN**: Quechua term for military officer deputy commander of a unit of 5,000 men.

**HATUN COLLA:** Major Inca administrative center south of Cuzco on the altiplano near Lake Titicaca.

**HATUN CUZQUI:** Quechua name for the sixth month of the year in the Inca calendar. It corresponds approximately to the month of May in the Western calendar.

**HATUN PUQUY:** Quechua name for the third month of the year in the Inca calendar. It corresponds approximately to the month of February in the Western calendar.

**HATUN RUNA:** Quechua term for taxable male head of a household in the Inca social system. It literally means "big man."

**HATUN TOPA INCA:** Name of Viracocha Inca before his accession.

**HATUN XAUXA:** Major Inca administrative center in the Mantaro Valley north of Cuzco.

**HIWAYA:** Inca punishment consisting of dropping a heavy stone on a person's back.

**HOMA RAYMI PUCHAYQUIZ:** Quechua name for the eleventh month of the year in the Inca calendar. It corresponds approximately to the month of October in the Western calendar.

**HONCO PAMPA:** Archaeological site pertaining to the Wari Empire in the north central highlands of Peru.

**HUACA:** (also spelled wak'a and guaca) Animistic spirits embodied in mummies, stones, mountain peaks, or anything great or unusual in nature. These served as guardians of people, places, or things. This term is also often used to refer to sacred places and archaeological ruins.

**HUAMACHUCO:** Town in the north Peruvian highlands where there is a major pre-Inca archaeological site.

**HUAMAN POMA DE AYALA, FELIPE:** Native Peruvian author who wrote an illustrated letter to the King of Spain complaining of maltreatment of the Indians in the early colonial period.

**HUANACAURI:** A mountain on the edge of the Cuzco Valley that was sacred to the Incas. Also a sacred stone on this mountain believed to be the body of Ayar Ucho, one of the brothers of Manco Capac. Also a sacred war idol carried into battle by Inca armies.

**HUANCA PROVINCE:** Inca province inhabited by the Huanca ethnic group in the Mantaro Basin north of Cuzco.

**HUANUCO PAMPA:** Major Inca administrative center in the Peruvian highlands north of Cuzco.

**HUAOQUE:** a statue made to represent an Inca ruler or high-ranking lord. The size, form, and material used to make the statue varied according to the whim of the person being represented. They could be made of many different materials, including stone, wood, or precious metals.

**HUARA:** Quechua term for the breechclout worn by adult Inca men.

**HUARACHICOY:** Quechua term for puberty rites and the knighting ceremony for young Inca males.

**HUARI:** (also spelled Wari) Quechua term meaning sacred or revered. Also the name for an archaeological culture centered at the site of the same name in Ayacucho.

**HUARO:** Town about 45 kilometers southeast of Cuzco; site of a major center of the Wari Empire.

**HUASCAR:** The twelfth Inca and last independent, formally crowned Inca ruler before the Spanish Conquest. He ruled from A.D. 1525 to 1532 and was overthrown by his brother Atahuallpa.

**HUATANAY RIVER:** River flowing through the Valley of Cuzco.

**HUAOQUE:** (also spelled huauque) The Quechua term for brother. Also means a guardian spirit or a statue that could serve as a person's double.

**HUAYNA CAPAC:** The eleventh Inca; ruled from A.D. 1493 to 1525.

**HUAYRUR ACLLA:** Second rank of the *acllas* or "chosen women."

**HUMBOLDT CURRENT:** Cold-water current from Antarctica that sweeps up the Pacific coast of South America resulting in rich fisheries and coastal deserts.

**HUNU CURACA:** Quechua term for Inca administrative official responsible for 10,000 heads of households.

**HURINSAYA:** Quechua term for the lower moiety half of Inca society.

**ICHU:** A type of grass used to build roofs and cables for bridges.

**ILLAPA:** The Inca thunder god, believed to control the weather.

**ILYA-TIQSI VIRACOCHA PACHAYACACHIQ:** Complete title of the creator god, which means "ancient foundation, lord, instructor."

**INCA CAPAC YUPANQUI:** (also spelled Inca Capac Yupanki) Fifth ruler in the Inca dynasty.

**INCA CUSI YUPANQUI:** (sometimes called Inca Yupanqui or Inca Yupanki) Name used by Inca Pachacuti, ninth ruler, before his accession.

**INCA ROCA:** Sixth ruler in the Inca dynasty.

**INCA URCON:** Heir of Viracocha Inca who was killed by Pachacuti Inca.

**INCAWASI:** (Inca house) Major Inca administrative center in the south coastal valley of Cañete. Also used in modern times as a generic name for Inca ruins.

**INTI:** The sun god who was the Incas' special patron deity.

**INTI HUATANA:** *Huaca* stone sometimes called the "hitching post of the sun."

**INTI PATA:** Quechua term meaning "platform of the sun." Also the name of an Inca site near Machu Picchu.

**INTI RAYMI:** Inca festival of the winter solstice.

**INTIP CHURIN:** Quechua term that means "children of the sun."

**ITU RAYMI:** A solemn sacrificial rite, sometimes involving human sacrifice, performed to get the attention of the gods when help was needed.

**JINCAMOCCO:** Administrative site of the Wari Empire in the central highlands of Peru.

**K'APA:** Quechua term for measurement used by the Incas; the size of a palm, or 20 centimeters.

**K'ILLKE STYLE:** A ceramic style found in the Valley of Cuzco and its environs; in use from approximately A.D. 1100 to the early Spanish colonial period.

**KALLANKA:** Quechua term for the large niched halls built by the Incas.

**KANIWA:** A native Andean grain.

**KAY PACHA:** Quechua term meaning "this world"; used to define the middle level in the Inca cosmology.

**KENKO:** Quechua term meaning zigzag or crooked. It is the name of a major *huaca* above the city of Cuzco.

**KERO:** Quechua word for wood. Used generically to refer to drinking cups in modern times.

**KHOCOC:** Quechua term for an Inca unit of measure; the distance from the elbow to the tip of the hand, about 45 centimeters.

**KIWICHA:** A native Andean grain.

**LAKE TITICACA:** A large body of water on the modern border between Peru and Bolivia.

**LATE HORIZON:** Time period extending from A.D. 1476 to 1532.

**LATE INTERMEDIATE PERIOD:** Time period extending from A.D. 900 to 1476

**LLACTA:** Quechua word for "town."

**LLAMA:** Largest of the native Andean camelid species.

**LLOQUE:** Quechua word for "left."

**LLOQUE YUPANQUI:** Third ruler in the Inca dynasty.

**LUCRE:** Town in the Lucre Basin at the eastern end of the Valley of Cuzco.

**LUCRE BASIN:** Easternmost of the three basins of the Cuzco Valley.

**LUCRE STYLE:** Ceramic style of the Late Intermediate Period.

**LÚCUMA:** A tropical fruit grown in the lowlands.

**LUPACA:** Powerful kingdom located on the western side of Lake Titicaca subjugated by the Incas.

**LUQUE, HERNANDO DE:** A partner of Francisco Pizarro and Diego de Almagro who helped finance the Spanish Conquest of Peru.

**LUQURMATA:** Tiwanaku site located on the southeast shore of Lake Titicaca.

**LURIN VALLEY:** Valley on the central coast of Peru containing the modern city of Lima.

**MACANA:** Quechua term for an Inca war club made of *chonta* palm wood and shaped like a sword, about 1.2 meters in length.

**MACHU PICCHU:** One of the royal estates of Inca Pachacuti made famous by the explorations of Hiram Bingham.

**MAIZE:** Corn.

**MALA VALLEY:** Valley on the central coast of Peru.

**MALLQUI:** Quechua word for mummy.

**MAMA:** Quechua term that was used by the Incas as a title or honorific equivalent to "lady."

**MAMA COCA:** Wife of the second ruler in the Inca dynasty, Sinchi Roca.

**MAMA CORA:** One of the original Incas who emerged from Tambo Tocco; wife of Ayar Cachi and sister of Manco Capac.

**MAMA HUACO:** One of the original Incas who emerged from Tambo Tocco; wife of Ayar Auca and sister of Manco Capac.

**MAMA MICAY:** Wife of Inca Roca, the sixth ruler of the Incas.

**MAMA OCLLO:** One of the original Incas who emerged from Tambo Tocco; wife and sister of Manco Capac.

**MAMA RAHUA:** One of the original Incas who emerged from Tambo Tocco; wife of Ayar Ucho and sister of Manco Capac.

**MAMACOCHA:** Quechua name for the deity "Lady Sea."

**MAMACONA:** Chosen women who became virgins of the sun.

**MAMAQUILLA:** Quechua word meaning "Lady Moon"; Inca name for the moon and moon goddess.

**MAMAZARA:** Quechua word for the maize ritual carried out during the Inca month of Hatun Cuzqui.

**MANCO CAPAC:** Founder of the Inca dynasty; also known as Ayar Manco.

**MANCO INCA:** Second of the post-Conquest rulers. He reigned from A.D. 1533 to 1545 and led a general uprising against the Spaniards.

**MANCO SAPACA:** Son of Sinchi Roca and the second ruler in the Inca dynasty.

**MANTA:** Town on the coast of Ecuador from where the creator Viracocha departed out to sea.

**MANTARO:** River basin in the central highlands of Peru.

**MARAS:** Town and ethnic group just to the north of Cuzco.

**MARAS TOCCO:** One of the three caves at Tambo Tocco, the Incas' legendary origin place.

**MARCAVALLE:** Archaeological culture in Cuzco dating to the Early Horizon time period.

**MASCAPAYCHA:** A fringed headdress worn over the eyebrows by the Inca emperor. The equivalent of the Inca crown.

**MASHUA:** Edible tuber

**MAULE RIVER:** River in modern Chile that marked the southern boundary of the Inca Empire.

**MAYMI:** Archaeological site on the south coast of Peru pertaining to the Wari Empire.

**MAYO:** Quechua word for river.

**MAYTA CAPAC:** Fourth ruler in the Inca dynasty.

**MESTIZO:** Spanish term for persons of mixed European and native Andean parentage.

**MIDDLE HORIZON:** Time period extending from A.D. 540 to 900.

**MIDDLE MARANON RIVER BASIN:** River basin in the north highlands of Peru.

**MINK'A:** Quechua term for calling upon exchange partners to perform labor that is owed.

**MIT'A:** Quechua term for a fixed period of labor that was performed as the payment of tax.

**MITAYOQ:** Quechua word for one who is performing *mit'a*.

**MITIMA:** (also spelled mitmaq) Groups of people relocated within the Inca Empire by the government for state purposes.

**MOCHA:** Quechua word for an Inca gesture of reverence.

**MOCHE:** River valley on Peru's north coast. Also the name of an archaeological culture centered in this valley.

**MOIETY:** One half of a society ritually divided into two parts. Inca society was divided into an upper and a lower moiety.

**MOLINA DE SANTIAGO, CRISTOBAL DE:** An eyewitness to the Spanish Conquest who wrote his account in A.D. 1556.

**MONTANA:** Cloud forest eco-zone on the eastern slopes of the Andes.

**MONTESINOS, FERNANDO DE:** A Spanish chronicler who wrote an account of the Incas around A.D. 1642; the account was notable for its inclusion of a lengthy and detailed list of Inca kings and those of earlier dynasties.

**MOQUEGUA:** River valley on the south coast of Peru.

**MUYNA:** (also spelled Muina or Mohina) Ancient name for the Lucre Basin of the Valley of Cuzco.

**ÑANA:** Quechua term that a woman would use in referring to her sister or female cousin.

**NAPA:** A pure white llama; symbol of the Inca Empire.

**NAZCA VALLEY:** River valley on the south coast of Peru. Also the name of an archaeological culture centered in the valley.

**NINACUMBI ISLAND:** An island off the coast of Ecuador (possibly in the Galápagos Islands) said to have been visited by Topa Inca.

**NINAN CUYOCHI:** Heir apparent to the Inca Huayna Capac.

**OCAS:** Andean tuber similar to a sweet potato.

**OCLLO:** Quechua word that means pure.

**OLLANTAY:** Name of a drama that is possibly Inca in origin.

**OLLANTAYTAMBO:** Royal estate of Inca Pachacuti located in the Urubamba Valley.

**OMASAYOS PROVINCE:** Inca province southwest of Cuzco.

**OREJONES:** Spanish name for Inca nobles who wore large earplugs. It literally means "big ears."

**OROPESA:** The middle basin of the Cuzco Valley containing a town of the same name. Derives from the Spanish Marques de Oropesa.

**OROYA:** Quechua name for a device for crossing rivers consisting of a basket slung beneath a rope.

**PACARINA:** Quechua word for a tribal origin place.

**PACARIQTAMBO:** Town believed to be the origin place of the Incas.

**PACAYOQ:** Quechua word for the nobles who wore large earplugs.

**PACHA:** Quechua term for earth, time, or space.

**PACHACA CAMAYOC:** Quechua term for Inca military officer responsible for 100 soldiers.

**PACHACA CURACA:** Quechua term for Inca administrative officer responsible for 100 heads of households.

**PACHACAMAC:** A creator deity in the ancient Andean pantheon who was revered on the coast.

**PACHACAMAC, SHRINE OF:** One of the holiest shrines and oracles in ancient Peru, located just to the south of the modern city of Lima and dedicated to the creator deity of the same name.

**PACHACUTI:** The ninth ruler in the Inca dynasty. He is credited with founding the Inca Empire.

**PACHACUTI:** Quechua term for the end of an epoch. It literally means "cataclysm" or "overturning of earth, time, and space."

**PACHAMAMA:** The earth-mother goddess of the Andean peoples.

**PACO ACLLA:** Quechua term for a class of *aclla* who were used by the Inca emperor to reward *curacas* and other important officials with wives.

**PAHUAC GUALPA:** Assassinated heir of Inca Yahuar Huacac.

**PAJCHIRI:** Administrative center of the Tiwanaku state located near southern shore of Lake Titicaca.

**PANA:** Quechua term used by a male to refer to his sister or female cousin.

**PANACA:** Quechua term for an Inca emperor's lineage corporation that excludes his heir.

**PAQCHA:** Quechua for a special container for liquid offerings.

**PARIA:** Inca administrative center in central Bolivia.

**PATA:** Quechua term for terrace or platform.

**PATALLACTA:** An Inca site in the Urubamba Valley built by Inca Pachacuti. It literally means "terrace town."

**PAUCAR HUARAY:** Quechua name for the fourth month of the year in the Inca calendar. It corresponds approximately to the month of March in the Western calendar.

**PAUCARTAMBO:** Inca and modern town to the southeast of Cuzco.

**PAULLU INCA:** Brother of Manco Inca whom the Spanish installed as Inca after Manco led the rebellion against them. He ruled from A.D. 1537–1549.

**PHILLIP III, KING OF SPAIN:** Spanish monarch at the time of the conquest of Peru.

**PHUYUPATAMARCA:** Town that served as a way station and mountain worship site on the Inca road to Machu Picchu. The name in Quechua means "cloud terrace town."

**PIKILLACTA:** Quechua name meaning "flea town" for the Wari imperial administrative center located in the Lucre Basin of the Valley of Cuzco.

**PINAGUA:** Ethnic group that resided in the eastern end of the Valley of Cuzco at the beginning of the Inca Empire.

**PIRCA:** Quechua word for construction of rough fieldstone.

**PISAC:** (also spelled Pisaq) Royal estate of Inca Pachacuti located in the Urubamba Valley near Cuzco.

**PISCA CHUNCA CAMAYOC:** Quechua term for an Inca military officer who led groups of fifty soldiers.

**PISCA PACHACA CURACA:** Quechua term for an Inca administrative official responsible for 500 heads of households.

**PISCA WARANGA CURACA:** Quechua term for an Inca administrative official responsible for 5,000 heads of households.

**PISCO VALLEY:** River valley on the south coast of Peru.

**PIURA:** Town on the north coast of Peru.

**PIZARRO, FRANCISCO:** Leader of the Spanish expedition to conquer the Inca Empire.

**PIZARRO, GONZALO:** Younger brother of Francisco Pizarro who took part in the conquest of the Incas and later rebelled against the Spanish crown.

**PIZARRO, HERNANDO:** Eldest brother of Francisco Pizarro. He took part in the conquest of the Incas and was later imprisoned in Spain.

**PIZARRO, JUAN:** Youngest of the Pizarro brothers. He was killed during the revolt of Manco Inca.

**PIZARRO, PEDRO:** Cousin of the Pizarro brothers. He took part in the conquest of the Incas and later wrote an eyewitness account.

**POLO DE ONDEGARDO, JUAN:** An early Spanish colonial official at Cuzco who wrote valuable observations of the Incas and their customs.

**PUMAP CHUPAN:** Quechua term meaning "tail of the puma." It refers to the sector of the city of Cuzco that lies between the Tullu and Saphi rivers at their confluence.

**PUMAPUNKU:** One of the great temples at the site of Tiwanaku in Bolivia.

**PUMPU:** A major Inca administrative center at Lake Junin in the central highlands of Peru.

**PUNA:** Quechua word for the high-altitude eco-zone above the tree line in the Andes.

**PUNCHAO:** Quechua word for "day." Also the name of a golden idol of the sun kept in the Coricancha temple in Cuzco.

**PURAPUCYO:** Quechua term for an annual festival held at the confluence of the Tullu and Saphi rivers in Cuzco.

**PURUAUCA:** Quechua word for stones that Pachacuti claimed had turned to warriors to help him defeat the Chanca armies at Cuzco.

**PUTUTU:** Quechua word for a trumpet made from a *Strombus* shell.

**QOLQA:** (also spelled colca) Quechua word for granary or storage structure.

**QOLQA CONSTELLATION:** Quechua name for the Pleiades.

**QOTAKALLI:** A Cuzco ceramic style during the Middle Horizon time period.

**QUECHUA:** Post-Conquest name for the Inca language Runasimi. Name of an ethnic group living northwest of Cuzco at the beginning of the Inca expansion. Also means warm frost-free lower valleys of the highland zone, excellent for the production of maize and other crops.

**QUELCCAYA GLACIER:** High-altitude glacier located about midway between Cuzco and Lake Titicaca. Ice cores from this glacier have been used to reconstruct past climatic events in the Andes.

**QUICUCHICOY:** Quechua word for Inca female puberty rites.

**QUINOA:** (also spelled Quinua) Edible grain grown at high altitudes in the Andes.

**QUIPOCAMAYOC:** Quechua term for a person who makes and reads *quipus*.

**QUIPU:** Quechua term for Inca recording device consisting of knotted cords.

**QUISHUARCANCHA:** The temple in Cuzco where the Incas kept a statue of the creator god Viracocha.

**QUISPE YUPANKI:** (also spelled Quispe Yupanqui) Designated heir to Inca Capac Yupanqui. Assassinated before taking office.

**QUISPIGUANCA:** Royal estate of Huayna Capac in the Urubamba Valley.

**QUITO:** Capital of modern Ecuador.

**RAQCHI:** Location of Inca temple of Viracocha in the district of San Pedro de Cacha about 110 kilometers southeast of Cuzco.

**RECIPROCITY:** Even exchange; fundamental principle of labor exchange in the Andes.

**RIKRA:** Quechua term for Inca unit of measure equal to the distance of a man's outstretched arms; about 162 centimeters.

**ROK'ANA:** Quechua term for Inca unit of measure equal to a finger.

**ROSTWOROWSKI DE DIEZ CANSECO, MARIA:** One of the foremost Peruvian ethnohistorians.

**ROWE, JOHN H.:** Most prominent Inca scholar of the twentieth century.

**RUNAKUNA:** Quechua term for "men."

**RUNASIMI:** Quechua term for the Inca language, it means "men's speech."

**RUNTU RACCAY:** Archaeological ruin of an Inca way station on the road to Machu Picchu.

**RUTUCHICOY:** Inca naming and first hair-cutting ceremony.

**SACSAYHUAMAN:** (also spelled Sacsahuaman) An enormous megalithic structure located on the hill just above the city of Cuzco.

**SANCHO DE LA HOZ, PEDRO:** One of Pizarro's soldiers who wrote an early eyewitness account of the conquest of the Incas.

**SANKACANCHA:** Quechua name for a pit in Cuzco said to be filled with wild animals and used for execution of criminals.

**SANTA CRUZ PACHACUTI YAMQUI SALCAMAYGUA, JOAN DE:** A native Andean author who published an account of the Incas in A.D. 1615.

**SANU:** Inca town where pottery was produced (modern San Sebastián), located about 5 kilometers east of Cuzco.

**SAPA INCA:** Quechua title for the Inca emperor. It means "sole or unique Inca."

**SAPHI:** One of the two rivers between which Cuzco lies.

**SARMIENTO DE GAMBOA, PEDRO:** Spanish author who wrote an account of the Incas at the command of the Viceroy Toledo.

**SARPAY:** Quechua title of a priestess who spoke for the idol of the Apurimac *huaca.*

**SAUSERO:** The sacred maize field dedicated to the sun and ceremonially planted at the beginning of the growing season.

**SAYA:** Quechua term for a moiety division of Inca society.

**SAYACMARCA:** Inca way station on the road to Machu Picchu.

**SAYRI TUPAC INCA:** (also spelled Sayri Topa Inca) Younger son of Manco Inca, reigned after the Conquest from A.D. 1545 to 1558.

**SIKYA:** Quechua term for an Inca unit of measure one half of the length of a *rikra,* about 81 centimeters.

**SINCHE:** (also spelled sinchi) Quechua term for the elective office of a community war leader held temporarily in times of emergency.

**SINCHI ROCA:** Second ruler in the Inca dynasty.

**SONCOYOC:** Quechua term for healer.

**SORAS PROVINCE:** Inca province near Cuzco and to the west.

**SPONDYLUS PRINCEPS:** A type of oyster whose shell is highly valued by Andean peoples for offerings made to the supernatural for water. It is characterized by long, sharp spines and a bright red or pink and white color.

**SUCANCA:** Quechua term referring to the pillars or towers erected on the hills above Cuzco and used for making solar observations.

**SUNI:** Andean ecological zone at 3,200 meters to 4,000 meters above sea level.

**SUNTURPAUCAR:** Quechua term for one of the symbols of Inca royal authority. It consisted of an elaborate tassel on a staff.

**SUTIC TOCCO:** Quechua name of one of the three caves at the Inca origin place of Tambo Tocco.

**SUYU:** Quechua term for geographic quarter or region. The whole of the Inca Empire was made up of four *suyus*.

**TALCA:** Town at the Chilean terminus of the Inca coastal highway.

**TAMBO COLORADO:** Quechua name of an Inca administrative center in the Pisco Valley on the south coast of Peru.

**TAMPU:** (also spelled *tambo*) Quechua word for a lodging facility on the Inca highway and in other locales. The Spanish translated it as "inn." Also the name of an ethnic group who lived near the modern town of Pacariqtambo and also in the Urubamba Valley.

**TAQUI ACLLA:** Quechua term for a class of *aclla,* or chosen women, selected for talent in playing music and singing. Their job was to entertain at festivals and feasts of the royal court.

**TARCO HUAMAN:** An Inca ruler who was apparently deposed by Capac Yupanki, the fifth king in the Inca dynasty. He was removed from Inca histories of the dynastic succession.

**TARMA:** Inca province in the central Peruvian highlands.

**TARPUNTAY:** Inca *ayllu* that provided priests of the sun. The name of this lineage became synonymous with the priesthood.

**TAWANTINSUYU:** Quechua word meaning "four parts together." The Inca name for their empire.

**THATKIY:** Quechua term for an Inca unit of distance measure of about 130 centimeters.

**THUNUPA:** Name of the god of thunder and lightning in the altiplano region of southern Peru and Bolivia. The Incas called this god Illapa.

**TIANA:** Quechua word for the low, carved wooden stool on which only the Inca emperor and his highest officials were allowed to sit.

**TINCUY:** Quechua term for the joining of two parts such as where two rivers meet. Believed to be a sacred spot.

**TITICACA:** Name of the large high-altitude lake located on the border between modern Peru and Bolivia.

**TITU CUSI:** Sixth ruler after the Spanish Conquest. He ruled from A.D. 1558 to 1571 and led the resistance to the Spanish.

**TITU CUSI HUALLPA:** Son and successor of Topa Inca who assumed the name of Huayna Capac upon accession to the throne.

**TIWANAKU:** (also spelled Tiahuanaco and Tihuanaco) Archaeological site at the southern end of Lake Titicaca in Bolivia. It was the capital of the Tiwanaku state during the Middle Horizon.

**TOCAPU:** Quechua name for the small, colorful rectangular designs woven into garments worn by Inca royalty.

**TOCAY CAPAC:** Ruler of the Ayarmaca ethnic group in Cuzco during the reign of Inca Roca.

**TOCORI:** Quechua name for the *huaca* that presided over the irrigation systems of Inca Cuzco.

**TOCOYRICOQ:** Quechua term meaning "he who sees all." An Inca official inspector was chosen from close family members of the ruler and went about the empire checking on how well administrators were performing their jobs.

**TOCRICOQ:** Quechua term for an Inca provincial governor.

**TOLEDO, FRANCISCO DE:** The viceroy who ruled Peru for the Spanish crown from 1569 to 1581.

**TOMAY HUARACA:** One of the two generals of the Chanca army that attacked Cuzco in A.D. 1438.

**TOMEBAMBA:** (also spelled Tumibamba or Tumipampa) Northern capital of the Incas established near modern Cuenca, Ecuador, by Inca Huayna Capac.

**TOPA HUALLPA:** First of the Inca rulers after the Spanish Conquest. He was placed on the throne by Pizarro in A.D. 1533 and died shortly afterward.

**TOPA INCA:** (also spelled Thopa Inca, also known as Tupac Inca Yupanqui) The tenth ruler of the Inca dynasty, who reigned from A.D. 1471 to 1493.

**TOPO:** Quechua for an Inca measure of distance of 6,000 paces, or 7.8 kilometers. Also an Inca measure of area of 25 *rikra* by 50 *rikra,* or about 3, 280 square meters.

**TOPO:** (also spelled *tupu*) Quechua term for spatulate-headed pins made of various metals that were used by Andean women to fasten their clothing.

**TORA:** Quechua term used by a woman to refer to her brother or male cousin.

**TULLU:** (also spelled Tullumayo) One of the two rivers between which Cuzco lies.

**TUMBES:** The place on the far north coast of Peru where Pizarro's expedition landed.

**TUPAC AMARU:** Seventh and last Inca ruler after the Spanish Conquest. He reigned from A.D. 1571 to 1572.

**UCHO:** Quechua word for chili pepper.

**UKHU PACHA:** Quechua term meaning "the world below," referring to the lowest level of the three tiers in Inca cosmology.

**ULLUCO:** An edible Andean tuber.

**URCUCHILLAY:** Quechua name for the constellation Lira.

**URUBAMBA:** Major tributary of the Amazon River that flows through the Inca heartland.

**USCOVILCA:** Sacred ancestral mummy of the Chanca tribe.

**USHNU:** Quechua term for a stagelike platform structure found in the main plazas of Inca centers from which the emperor or his surrogates could preside over ceremonies.

**VERTICALITY:** The concept of exploiting a variety of altitudinal eco-zones.

**VICEROY:** The representative of the Spanish crown who ruled colonial Peru.

**VICUNA:** One of the four camelid species of the Andes. A smaller cousin of the llama and alpaca that produces very fine wool.

**VILCABAMBA:** A wild region of the *montaña* northwest of Cuzco where the Incas resisting the Spanish Conquest built their last capital.

**VILCANOTA:** Name of the river that becomes the Urubamba River after passing Cuzco.

**VILCAS:** Inca province to the west of Cuzco.

**VILCASHUAMAN:** Inca administrative center in the province of Vilcas.

**VILLAC UMU:** Quechua title of the Inca head priest.

**VIRACOCHA:** (also spelled Wiracocha; also known as Ilya-Tiqsi Viracocha Pachayacachiq) The Andean creator god worshipped by the Incas. This term also came to be applied to Europeans by the natives of the Andes.

**VIRACOCHA INCA:** The eighth ruler in the Inca dynasty, who reigned until being overthrown by Pachacuti Inca in A.D. 1438.

**VIRACOCHA PAMPA:** Large archaeological site in the north-central highlands of Peru that contains the remains of a Wari imperial administrative center.

**VITCOS:** Town in the Vilcabamba region where Incas resisting the Spanish sought refuge.

**WAMANI:** A sacred mountain peak, an administrative division of the Inca empire, and an Inca unit of distance consisting of 30 *topos* or 234 kilometers.

**WARANQA CAMAYOC:** Quechua term for an Inca military officer who led 1,000 men.

**WARANQA CURACA:** Quechua term for an Inca administrative officer in charge of 1,000 households.

**WARI:** (also spelled Huari and Guari) Quechua word for "sacred." It is also the name of a pre-Inca culture known as the Wari Empire that was centered at the archaeological site of Wari near the modern city of Ayacucho in the central Peruvian highlands.

**WARI WILKA:** Name of a famous oracle during the Inca period. It was located at an earlier temple belonging to the Wari Empire near the modern city of Huancayo in the central Peruvian highlands.

**WIMPILLAY:** Archaeological site in the Cuzco Basin.

**WINAY WAYNA:** Inca archaeological ruin located next to Machu Picchu.

**XEREZ, FRANCISCO DE:** One of Pizarro's soldiers who wrote an eyewitness account immediately after the conquest of the Incas.

**YACHAYWASI:** (also spelled Yachayhuasi) Quechua term for the school maintained in Cuzco to educate sons of both Inca and provincial nobility.

**YAHUAR HUACAC:** Seventh ruler in the Inca dynasty.

**YANA ACLLA:** Quechua term for a class of *aclla*, or chosen women, that consisted of the least desirable girls, who became servants.

**YANACONA:** (also spelled *yanacuna*) A special class of people outside of the normal Inca hierarchy who were exempt from taxation and worked as retainers for the nobility.

**YAPAQUIS:** Quechua name for the ninth month of the year in the Inca calendar. It corresponds approximately to the month of August in the Western calendar.

**YAUYOS:** An Inca province on the central coast of Peru near modern Lima.

**YUCAY:** A town in the Urubamba Valley near Cuzco.

**YUKU:** Quechua term for an Inca unit of measure consisting of the distance between the thumb and forefinger of an outstretched hand; about 12–14 centimeters.

**YUNGAS:** Quechua term for coastal midvalley zones between 500 and 2,500 meters in elevation.

**YUPAY:** Quechua verb meaning "to count."

**YURAC ACLLA:** The highest-ranking category of chosen women; consisted of young women of Inca blood who were consecrated as virgins to Inti the sun god.

**ZUIDEMA, R. TOM:** Influential and important Inca scholar associated with the structuralist approach to interpreting Inca history.

# Resources for Further Study

Acosta, José de.
    1986. *Historia natural y moral de las Indias*. Madrid: Historia 16. (A classic and very influential early history of Spanish America first published in 1590 by a Jesuit missionary who spent seventeen years in Peru and Mexico.)

    2002. *Natural and Moral History of the Indies*. Edited by Jane E. Mangan. Translated by Frances López-Morillas. Durham, NC: Duke University Press. (A new English translation of Acosta's classic work.)

Adamska, Anna, and Adam Michcznski.
    1996. "Towards Radiocarbon Chronology of the Inca State." *Andes: Boletín de la Misión Arqueológica Andina* 1: 35–58. (This article considers the problems of dating the Inca chronology using the radiocarbon method. The authors conclude that traditional chronology of the chronicles is supported.)

Adorno, Rolena.
    1986. *Guaman Poma: Writing and Resistance in Colonial Peru*. Austin: University of Texas Press. (The author analyzes the work of the native author Guaman Poma, who wrote to the king of Spain protesting the conditions of Spanish colonial rule in the period following the European Conquest.)

Agurto Calvo, Santiago.
    1980. *Cuzco—Traza Urbano de la ciudad Inca*. Proyecto 39, UNESCO, Instituto Nacional de Cultura, Perú. Cuzco: Imprenta Offset Color, S.R.I. (UNESCO-sponsored study delimiting the surviving Inca architecture in Cuzco.)

    1987. *Estudios acerca de la construcción, arquitectura, y planeamiento incas*. Lima: Cámera Peruana de la Construcción. (A study of Inca architecture, site planning, and construction techniques.)

Alcina Franch, José.
    1976. *Arqueología de Chinchero 1: La Arquitectura*. Madrid: Ministerio de Asuntos Exteriores. (Report of the Spanish archaeological mission's work at Topa Inca's royal estate at Chinchero near Cuzco.)

    1978. "Ingapirca: arquitectura y areas de asentamiento." *Revista Española de Antropología Americana* 8: 127–146. (Study of architecture and settlement planning at the Inca site of Ingapirca in Ecuador.)

Alcina Franch, José, Miguel Rivera, Jesus Galván, María Carmen García Palacios, Mercedes Guinea, Balbina Martínez-Caviró, Luis J. Ramos, and Tito Varela.
   1976. *Arqueología de Chinchero*. Vol. 2, *Cerámicas y otros materials.* Madrid: Ministerio de Asuntos Exteriores. (Second volume of the authors' report of the results of the Spanish archaeological misson's work at the royal estate of Chinchero. This volume deals with ceramic and other types of artifacts.)

Angeles Vargas, Victor.
   1970. *P'isaq: Metrópoli inka.* Lima: Industrial Gráfica. (The author presents his views and drawings of the Inca royal estate at Pisaq in the Sacred Valley of the Incas.)

   1972. *Machupijchu: Enigmática ciudad inka.* Lima: Industrial Gráfica. (The author presents his interpretation of Machu Picchu and its mysteries.)

   1980. *Historia del Cuzco incaico.* Lima: Industrial Gráfica. (The author presents his history of the Inca capital of Cuzco.)

Anonymous Conqueror.
   1929. *The Conquest of Peru as Related by a Member of the Pizarro Expedition.* Edited and translated by Joseph H. Sinclair. New York: New York Public Library. (An English translation of one of the few eyewitness accounts of the Spanish Conquest of the Incas.)

Arriola, C., and R. Bustinza.
   1999. "Kañaraqay." Thesis for licentiate in archaeology, Universidad Nacional San Antonio Abad del Cuzco. (A study of the Inca site of Kañaraqay in the Lucre Basin at the eastern end of the Valley of Cuzco. This site is believed to have been both the birthplace and later the royal estate of the last Inca ruler, Huascar.)

Arroyo Abarca, P., and G. Choque Centeno.
   1992. "Mamaqolla y la ocupación Inka del área de la laguna de Muyna." Thesis for licentiate in archaeology, Universidad Nacional San Antonio Abad del Cuzco. (A study of Mamaqolla, a sacred mound built on a natural promontory in the Lucre Basin at the eastern end of the Valley of Cuzco. The Mamaqolla site dates from at least the Middle Horizon if not earlier. The authors also discuss the Inca occupation of the Lucre Basin.)

Ascher, Marcia, and Robert Ascher.
   1981. *Code of the Quipu.* Ann Arbor: University of Michigan Press. (The classic work on the knotted cord devices called *quipu* that were used by the Incas for record keeping. The authors discuss *quipu* making, the role of *quipu* readers in Inca society, how *quipus* work, how to make a *quipu*, and other related topics.)

   1997. *Mathematics of the Incas: Code of the Quipu.* New York: Dover. (A recent reprint and update of the authors' previously cited work.)

Astete Victoria, F.
   1974. "Las obras hidraúlicas del valle del Cusco." Thesis for licentiate in archaeology, Universidad Nacional San Antonio Abad del Cuzco. (This study of the hydraulic works of the Valley of Cuzco is mainly descriptive.)

Aveni, Anthony F.
 1981. "Horizon Astronomy in Incaic Cuzco." In *Archaeoastronomy in the Americas*, edited by Ray A. Williamson, 305–318. Los Altos, CA: Ballena. (A discussion of the use of horizon markers in Inca astronomy.)

Bandelier, Adolf.
 1910. *The Islands of Titicaca and Coati*. New York: Hispanic Society of America. (Classic description of the islands of Titicaca—also known as the Island of the Sun—and Coati located in Lake Titicaca between Bolivia and Peru. These islands were sacred to the Incas and contain impressive architectural remains and shrines.)

Barnes, Monica, and Daniel Slive.
 1993. "El Puma de Cuzco: ¿plano de la ciudad Ynga o noción europea?" *Revista Andina* 11(1): 79–102. (Authors discuss whether the plan to lay out the city of Cuzco in the shape of a puma was an Inca or European idea.)

Barreda M., Luis.
 1973. "Las culturas Inca y pre-Inca de Cuzco." Ph.D. dissertation, Universidad San Antonio Abad del Cuzco. (A description of the prehistoric culture sequence in Cuzco.)

 1982. "Asentiamento Humano de los Qotakalli de Cuzco." In *Arqueologia de Cuzco*, 13–20. Cuzco: Instituto Nacional de Cultura region Cuzco. (This work describes the pre-Inca Qotakalli culture of Cuzco and illustrates its ceramic style.)

Baudin, Louis.
 1928. *L'Empire socialiste des Inka*. Paris: Institut d'Ethnologie. (A famous work arguing that the Inca state was socialist in political structure.)

Bauer, Brian S.
 1989. "Muyu Orqo Y Ccoipa: Dos Nuevos Tipos de Ceramica para la Region del Cusco." *Revista Andina* 7(2): 537–542. (A description of two non-Inca ceramic styles found in the province of Cuzco.)

 1990. "State Development in the Cusco Region: Archaeological Research on the Incas in the Province of Paruro." Ph.D. dissertation, University of Chicago. (The author attempts to trace the rise of the Inca state using data from the province of Paruro, wherein lies Pacariqtambo, the legendary origin place of the Incas. Using surface collections of K'illke-related ceramic styles, he argues in favor of a processualist model of Inca state formation.)

 1991. "Pacariqtambo and the Mythical Origins of the Inca." *Latin American Antiquity* 2: 7–26. (An examination of Inca origin myths and the town of Pacariqtambo, which is said to be the origin place of the Incas.)

 1992. "Ritual Pathways of the Inca: An Analysis of the Collasuyu Ceques in Cuzco." *Latin American Antiquity* 3: 183–205. (A discussion of the author's work on the Inca *ceqe* system, a series of shrines arranged on imaginary lines radiating from the Coricancha temple in Cuzco.)

1992. *The Development of the Inca State.* Austin: University of Texas Press. (Published version of the author's dissertation mentioned above.)

1996. "The Legitimization of the Inca State in Myth and Ritual." *American Anthropologist* 98(2): 327–337. (A discussion of Inca techniques for justifying their rule and the role of ideology in the development and maintenance of stratified societies.)

1998. *The Sacred Landscape of the Incas: The Cuzco Ceque System.* Austin: University of Texas Press. (Book-length version of the author's work on the Inca *ceqe* system, a series of shrines arranged on imaginary lines radiating from the Coricancha temple in Cuzco. He argues that the *ceqes* were not perfectly straight lines, as most scholars believe.)

1999. *The Early Ceramics of the Inca Heartland.* Fieldiana Anthropology, n.s. no. 31. Chicago: Field Museum of Natural History. (Author presents a discussion of the pre-Inca ceramic styles of the province of Paruro based on his surveys in the region.)

2004. *Ancient Cuzco: Heartland of the Inca.* Austin: University of Texas Press. (A general synthesis of Cuzco archaeology.)

2004. "Archaeological Investigations at Maukallaqta and Puma Orco, Department of Cuzco, Peru." *Ñawpa Pacha* 25–27: 207–250. Institute of Andean Studies, Berkeley, California. (Reports on the excavations at these two sites that are located near the mythical Inca origin place of Pacariqtambo. Useful for descriptions and illustrations of Inca architecture and ceramics.)

Bauer Brian S., and R. Alan Covey.
2002. "Processes of State Formation in the Inca Heartland (Cuzco, Peru)." *American Anthropologist* 104(3): 846–864. (The authors present a processual model of Inca state formation based on surface surveys in the Cuzco region.)

Bauer, Brian S., and David S. P. Dearborn.
1995. *Astronomy and Empire in the Ancient Andes.* Austin: University of Texas Press. (The authors present a model of Inca cosmology based on a solar calendar.)

Bauer, Brian S., and Charles Stanish.
1990. "Killke and Killke-related pottery from Cuzco, Peru, in the Field Museum of Natural History." In Fieldiana Anthropology, no. 15. Chicago: Field Museum of Natural History. (A description of the collection of vessels from Late Intermediate Period Cuzco held by the Field Museum of Chicago.)

Bauer, Thomas W., and Brian S. Bauer.
1987. "Selected aspects of skulls found by the Pikillacta Archaeological Project 1982." In Appendix II of *The Middle Horizon in the Valley of Cuzco, Peru: The Impact of the Wari Occupation of Pikillacta in the Lucre Basin,* by Gordon McEwan. BAR International Series, vol. 372. Oxford: British Archaeological Reports, International Series, no. 372. (Technical description of the human skulls found in an offering at the Wari site of Pikillacta in Cuzco.)

Bejar Navarro, Raymundo.

1990. *El templo del sol o Qorikancha*. Cuzco: Imprenta Yarez. (A report of excavations carried out in the Coricancha temple during the 1970s.)

Bejar, S. I., and M. Colque.

1997. *Arqueologia de Piñipampa: Introduccin a su estudio*. Thesis for licentiate in archaeology, Universidad Nacional San Antonio Abad del Cuzco. (Discusses the Inca archaeological site of Piñipampa located in the Rumiqolqa quarry at the eastern end of the Valley of Cuzco.)

Bengtsson, Lisbet.

1998. *Prehistoric Stonework in the Peruvian Andes: A Case Study at Ollantaytambo*. Göteborg, Sweden: Etnografisca Museet, Göteberg University. (A study of Inca stonework at the royal estate of Ollantaytambo in the Sacred Valley of the Incas.)

Bennett, Wendell C.

1946. "The Archaeology of the Central Andes." In *Handbook of South American Indians*, edited by Julian Steward, Bureau of American Ethnology, bulletin 143, vol. 2, 61–147. Washington, DC: Smithsonian Institution. (An overview of the state of archaeological knowledge of the central Andes just after World War II. In this work, Bennett presents a new chronological scheme for ancient Peru.)

1948. "The Peruvian Co-Tradition." In *A Reappraisal of Peruvian Archaeology*, edited by Wendell C. Bennett, Society for American Archaeology memoir, 4, 1–7. (A classic work in which Bennett presents a revised scheme of ancient Peruvian chronology.)

Bennett, Wendell C., ed.

1948. *A Reappraisal of Peruvian Archaeology*. Society for American Archaeology memoir, 4. (A classic work that charted the course of studies for the post–World War II era in Peruvian archaeology. It contains contributions by most of the prominent scholars of the day. An important work for understanding the evolution of chronological schemes for ancient Peru.)

Berthelot, Jean.

1986. "The Extraction of Precious Metals at the Time of the Inka." In *Anthropological History of Andean Polities*, edited by John V. Murra, Nathan Wachtel, and Jacques Revel, 69–88. Cambridge: Cambridge University Press. (Inca mining and metallurgy are discussed.)

Bertonio, Ludivico.

1956. *Vocabulario de la lengua Aymara*. La Paz: Facsimile Edition. (Important early dictionary from 1612 of the Aymara language spoken in the southern part of the Inca Empire.)

Betanzos, Juan de.

1968. *Suma y Narración de los Incas*, no. 209. Madrid: Biblioteca de Autores Españoles. (Important early description of the Incas by one of the Spanish conquistadores who married into the family of Inca Pachacuti. First published in 1551.)

1996. *Narrative of the Incas.* Translated and edited by Roland Hamilton and Dana Buchanan. Austin: University of Texas Press. (Recent English translation of the previously cited work.)

Bingham, Hiram.
1910. "The Ruins of Choqquequirao." *American Anthropologist* 12: 505–525. (A description of the author's exploration of the Inca site of Choqquequirao, an impressive monument similar to but smaller than Machu Picchu.)

1913. "In the Wonderland of Peru: The Work Accomplished by the Peruvian Expedition of 1912, under the Auspices of Yale University and the National Geographic Society." *National Geographic* 24(4): 387–574. (The classic article by Hiram Bingham that made Machu Picchu and *National Geographic* famous.)

1914. "The Ruins of Espiritu Pampa, Peru." *American Anthropologist* 16: 185–199. (Bingham describes the Inca site at Espiritu Pampa, not far from Vilcabamba, the last refuge of the Incas during the Spanish Conquest.)

1915. "Types of Machu Picchu Pottery." *American Anthropologist* 17: 257–271. (A description of Inca pottery found at Machu Picchu.)

1922. *Inca Land: Explorations in the Highlands of Peru.* Boston: Houghton Mifflin. (The author's description of various Inca sites in and around Cuzco.)

1930. *Machu Picchu: A Citadel of the Incas: Report of the Explorations and Excavations made in 1911, 1912 and 1915 under the Auspices of Yale University and the National Geographic Society.* New Haven, CT: Yale University Press. (Hiram Bingham's report of the expeditions that investigated and cleared the royal Inca estate at Machu Picchu.)

1948. *Lost City of the Incas: The Story of Machu Picchu and Its Builders.* New York: Duell, Sloan and Pearce. (Bingham's popular book describing his discovery of Machu Picchu.)

Bingham, Hiram, III.
2004. "The Discovery of Machu Picchu." In *Machu Picchu: Unveiling the Mystery of the Incas,* edited by Richard L. Burger and Lucy Salazar, 7–20. New Haven, CT: Yale University Press. (Bingham's account of the discovery of Machu Picchu reprinted from *Harper's Monthly.*)

Bram, Joseph.
1941. *An Analysis of Inca Militarism.* New York: American Ethnological Society, monograph no. 4. (A published version of the author's dissertation on Inca armies, fighting methods, and strategy.)

Bray, Tamara L.
1991. "The Effects of Inca Imperialism on the Northern Frontier." Ann Arbor, MI: University Microfilms. (The author's doctoral dissertation which examines the impact of the Inca expansion into Ecuador.)

1993. "Archaeological Survey of Northern Highland Ecuador: Inca Imperialism and the País Caranqui." *World Archaeology* 24(2): 218–233. (Presentation of survey data relating to the Inca occupation of Ecuador.)

2000. "Imperial Inca Iconography: The Art of Empire in the Andes." *RES: Anthropology and Aesthetics* 38: 168–178. (A look at the iconography used by the Incas in promoting their empire.)

2003. "Inca Pottery as Culinary Equipment: Food, Feasting, and Gender in Imperial State Design." *Latin American Antiquity* 14(1): 1–22. (The author discusses the functions of various Inca vessel forms and points out the links between food, politics, and gender in state formation.)

Brown, David O.
1991. "Administration and Settlement Planning in the Provinces of the Inka Empire: A Perspective from the Inca Provincial Capital of Pumpu on the Junin Plain in the Central Highlands of Peru." Ann Arbor, MI: University Microfilms. (The author's doctoral dissertation based on work at the Inca provincial capital of Pumpu, one of the largest Inca highland administrative centers.)

Brundage, Burr C.
1963. *Empire of the Inca.* Norman: University of Oklahoma Press. (A very readable synthesis of Inca history based on the traditional accounts of the Spanish chronicles and archaeological evidence available at that time.)

1967. *Lords of Cuzco: A History and Description of the Inca People in Their Final Days.* Norman: University of Oklahoma Press. (A very readable description of Inca society at the time of the European Conquest.)

Burger, Richard L.
2004. "Scientific Insights into Daily Life at Machu Picchu." In *Machu Picchu: Unveiling the Mystery of the Incas,* edited by Richard L. Burger and Lucy Salazar, 85–106. New Haven, CT: Yale University Press. (The author discusses what scientists have learned about life at Machu Picchu.)

Burger, Richard L., and Lucy Salazar, eds.
2004. *Machu Picchu: Unveiling the Mystery of the Incas.* New Haven, CT: Yale University Press. (A collection of scholarly essays on Machu Picchu published as a catalog of the Yale Machu Picchu exhibit at the Peabody Museum.)

Bürgi, Peter.
1993. "The Inka Empire's Expansion into the Coastal Sierran Region West of Lake Titicaca." Ph.D. dissertation, University of Chicago. (The author examines Inca control of the area between Lake Titicaca and the Pacific Ocean.)

Cabello Valboa, Miguel.
1951. *Miscelánea antártica: una historia del Perú antiguo.* Lima: Universidad Mayor de San Marcos, Instituto de Etnología y Arqueología. (Written about 1586, this manuscript is considered by scholars to be one of the best accounts of Inca history.)

Callapiña, Supno y Otros Quipucamayos.
1974. *Relación de los quipucamayos*. Edited by Juan José Vega. Lima: Biblioteca Universitaria. (*Quipucamayos* were men trained to make and read the knotted cord records called *quipus* by the Incas. This work gives the testimony of a group of elderly *quipucamayos* who had lived under Inca rule before the Spanish Conquest. It is thus a rare and valuable source of pre-Conquest Inca history.)

Carrasco, Pedro.
1982. "The Political Economy of the Aztec and Inca States." In *The Inca and Aztec States 1400–1800: Anthropology and History*, edited by George A. Collier, Renato I. Rosaldo, and John D. Wirth, 23–40. New York: Academic Press. (A comparative discussion of the economic underpinnings of the Inca and Aztec states.)

Chávez Ballón, Manuel.
1970. "Ciudades incas: Cuzco capital del imperio." *Wayka* 3:1–15. (A description of the Inca capital city of Cuzco by one of the great Peruvian archaeologists.)

Cieza de León, Pedro de.
1947. *La crónica del Perú*. Madrid: Biblioteca de Autores Españoles. (One of the most valuable and reliable early accounts of the Incas written by a Spanish soldier who arrived in Peru shortly after the Conquest and first published in 1553.)

1959. *The Incas of Pedro de Cieza de León*. Translated by Harriet de Onis and edited by Victor W. von Hagen. Norman: University of Oklahoma Press. (A good English translation of the 1947 work mentioned above.)

Classen, Constance.
1993. *Inca Cosmology and the Human Body*. Salt Lake City: University of Utah Press. (A published version of the author's doctoral dissertation, in which she argues that the Incas used the same organizational model for conceptualizing both the human body and the cosmos.)

Cobo, Bernabé.
1979. *History of the Inca Empire: An Account of the Indians' Customs and their Origin Together with a Treatise on Inca Legends, History, and Social Institutions*. Translated and edited by Roland Hamilton. Austin: University of Texas Press. (A good English translation of this very important early account of Inca history first published in 1653.)

Cobo, Bernabé.
1990. *Inca Religion and Customs*. Translated and edited by Roland Hamilton. Austin: University of Texas Press. (A good English translation of the most important early work describing Inca culture and behavior.)

Conrad, Geoffrey W.
1981. "Cultural Materialism, Split Inheritance, and the Expansion of Ancient Peruvian Empires." *American Antiquity* 46: 3–26. (Conrad argues that the Inca imperial expansion was in part motivated by the practice of split inheritance, in which a newly crowned emperor inherited control of the state but not any of his predecessor's wealth. Thus the first order of imperial business during a new reign was to conquer new territories to fill the treasury.)

Conrad, Geoffrey W., and Arthur Demarest.
   1984. *Religion and Empire.* Cambridge: Cambridge University Press. (The authors compare and contrast the role of religion in the development and expansion of the Aztec and the Inca empires.)

Cook, Noble David.
   1975. *Tasa de la visita general de Francisco de Toledo.* Lima: Universidad Nacional de San Marcos. (An account of the inspection tour made by the viceroy Francisco Toledo between 1570 and 1575. This account contains census data and much other useful information about the population of Peru in the late sixteenth century.)

   1981. *Demographic Collapse: Indian Peru, 1520–1620.* Cambridge: Cambridge University Press. (An analysis of the demographic collapse of the native Peruvian population that resulted from the European invasion. Diseases, wars, and cultural disruption decimated the populace, making it very difficult for scholars to accurately calculate the pre-Conquest population of the Inca domain.)

Cornejo Guerrero, Miguel A.
   2000. "An Inka Province: Pachacamac and the Ischma Nation." Ph.D.dissertation, Australian National University, Canberra. (Work discusses the coastal polity of Ischma, which was centered at the famous shrine site of Pachacamac, south of modern Lima. This polity became an Inca province after its conquest by the Inca Empire.)

Costin, Cathy L.
   1986. "From Chiefdom to Empire State: Ceramic Economy among the Prehispanic Wanka of Highland Peru." Ph.D. dissertation, University of California at Los Angeles. (Costin studies the effects of the Inca conquest of the Wanka chiefdoms through an analysis of their ceramics.)

   1993. "Textiles, Women, and Political Economy in Late Prehispanic Peru." *Research in Economic Anthropology* 14: 3–28. (The role of women and textile production in the Inca political economy are examined.)

   2001. "Production and Exchange of Ceramics." In *Empire and Domestic Economy,* by T. D'Altroy, C. Hastorf, and Associates, 203–242. New York: Kluwer Academic. (The author discusses ceramic production and distribution in the Inca economy.)

Costin, Cathy L., Timothy K. Earle, Bruce Own, and Glen S. Russell.
   1989. "Impact of Inka Conquest on Local Technology in the Upper Mantaro Valley, Peru." In *What's New?: A Closer Look at the Process of Innovation,* edited by Sander van der Leeuw and Robin Torrance, 107–139. One World Archaeology Series, vol. 14. London: Unwin and Allen. (The authors discuss changes in local technology resulting from the Inca conquest of the Wanka ethnic group.)

Covey, R. Alan.
   2000. "Inca Administration of the Far South Coast of Peru." *Latin American Antiquity* 11(2): 119–138. (The author interprets Craig Morris's data on the Incas, arguing that administrative policies were adapted to local conditions.)

   2003. "A Processual Study of Inca State Formation." *Journal of Anthropological Archae-*

*ology* 22: 333–357. (An argument that a centralized Inca state emerged in Cuzco between A.D. 1000 and 1400, much earlier than most scholars believe.)

2003. "The Vilcanota Valley (Peru): Inca State Formation and the Evolution of Imperial Strategies." Ph.D. dissertation, University of Michigan. (The author tries to make a processual argument for the early formation of the Inca state using survey data from only part of the Valley of Cuzco.)

Cummins, Thomas B. F.
1988. "Abstraction to Narration: Kero Imagery of Peru and Colonial Alteration of Native Identity." Ph.D. dissertation, University of California, Los Angeles. (Cummins discusses and analyzes the function of the decoration on Inca drinking vessels (called *keros*). He attempts to explain why the motifs changed from abstract engraved designs before the Conquest to painted narrative images after the Conquest.)

D'Altroy, Terrence N.
1992. *Provincial Power in the Inka Empire.* Washington, DC: Smithsonian Institution. (This study presents archaeological evidence for the Inca conquest of the Xauxa and Wanka people in the Mantaro Valley of central Peru, which took place around A.D. 1460. The author reports the results of archaeological work in the Mantaro region and discusses Inca military strategy and tactics and the impact of Inca rule on communities in the Mantaro river drainage.)

1994. "Public and Private Economy in the Inka Empire." In *The Economic Anthropology of the State,* edited by Elizabeth Brumfield, 171–222. Society for Economic Anthropology Monograph 11. Lanham, MD: University Press of America. (A discussion of varying economic modes under Inca rule.)

2002. *The Incas.* Oxford: Blackwell. (A recent general work in which the author attempts a synthesis of the present state of knowledge about the Incas. The author's point of view from his research outside of the Cuzco heartland of the Incas provides some novel interpretations of certain aspects of Inca history and culture.)

D'Altroy, Terrence N., and Ronald A. Bishop.
1990. "The Provincial Organization of Inka Ceramic Production." *American Antiquity* 55: 120–138. (The authors discuss the organization of production and distribution of Inca ceramics.)

D'Altroy, Terrence N., and Timothy K. Earle.
1985. "Staple Finance, Wealth Finance, and Storage in the Inka Political Economy." *Current Anthropology* 25: 187–206. (The authors discuss finance and wealth management in a nonmoney economy.)

D'Altroy, Terrence N., and Christine Hastorf.
1984. "The Distribution and Contents of Inca State Storehouses in the Xauxa Region of Peru." *American Antiquity* 49: 334–349. (This article examines the functions of Inca state storehouses and how their distribution and contents reflect central management. It also presents the results of excavations in six storehouses.)

D'Altroy, Terrence N., Ana María Lorandi, Verónica I. Williams, Christine Hastorf, Eliabeth DeMarrais, Milena Calderari, and Melissa Hagstrum.
2000. "Inka Imperial Rule in the Valle Calchaquí, Argentina." *Journal of Field Archaeology* 27: 1–26. (Evidence for Inca imperial control of northwest Argentina is discussed.)

D'Altroy, Terrence N., and Katharina Schreiber.
2004. "Andean Empires." In *Andean Archaeology,* edited by Helaine Silverman. Oxford: Blackwell. (Discussion comparing and contrasting the Inca and Wari empires of ancient Peru.)

Davies, Nigel.
1995. *The Incas.* Niwot: University Press of Colorado. (A recent general work attempting a synthetic overview of knowledge about the Incas. Recapitulates earlier similar works and is marred by confusion of place names, such as substituting Paucartambo for Pacariqtambo and other editorial errors.)

Dearborn, David S., and Katharina J. Schreiber.
1986. "Here Comes the Sun: The Cuzco-Machu Picchu Connection." *Archaeoastronomy* 9: 15–37. (The authors discuss solar observations at Machu Picchu.)

Dearborn, David S. P., and Katharina J. Schreiber.
1989. "Houses of the Rising Sun." In *Time and Calendars in the Inca Empire,* edited by Mariusz S. Ziòlkowski and Robert M. Sadowski, 49–74. Oxford: British Archaeological Reports, International Series, no. 479. (The authors discuss solar observations and special observatories of the Incas.)

Dearborn, David S. P., Katharina J. Schreiber, and Raymond E. White.
1987. "Intimachay, A December Solstice Observatory." *American Antiquity* 52: 346–352. (The authors present evidence that the Intimachay cave at Machu Picchu was a solar observatory with a structure built by the Incas at its entrance that admitted light from the sunrise only on and near the December solstice.)

Dearborn, David S. P., and Raymond E. White.
1983. "The 'Torreón' at Machu Picchu as an Observatory." *Archaeoastronomy* 5: 37–49. (The authors present evidence that the building known as the "Torreón," or tower, at Machu Picchu was used as a solar observatory for determining the June solstice.)

Demarest, Arthur A.
1981. *Viracocha: The Nature and Antiquity of the Andean High God.* Cambridge, MA: Harvard University, Peabody Museum of Archaeology and Ethnology, monograph no. 6. (A Mayanist attempts to explain the Andean creator deity.)

Dillehay, Tom D.
1975. "Tawantinsuyu Integration of the Chillon Valley, Peru: A Case of Inca Geopolitical Mastery." *Journal of Field Archaeology* 4(4): 397–405. (The author discusses the Inca occupation of the coastal Chillon Valley of Peru.)

Dillehay, Tom D., and Patricia J. Netherly, eds.

1988. *La Frontera del Estado Inca.* Oxford: British Archaeological Reports, International Series, no. 442. (The authors discuss the frontiers of the Inca state.)

Duviols, Pierre.

1976. "La capacocha: mecanismo y función del sacrificio humano, su proyección, su papel de la política integracionista y en la economía redistributive de Tawantinsuyu." *Allpanchis Phuturinqa* 9: 11–57. (The author describes the Inca human sacrifice of children called the Capac Ucha. He examines its function and role in political integration and the redistributive economy of the Inca Empire.)

1976. "Punchao, idolo mayor de Coricancha. Historia y tipología." *Antropología Andina* 1–2: 156–183. (Duviols describes the principal Inca idol of the sun, or Punchao, that was located in the Coricancha sun temple in Cuzco.)

1979. "La dinastía de los Incas: ¿monarquía o diarquía? Argumentos heurísticos a favor de una tesis estructuralista." *Journal de la Société des Americanistes* 64: 67–83. (The author makes a structuralist argument that the Inca dynasty was structured as a diarchy.)

Dwyer, Edward B.

1971. "The Early Inca Occupation of the Valley of Cuzco, Peru." Ph.D. dissertation, University of California at Berkeley. (Dwyer deals with the pre-Inca K'illke ceramic style in Cuzco.)

Earle, Timothy K.

1994. "Wealth Finance in the Inka Empire: Evidence from the Calchaquí Valley, Argentina." *American Antiquity* 59(3): 443–460. (The author presents evidence from the Northwest of Argentina that the Incas were expropriating locally manufactured high-status goods for use elsewhere in the empire.)

Earle, Timothy K., and Terrence N. D'Altroy.

1989. "The Political Economy of the Inka Empire: The Archaeology of Power and Finance." In *Archaeological Thought in America,* edited by Carl C. Lamberg-Karlovsky, 183–204. Cambridge: Cambridge University Press. (The authors argue that to understand the evolution of the Inca state, it is necessary to understand how resources are used to finance activities of new institutions.)

Earle, Timothy K., Terrence N. D'Altroy, Christine Hastorf, Catherine J. Scott, Cathy L. Costin, Glenn S. Russell, and Elsie Sandefur.

1987. *Archaeological Field Research in the Upper Mantaro, Peru, 1982–1983: Investigations of Inka Expansion and Exchange.* Los Angeles: Institute of Archaeology, University of California, Monograph 28. (A report on authors' fieldwork investigating Inca expansion into the Upper Mantaro drainage.)

Eaton, George F.

1916. *The Collection of Osteological Material from Machu Picchu.* Memoir No. 5, Connecticut Academy of Arts and Sciences. (The first report on the skeletal material recovered at Machu Picchu. Eaton was the osteologist with Bingham's expedition that found and cleared Machu Picchu.)

Espinosa S., Waldemar.
  1975. "El Habitat del Etnia Pinagua, Siglos XV y XVI." *Revista del Museo Nacional* XL: 157–220. (A discussion of the Pinagua ethnic group, who were early rivals to the developing Inca state. Author argues that the Pinagua capital was at the site of Tipon, a belief rejected by most other scholars.)

  1980. "Acerca de la historia militar Inca." *Allpanchis Phuturinqa* 14(16): 171–186. (A description of the military history of the Incas.)

  1990. *Los Incas: Economia sociedad y estado en la era del Tahuantinsuyo.* Lima: Amaru Editores. (The author describes Inca history and culture focusing on economics and social structure of the empire.)

Espinosa S., Waldemar, ed.
  1978. *Los modos de producción en imperio de los Incas.* Lima: Editorial Mantaro-Gratifal. (An examination of the modes of production in the Inca Empire.)

Estete, Miguel de.
  1918. "Noticia del Perú, o El descubriemiento y conquista del Perú." Published with introduction and notes by Carlos Larrea. *Boletín de la Sociedad Ecuatoriana de Estudios Históricos* 1(3): 300–350. (Important eyewitness account written by one of Pizarro's soldiers shortly after the Conquest.)

  1967. *La Relación del viaje que hizo el señor Capitán Hernando Pizarro por mandado del señor Gobernador, su hermano, desde el pueblo de Caxamalca a Pachacamac y de allí a Jauja.* Edited by Concepción Bravo. Madrid: Historia 16. (An account of the first visit by the Spaniards to the famous temple of Pachacamac written by a member of that expedition, published in 1532–1533.)

Farrington, Ian S.
  1983. "Prehistoric Intensive Agriculture: Preliminary Notes on River Canalization in the Sacred Valley of the Incas." In *Drained Field Agriculture in Central and South America,* edited by John Darch, 221–235. Oxford: British Archaeological Reports, International Series, no. 189. (The author discusses the canalization of the Vilcanota–Urubamba River in the so-called Sacred Valley of the Incas near Cuzco.)

  1992. "Ritual Geography, Settlement Patterns and the Characterization of the Provinces of the Inka Heartland." *World Archaeology* 23: 368–385. (A look at Inca patterns of settlement and provincial divisions in light of sacred ritual geography.)

  1995. "The Mummy, Estate, and Palace of Inka Huayna Capac at Quispiguanca." *Tawantinsuyu* 1: 55–65. (A description of the royal estate of Huayna Capac based on original research by the author.)

Fejos, Paul.
  1944. *Archaeological Explorations in the Cordillera Vilcabamba, Southeastern Peru.* New York: Viking Fund, Publications in Anthropology, no. 3. (A classic study of the area surrounding the Machu Picchu site, including the sites on the famous "Inca Trail" to Machu Picchu.)

Flores Ochoa, Jorge A.
2004. "Contemporary Significance of Machu Picchu." In *Machu Picchu: Unveiling the Mystery of the Incas,* edited by Richard L. Burger and Lucy Salazar, 109–123. New Haven, CT: Yale University Press. (The author discusses the significance of Machu Picchu to foreign visitors from around the world as well as to the native Peruvian population.)

Fresco, Antonio.
1984. "Excavaciones en Incapirca: 1978–1982." *Revista Española de Antropología Americana* 14: 85–101. (Reports on the author's excavations at the Inca site of Incapirca in southern Ecuador.)

Garcilaso de la Vega, El Inca.
1966. *Royal Commentaries of the Incas and General History of Peru, Parts One and Two.* Translated by Harold Livermore. Austin: University of Texas Press. (The most famous, but not most reliable, of the Spanish chronicles. First published in 1609.)

Gasparini, Graziano, and Luise Margolies.
1980. *Inca Architecture.* Translated by Patricia J. Lyon. Bloomington: University of Indiana Press. (A synthetic treatment of Inca architecture discussing most of the major Inca monuments and the techniques used to build them.)

Gibaja O., Arminda.
1973. "Arqueologia de Choquepujyo." B.A. thesis, Universidad Nacional San Antonio Abad del Cuzco. (The author's thesis reports on her excavations at the important site of Chokepukio in the eastern end of the Valley of Cuzco.)

1983. Arqueologia de Choquepugio. *Arqueologia Andina:* 29–44. (A summary of the work at Chokepukio reported in the author's thesis.)

1984. "Excavaciones en Ollantaytambo, Cusco." *Gaceta Arqueológica Andina* 3(9): 4–5. (The author reports on her excavations in the royal Inca estate of Ollantaytambo in the so-called Sacred Valley of the Incas.)

2004. "Dos ofrendas al agua de Ollantaytambo." *Ñawpa Pacha* 25: 176–188. (A description of two Inca water offerings excavated by the author at the Inca site of Ollantaytambo.)

Glynn, William Burns.
1981. "La Escritura de Los Incas." *Boletin de Lima,* 12–14: 1–32. (The author discusses attempts to decipher the Inca motifs known as *tocapu* and show that they constituted a written language.)

González, Alberto R.
1983. "Inca Settlement Patterns in a Marginal Province of the Empire: Socio-cultural Implications." In *Prehistoric Settlement Patterns: Essays in Honor of Gordon R. Willey,* edited by Evon Z. Vogt and Richard Leventhal, 337–360. Cambridge, MA: Harvard University Press. (The author discusses the pattern of Inca settlement on the Argentine frontier.)

González Carré, Enrique, Jorge Cosmopolis A., and Jorge Lévano P.
   1981. *La ciudad inca de Vilcashuaman.* Ayacucho, Peru: Universidad Nacional de San Cristóbal de Huamanga. (The authors discuss their work at the Inca monument of Vilcashuaman in the modern province of Ayacucho, Peru.)

González Corrales, José.
   1984. "La arquitectura y ceramica Killke del Cusco." In *Current Archaeological Projects in the Central Andes,* edited by A. Kendall, 189–204. Oxford: British Archaeological Reports, International Series, no. 210. (Author discusses excavations in Cuzco that revealed a wall foundation that he believes represents pre-Inca K'illke architecture.)

Gose, Peter.
   1993. "Segmentary State Formation and the Ritual Control of Water Under the Incas." *Comparative Study of Society and History* 35: 480–514. (The author discusses the role of water ideology in the formation and functioning of the Inca state.)

   1996. "Oracles, Divine Kingship, and Political Representation in the Inca State." *Ethnohistory* 43(1): 1–32. (An examination of the ideology of divine kingship and its mediation by oracles in the Inca Empire.)

   1996. "The Past Is a Lower Moiety: Diarchy, History, and Divine Kingship in the Inca Empire." *History and Anthropology* 9(4): 383–414. (The author argues in favor of the Inca government being organized as a monarchy rather than a diarchy as some scholars recently suggest.)

Gregory, Herbert E.
   1916. "A Geological Reconnaissance of the Cuzco Valley, Perú." *American Journal of Science* XLI(241): 1–100. (Gregory was the geologist on the Yale–Machu Picchu expedition of Hiram Bingham. He provides a description of the geology of the Valley of Cuzco based on his own work there.)

Guaman Poma de Ayala, Felipe.
   1936. *Nueva corónica y buen gobierno.* Paris: Travaux et Mémoires de L'Institut d'Ethnologie 22. (First facsimile edition, and still one of the best, of this famous work by a native Peruvian author of the early colonial period. This work, written about 1613, is deemed most valuable for its numerous detailed drawings showing Inca dress and customs.)

   1987. *Nueva Crónica y Buen Gobierno.* Madrid: Crónicas de América 29, Historia 16. (A more recent reproduction of the author's work cited above.)

Hampe, M. T.
   1982. "Las momias de los Incas en Lima." *Revista del Museo Nacional* (Peru) 46: 405–418. (Hampe relates that after the European Conquest, the extant royal Inca mummies were rounded up by the Spaniards and taken to Lima, where they were buried.)

Hardoy, Jorge. E.
   1964. *Ciudades Precolombinas.* Buenos Aires: Ediciones Infinito. (A comparative study of pre-Columbian cities including those of the Incas.)

Harth-Terre, Emilio.
    1964. "El pueblo de Huánuco Viejo." *Arquitecto Peruano* 320(21): 1–20. (A discussion of the Inca imperial administrative center at Huánuco Viejo in northern Peru.)

Heath, Ian.
    1999. *The Armies of the Aztec and Inca Empires, Other Native Peoples of the Americas, and the Conquistadores 1450–1608.* Vol. 2, *Armies of the Sixteenth Century.* Guernsey, England: Foundry. (The author examines the armies and weapons of the native peoples of America and compares them to those of the European conquerors.)

Heffernan, Kenneth J.
    1989. "Limatambo in Late Prehistory: Landscape Archaeology and Documentary Images of Inca Presence in the Periphery of Cuzco." Ph.D. dissertation, Australian National University, Canberra. (An important work examining the archaeological remains of a large Inca site in the vicinity of the city of Cuzco.)

    1996. *Limatambo: Archaeology, History, and the Regional Societies of Inca Cusco.* Oxford: British Archaeological Reports, International Series, no. 644. (Published version of the author's thesis.)

Helsley-Marchbanks, Anne M.
    2004. "The Inca Presence in Chayanta, Bolivia: The Metallurgical Component." *Ñawpa Pacha* 25–27: 251–260. (The author reports on her excavations that produced ceramic molds for casting of Inca style metal objects.)

Hemming, John.
    1970. *The Conquest of the Incas.* London: MacMillan. (Highly readable classic modern account of the Spanish Conquest of the Incas.)

Hemming, John, and Edward Ranney.
    1992. *Monuments of the Inca.* Albuquerque: University of New Mexico Press. (Pictures and descriptions of the major Inca monuments.)

Hiltunen, Juha J.
    1999. *Ancient Kings of Peru: The Reliability of the Chronicle of Fernando de Montesinos: Correlating the Dynasty Lists with Current Prehistoric Periodization in the Andes.* Helsinki: Suomen Historiallinen Seura. (An important reexamination of the chronicle of Fernando Montesinos. Published version of the author's dissertation.)

Hiltunen, Juha J., and Gordon F. McEwan.
    2004. "Knowing the Inca Past." In *Andean Archaeology,* edited by Helaine Silverman, 237–254. Oxford: Blackwell. (Authors discuss problems and approaches to learning about the Inca past.)

Huamán Poma de Ayala, Don Felipe.
    1978. *Letter to a King: A Peruvian Chief's Account of Life under the Incas and under Spanish Rule.* Translated by Christopher Dilke. New York: E. P. Dutton. (An English translation of the famous work by Guaman Poma mentioned above.)

Hyslop, John.

1979. "El area Lupaqa bajo el dominio incaico, un reconocimiento arqueológico." *Histórica* 3(1): 53–81. (Hyslop describes an archaeological reconnaissance of the Lupaca area of the altiplano and evidence of the Inca occupation.)

1984. *The Inca Road System.* New York: Academic. (A comprehensive study of the Inca highway system.)

1985. *Inkawasi: The New Cuzco.* Oxford: British Archaeological Reports, International Series, no. 234. (An examination of the Inca site called Inkawasi that was reportedly built to replicate the capital of Cuzco.)

1990. *Inka Settlement Planning.* Austin: University of Texas Press. (The author discusses the principles of Inca settlement planning throughout the empire.)

1993. "Factors Influencing the Transmission and Distribution of Inka Cultural Materials throughout Tawantinsuyu." In *Latin American Horizons,* edited by Don. S. Rice, 337–356. Washington DC: Dumbarton Oaks. (Hyslop discusses which elements of Inca material culture were distributed throughout the empire, and how and why they were distributed.)

Isbell, Billie Jean.

1978. *To Defend Ourselves: Ecology and Ritual in an Andean Village.* Austin: University of Texas Press. (Modern study of Quechua society in the Ayacucho province of the central highlands of Peru.)

Isbell, William H.

1978. "Environmental Perturbations and the Origin of the Andean State." In *Social Archaeology: Beyond Subsistence and Dating,* edited by C. Redman et al., 303–313. New York: Academic Press. (The author argues that a feature of Inca statecraft—that is, state-level storage or energy averaging—was previously used by the Wari Empire and helps explain the rise of the Wari state.)

Julien, Catherine.

1982. "Inca Decimal Administration in the Lake Titicaca Region." In *The Inca and Aztec States,* edited by George A. Collier, Renato I. Rosaldo, and John D. Wirth, 119–151. New York: Academic. (Julien discusses how the Incas grouped subject peoples into decimal units for the purpose of administration and as a means to effectively limit the power of local elites.)

1983. *Hatunqolla: A View of Inca Rule from the Lake Titicaca Region.* Publications in Anthropology, vol. 15. Berkeley: University of California Press. (Published version of the author's doctoral dissertation studying the major Inca administrative center of Hatunqolla from which the Incas ruled the Lake Titicaca region.)

1988. "How Inca Decimal Administration Worked." *Ethnohistory* 35: 257–279. (The author discusses the functioning of the decimal administrative system and compares the ideal against the reality.)

1992. *Condesuyu: The Political Division of Territory under Inca and Spanish Rule.* Vol. 19. Bonn: Bonner Amerikanistische Studien. (A comparison of Inca and Spanish territorial divisions in the Andes.)

1993. "Finding a Fit: Archaeology and Ethnohistory of the Incas." In *Provincial Inca: Archaeological and Ethnohistorical Assessment of the Impact of the Inca State,* edited by Michael Malpass, 177–233. Iowa City: University of Iowa Press. (The author discusses the problems of matching the archaeological record to the ethnohistorical record.)

2000. *Reading Inca History.* Iowa City: University of Iowa Press. (An important work discussing techniques for interpreting the history of the Incas related in the Spanish chronicles.)

2004. "Las tumbas de Sacsahuaman y el estilo Cuzco-Inca." *Ñawpa Pacha* 25–27: 1–126. (An important work describing the Cuzco-Inca ceramic style based on grave lots from the Inca site of Sacsayhuaman in Cuzco.)

Kauffmann Doig, F.
1980. *Manual de arqueologia Peruana.* Lima: Iberia S.A. (A comprehensive overview of Peruvian archaeology that gives major attention to the Incas.)

Kendall, Ann.
1974. *Aspects of Inca Architecture.* Ph.D. dissertation, Institute of Archaeology, University of London. (A survey and catalog of Inca imperial architecture in the Cuzco region.)

1976. "Descripción e Inventario de las formas arquitectónicas Incas: Patrones de distribución e inferencia cronológicas." *Revista del Museo Nacional* 42: 13–96. (Describes the architecture of the Incas and makes chronological inferences based on the distribution of Inca architectural forms.)

1985. *Aspects of Inca Architecture—Description, Function, and Chronology.* Oxford: British Archaeological Reports, International Series, no. 242. (Published version of the author's doctoral dissertation mentioned above.)

Kendall, A., R. Early, and B. Sillar.
1992. "Report on Archaeological Field Season Investigating Early Inca Architecture at Juchuy Coscco (Q'aqya Qhawana) and Warq'ana, Province of Calca, Dept. of Cuzco, Peru." In *Ancient America: Contributions to New World Archaeology,* edited by N. J. Saunders, 189–255. Oxbow Monograph 24. (A description of early Inca-style architecture at the royal estate of Viracocha Inca.)

Kubler, George.
1945. "The Behavior of Atahualpa, 1531–1533." *The Hispanic American Historical Review* 25(4): 413–427. (Kubler discusses the last three years of the life of the last Inca ruler.)

Lagos M., C. R.
1987. "Mamaqollapata: Importante Centro Religioso de la Cuenca de Lucre." B.A. thesis, Universidad Nacional San Antonio Abad del Cuzco. (The author examines the

Huaca of Mamaqolla located in the Lucre Basin at the eastern end of the Valley of Cuzco.)

Lanning, Edward P.
1967. *Peru before the Incas*. Englewood Cliffs, NJ: Prentice-Hall. (An overview of Peruvian prehistory before the Inca conquests.)

Lee, Vincent R.
1988. *The Lost Half of Inca Architecture*. Wilson, WY: Sixpack Manco. (A study of Inca architecture and the roofing systems for Inca buildings.)

1989. *Chanasuyu: The Ruins of Inca Vilcabamba*. Wilson, WY: Sixpack Manco. (A report on the famous site of Vilcabamba based on the author's own explorations.)

1989. *The Building of Sacsayhuaman and Other Papers*. Wilson, WY: Sixpack Manco. (The author, an architect, discusses Inca building techniques and seeks to explain how megalithic buildings were constructed.)

1996. *Design by the Numbers: Architectural Order among the Incas*. Wilson, WY: Sixpack Manco. (Lee discusses possible ways that the Incas transmitted architectural plans and information without the benefit of writing.)

2000. *Forgotten Vilcabamba*. Wilson, WY: Sixpack Manco. (A report on the author's explorations in the last Inca refuge of Vilcabamba.)

LeVine, Terry Y.
1987. "Inka Labor Service at the Regional Level: The Functional Reality." *Ethnohistory* 34: 14–46. (A study of the Inca system of labor tax and how it functioned.)

LeVine, Terry Y., ed.
1992. *Inka Storage Systems*. Norman: University of Oklahoma Press. (Articles regarding Inca state storage of commodities.)

Lothrop, Samuel K.
1938. *Inca Treasure as Depicted by Spanish Historians*. Los Angeles: The Southwest Museum. (A look at the Spanish reaction to and description of their loot from the Inca Empire.)

Lounsberry, Floyd G.
1986. "Some Aspects of the Inka Kinship System." In *Anthropological History of Andean Polities*, edited by John V. Murra, Nathan Wachtel, and Jacques Revel, 121–136. Cambridge: Cambridge University Press. (A discussion of Inca kinship.)

Lumbreras, Luis G.
1974. *The Peoples and Cultures of Ancient Peru*. Washington, DC: Smithsonian Institution. (An overview of Peruvian prehistory, including the Inca Empire.)

Lunt, Sara W.
1984. "An Introduction to the Pottery from the Excavations at Cusichaca, Department of Cuzco, Peru." In *Current Archaeological Projects in the Central Andes: Some Approaches and Results*, edited by Ann Kendall, 307–322. Oxford: British Archaeological

Reports, International Series, no. 210. (A description of ceramic remains found during the excavations at the Inca site of Cusichaca in the Urubamba Valley.)

1987. "Inca and Pre-Inca Pottery: Pottery from Cusichaca, Department of Cuzco, Peru." Ph.D. dissertation, Institute of Archaeology, University of London. (An analysis of the ceramic artifacts recovered from the excavations at the Inca site of Cusichaca.)

Lyon, Patricia J.
1978. "Informe Sobre Las Labores de la Temporada de 1978." Unpublished report to the Instituto Nacional de Cultura, Regional Cuzco. (Important work that reports the discovery of the pre-Inca Qotakalli ceramic style at the site of Qotakalli in Cuzco.)

MacCormack, Sabine.
1991. *Religion in the Andes: Vision and Imagination in Early Colonial Peru.* Princeton, NJ: Princeton University Press. (The author examines the persistence of Andean religion and the impact of Catholicism after the European Conquest.)

MacLean, Margaret G.
1986. "Sacred Land, Sacred Water: Inca Landscape Planning in the Cuzco Area." Ph.D. dissertation, University of California at Berkeley. (Author describes in detail the architecture of major Inca sites along the Inca trail to Machu Picchu.)

Malpass, Michael A.
1996. *Daily Life in the Inca Empire.* Westport, CT: Greenwood. (The Inca Empire and culture described for a popular audience.)

Malpass, Michael A., ed.
1993. *Provincial Inca: Archaeological and Ethnohistorical Assessment of the Impact of the Inca State.* Iowa City: University of Iowa Press. (A compilation of papers devoted to showing how the Inca state influenced the various areas that it conquered.)

Matheus C., M.
1984. *Estados Regionales: Una interpretación sobre el señorío Lucre.* Thesis for licentiate in archaeology, Universidad Nacional San Antonio Abad del Cuzco. (The author argues that a Lucre polity existed that can be described as a regional state.)

Matos M., Ramiro.
1994. *Pumpu: Centro Administrative Inka de la Puna de Junin.* Lima: Editorial Horizonte. (An important study of the major Inca administrative center of Pumpu in the Junin region of Peru.)

McEwan, Colin, and María Isabel Silva.
1989. "¿Que fueron a hacer los Incas en la costa central del Ecuador?" In *Proceedings of the 46th International Congress of Americanists,* 163–185. Oxford: British Archaeological Reports, International Series no. 503. (This work examines why the Incas went to the coast of Ecuador.)

McEwan, Colin, and Maarten van de Guchte.
1992. "Ancestral Time and Sacred Space in Inca State Ritual." In *The Ancient Americas: Art from Sacred Landscapes,* edited by Richard F. Townsend, 359–373. Chicago: Art

Institute of Chicago. (The authors discuss the Capac Ucha ritual of human sacrifice and its symbolic meaning for Incas in terms of their concept of a sacred landscape.)

McEwan, Gordon F.
1984. "Investigaciones en la cuenca del Lucre, Cusco." *Gaceta Arqueologica Andina* 3(9): 12–15. Instituto Andino de Estudios Arqueológicos, Apartado 11279, Lima. (A report on original research in the Valley of Cuzco in the Inca heartland.)

1984. "The Middle Horizon in the Valley of Cuzco, Peru: The Impact of the Wari Occupation of Pikillacta in the Lucre Basin." Ph.D. dissertation, University of Texas at Austin. (Author reports original research on the impact of the Wari Empire's occupation of Cuzco on the later rise of the Inca state.)

1987. *The Middle Horizon in the Valley of Cuzco, Peru: The Impact of the Wari Occupation of Pikillacta in the Lucre Basin.* Oxford: British Archaeological Reports, International Series, S-372. (The published version of author's dissertation, mentioned above.)

1995. "The Incas." In *Encyclopedia of Latin American History and Culture,* vol. 3, 247–250. New York: Charles Scribner's Sons. (A brief overview of the Incas.)

1996. "Archaeological Investigations at Pikillacta, a Wari Site in Peru." *Journal of Field Archaeology* 23(2): 169–186. (A report of further research on the Wari impact on the Inca heartland.)

2000. "Cultural Background: Inca Heritage." In *Machu Picchu: A Civil Engineering Marvel,* edited by Kenneth R. Wright and Alfredo Valencia Zegarra, 79–87. Reston, VA: ASCE. (A brief discussion of Inca culture and history.)

McEwan, Gordon F., Melissa Chatfield, and Arminda Gibaja O.
2002. "The Archaeology of Inca Origins: Excavations at Chokepukio, Cuzco, Peru." In *Andean Archaeology,* edited by W. Isbell and H. Silverman, 287–302. New York: Kluwer Academic. (A report on the archaeological evidence for Inca origins.)

McEwan, Gordon F., Arminda Gibaja, and Melissa Chatfield.
1995. "Archaeology of the Chokepukio Site: An Investigation of the Origin of the Inca Civilization in the Valley of Cuzco, Peru: A Report on the 1994 Field Season." *TAWATINSUYU: International Journal of Inka Studies* 1: 11–17. (Original research on the origin of the Inca state in the Valley of Cuzco.)

McIntyre, Loren.
1975. *The Incredible Incas and Their Timeless Land.* Washington, DC: National Geographic Society. (An excellent and well-illustrated account of the Incas aimed at a popular audience.)

Means, Philip Ainsworth.
1931. *Ancient Civilizations of the Andes.* New York: Scribners and Sons. (An important work from the last century on the Incas and earlier cultures of Peru.)

Mena, Cristóbal de (also known as El Anónimo Sevillano).
1937. "La conquista del Perú." In *Las realciones primitives de la conquista del Perú,*

*Cuadernos de historia,* edited by R. Porras Barrenechea. *Los cronistas de la conquista,* no. 1, vol. 2, 79–101. Paris: Les Presses Modernes. (One of the earliest eyewitness accounts of the Conquest by one of Pizarro's soldiers published in 1534.)

Menzel, Dorothy.
1959. "The Inca Occupation of the South Coast of Peru." *Southwestern Journal of Anthropology* 15(2): 125–142. (A classic article that points out that the Incas built administrative infrastructure in proportion to the preexisting complexity of a conquered province and that written sources and archaeology can be successfully used together.)

1977. *The Archaeology of Ancient Peru and the Work of Max Uhle.* Berkeley, CA: R. H. Lowie Museum. (This article covers a variety of topics on ancient Peru, including the Incas.)

Métraux, Alfred.
1969. *The History of the Incas.* New York: Schocken. (A synthetic overview of Inca history by an important French scholar.)

Miller, George R.
2004. "An Investigation of Cuzco-Inca Ceramics: Canons of Form, Proportion, and Size." *Ñawpa Pacha* 25–27: 127–150. (An important description of form, proportion, and size of five common shape categories of Cuzco-Inca ceramics.)

Molina, Cristóbal.
1943. "Fábulas y ritos de los Incas." In *Las crónicas de los Molinas,* vol. serie I, tomo IV, 1–84. Lima: Los pequeños grandes libros de historia americana. (An important early source on Inca customs, considered very accurate. First published in 1573.)

Montesinos, Fernando de.
1882. *Ophir de España. Memorias Antiguas Historiales y Politicas del Perú.* Cuidada por D. Marcos Jiménez de la Espada. Madrid: Imprenta de Miguel Ginesta. (One of the most controversial sources on the Incas, which also provides a detailed history and list of pre-Inca kings. First published in 1644.)

1920. *Ophir de España. Memorias Antiguas Historiales y Politicas del Peru,* second series, No. XLVIII. Translated and edited by Philip A. Means. London: Hakluyt Society. (English translation of the above work.)

Moore, Sally F.
1958. *Power and Property in Inca Peru.* New York: Columbia University Press. (An examination of ownership in the economy of the Incas.)

Moorehead, Elizabeth L.
1978. "Highland Inca Architecture in Adobe." *Ñawpa Pacha* 16: 65–94. (Although Inca architecture was most famous for its stonework, Moorehead examines the good portion of it that was constructed of adobe.)

Morris, Craig.
1967. "Storage in Tawantinsuyu." Ph.D. dissertation, University of Chicago. Ann

Arbor: University Microfilms. (A report of original research on the elaborate system of Inca state-level storage.)

1972. "State Settlement in Tawantinsuyu: A Strategy of Compulsory Urbanism." In *Contemporary Archaeology,* edited by Mark P. Leone, 393–401. Carbondale: Southern Illinois University Press. (Morris argues that the Incas rearranged the settlement patterns of conquered areas through a policy of forced urbanism.)

1974. "Reconstructing Patterns of Nonagricultural Production in the Inca Economy: Archaeology and Documents in Instituted Analysis." In *Reconstructing Complex Societies,* edited by Carol Moore. Supplement to the Bulletin of the American Schools of Oriental Research, vol. 20, 49–68. Chicago. (The author discusses the form of Inca economic production of products other than agriculture.)

1979. "Maize Beer in the Economics, Politics, and Religion of the Inca Empire." In *Fermented Food Beverages in Nutrition,* edited by Clifford F. Gastineau, William J. Darby, and Thomas B. Turner, 21–34. New York: Academic. (The author discusses the vital role of *chicha,* or corn beer, in almost all aspects of Inca political life.)

1982. "The Infrastructure of Inca Control in the Peruvian Central Highlands." In *The Inca and Aztec States 1400–1800: Anthropology and History,* edited by George A. Collier, Renato I. Resoldo, and John D. Wirth, 153–171. New York: Academic. (An argument that the large Inca administrative centers were designed to provide venues for ritual drinking and feasting and that these activities were larger extensions of local-level village rituals.)

1988. "Progress and Prospect in the Archaeology of the Inca." In *Peruvian Prehistory: An Overview of Pre-Inca and Inca Society,* edited by Richard W. Keatinge, 233–256. Cambridge: Cambridge University Press. (An important summary of the state of Inca archaeology as of the 1980s.)

1990. "Arquitectura y estructura del espacio en Huánuco Pampa." *Cuadernos Instituto Nacional de Antropología* 12: 27–45. (A discussion of the architecture and spatial layout of the large Inca administrative center of Huanuco Pampa.)

1991. "Signs of Division, Symbols of Unity: Art in the Inka Empire." In *Circa 1492: Art in the Age of Exploration,* edited by Jay A. Levenson, 521–528. Washington, DC, New Haven, CT, and London: National Gallery of Art and Yale University Press. (The author discusses the political role of art in the Inca Empire.)

1995. "Symbols of Power: Styles and Media in the Inka State." In *Style, Society and Person: Archaeological and Ethnological Perspectives,* edited by Christopher Carr and Jill E. Neitzel, 419–433. New York: Plenum. (A discussion of the symbolic values of artistic style and media among the Incas.)

1998. "Inka Strategies of Incorporation and Governance." In *Archaic State,* edited by Gary Feinman and Joyce Marcus, 293–309. Santa Fe, NM: School of American Research. (The author looks at a variety of strategies used by the Incas in constructing their imperial state.)

Morris, Craig, and Donald E. Thompson.
1985. *Huánuco Pampa: An Inca City and Its Hinterland.* London: Thames and Hudson. (The authors report original research at the major Inca administrative center of Huanuco Pampa.)

Moseley, Michael.
1992. *The Incas and Their Ancestors.* New York: Thames and Hudson. (Intended as an undergraduate textbook, this work presents a good overview of the Incas and the cultures that came before them.)

Murra, John V.
1958. "On Inca Political Structure." In *Proceedings of the Annual Spring Meeting of the American Ethnological Society,* 30–41. Seattle: University of Washington. (The author discusses his understanding of Inca political structure.)

1960. "Rite and Crop in the Inca State." In *Culture in History,* edited by Stanley Diamond, 393–407. New York: Columbia University Press. (Murra examines ritual and agriculture in the Inca Empire.)

1962. "Cloth and its Functions in the Inca State." *American Anthropologist* 64: 710–728. (The author discusses cloth, the most highly valued commodity in the Inca state, and the uses to which it was put.)

1965. "Herds and Herders in the Inca State." In *Man, Culture, and Animals,* edited by Anthony Leeds and Andrew P. Vayda, 185–215. Washington DC: American Association for the Advancement of Science, publication no. 78. (A look at the role of animal husbandry in the economy of the Inca state.)

1966. "New Data on Retainer and Servile Populations in Tawatinsuyu." In *XXXVI Congreso Internacional de Americanistas, Spain 1964,* vol. 2, 35–45. Seville: International Congress of Americanists. (Murra examines the status of the servant population of the Inca state in light of his original research.)

1972. "El 'control vertical' de un máximo de pisos ecológicos en la economía de las sociedades andinas." In *Visita de la Provincia de León de Huánuco en 1562, Iñigo Ortiz de Zúñiga, visitador,* edited by John V. Murra, vol. 2, 427–476. Huánuco, Peru: Universidad Nacional Hermilio Valdizán. (A classic work on the Inca economy highlighting the culture's exploitation of ecological diversity.)

1975. "El Trafico de Mullu de la Costa del Pacifico." In *Formaciones Economicas y Politicas del Mundo Andino.* Historia Andina, vol. 3, 62–85. Lima: Instituto de Estudios Peruanos. (Murra discusses mullu, or *Spondylus,* shells from the north Pacific coast of South America, which were an indispensable and highly valuable ritual commodity widely traded in the ancient Andes.)

1975. *Formaciones Economicas y Politicas del Mundo Andino.* Lima: Instituto de Estudios Peruanos. (A study of the relationship and form of economics and politics in the Andean world.)

1980. *The Economic Organization of the Inca State.* Greenwich, CT: JAI. (A classic study of the Inca imperial economy.)

1982. "The Mit'a Obligations of Ethnic Groups to the Inka State." In *The Inca and Aztec States 1400–1800: Anthropology and History,* edited by George A. Collier, Renato I. Resoldo, and John D. Wirth, 237–262. New York: Academic. (Murra discusses the labor tax extracted by the Incas and argues that production activities in the provinces tended to continue unchanged. The author discounts the impact of the decimal system of administration.)

1986. "The Expansion of the Inka State: Armies, War, and Rebellions." In *Anthropological History of Andean Polities,* edited by John V. Murra, Nathan Wachtel, and Jacques Revel, 49–58. Cambridge: Cambridge University Press. (An examination of the dynamics of Inca expansion and the reaction to it in military terms.)

Murúa, Martín de.
1986. *Historia general del Perú.* Edited by Manuel Ballesteros. Madrid: Historia 16. (A general history of the Incas deemed most valuable for its comments on Inca customs. First published in 1605.)

Niles, Susan A.
1987. *Callachaca: Style and Status in an Inca Community.* Iowa City: University of Iowa Press. (Niles describes the royal estate of Amaru Topa Inca at Callachaca near Cuzco and argues that physical layout of the planned community reflects the Inca idea of appropriate social order.)

1992. "Inca Architecture and the Sacred Landscape." In *The Ancient Americas: Art from Sacred Landscapes,* edited by Richard F. Townsend, 347–358. Munich, Germany: Prestel Verlag. (Niles argues that as the Inca Empire expanded, it continually revised its cosmology and mythic history to encompass new features of sacred geography that were encountered.)

1999. *The Shape of Inca History: Narrative and Architecture in an Andean Empire.* Iowa City: University of Iowa Press. (The author reports on original research on the estate of Inca Huayna Capac. She argues that new styles and innovations in the architecture reflect the political events of his reign.)

2004. "The Nature of Inca Royal Estates." In *Machu Picchu: Unveiling the Mystery of the Incas,* edited by Richard L. Burger and Lucy Salazar, 49–68. New Haven, CT: Yale University Press. (A good general discussion of the nature and function of Inca royal estates.)

2004. "Moya Place or Yours? Inca Private Ownership of Pleasant Places." *Ñawpa Pacha* 25–27: 189–206. (Niles discusses lands privately owned by individual Incas.)

Pachacuti Yamqui Salcamaygua, Joan de.
1968. *Relación de antigüedades deste Reyno del Perú.* Biblioteca de Autores Españoles, 209, 279–319. Madrid: Ediciones Atlas. (Important early-seventeenth-century account written by a native Andean author that is most valuable for its information on Inca religion and history.)

Pardo, Luis A.
1937. *Ruinas precolombinas del Cuzco.* Cuzco. (A description of the principal Inca monuments of Cuzco as they were in the 1930s.)

1957. *Historia y Arqueología del Cuzco.* Lima: Impresa Colegio Militar "Leoncio Prado." (An overview of the history and archaeology of Cuzco by an eminent Cuzco scholar of the last century.)

Parsons, Jeffrey R.
1998. "A Regional Perspective on the Inka Impact in the Sierra Central, Perú." *Tawantinsuyu* 5: 153–159. (The author discusses the results of the Inca conquest of the central highlands of Peru.)

Pärssinen, Martti.
1992. *Tawantinsuyu: The Inca State and Its Political Organization.* Helsinki: Societas Historica Finlandiae. (An overview of Inca politics by a scholar from Finland.)

Pärssinen, Martti, and Ari Siiriäinen.
1997. "Inca-Style Ceramics and Their Chronological Relationship to the Inca Expansion in the Southern Lake Titicaca Area (Bolivia)." *Latin American Antiquity* 8(3): 255–271. (Authors argue that Inca imperial ceramics were present in Bolivia earlier than the generally accepted historical dates for the Inca conquest of that region.)

Patterson, Thomas C.
1985. "Pachacamac—an Andean Oracle under Inca Rule." In *Recent Studies in Andean Prehistory and Protohistory: Paper from the Second Annual Northeast Conference on Andean Archaeology and Ethnohistory,* edited by D. Peter Kvietok and Daniel Sandweiss, 159–176. Ithaca: Cornell University Latin American Studies Program. (The author describes the function of the most famous Andean oracle under the Inca Empire.)

1991. *The Inca Empire: The Formation and Disintegration of a Pre-Capitalist State.* New York: Berg. (A general overview of the Inca Empire from a Marxist perspective.)

Pease G. Y., Franklin.
1982. "The Formation of Tawantinsuyu: Mechanisms of Colonization and Relationship with Ethnic Groups." In *The Inca and Aztec States 1400–1800: Anthropology and History,* edited by George A. Collier, Renato I. Resoldo, and John D. Wirth, 173–198. New York: Academic. (The author discusses the formation of the structure of the Inca Empire, comparing and contrasting the experiences of different ethnic groups brought into the empire. He concludes that the Inca state was not as monolithic as the chroniclers indicated.)

1991. *Los Incas.* Lima: Fondo Editorial, Pontificia Universidad Católica del Perú. (An overview of the Inca Empire by a prominent Peruvian scholar.)

Pizarro, Pedro.
1921. *Relation of the Discovery and Conquest of the Kingdoms of Peru.* Translated and edited by Philip Ainsworth Means. Boston: Milford House. (An English-language translation of an eyewitness account of the conquest of Peru written by a cousin of Francisco Pizarro who participated in the events. First published in 1571.)

1986. *Relación del descubrimiento y conquista de los reinos del Perú.* Edited by Gjillermo

Lohmann Villena. Lima: Pontificia Universidad Católica, Fondo Editorial. (A recent Spanish-language edition of Pizarro's work cited above.)

Polo de Ondegardo, Juan.
1873. *The Rites and Laws of the Incas.* Edited and translated by C. R. Markham. London: Hakluyt Society. (An English-language translation of a manuscript dealing with laws and customs of the Incas.)

1917. "La Relación del linaje de los Incas y como extendieron ellos sus conquistas." In *Colección de Libros y Documentos Referentes a la Historia del Perú,* edited by Horacio H. Urteaga, vol. 4, 45–94. Lima: Sanmartí. (A document written in 1567, some thirty years after the Conquest, that deals with Inca kinship and the Incas' conquests.)

Prescott, William Hickling.
1847. *History of the Conquest of Peru.* 2 vols. New York: Harper and Brothers Publishers. (Prescott's classic and very influential account of the conquest of the Incas.)

Protzen, Jean Pierre.
1985. "Inca Quarrying and Stone Cutting." *Ñawpa Pacha* 21: 183–214. (A report on original research and discoveries about Inca stone-working techniques.)

1986. "Inca Stonemasonry." *Scientific American* 254 (2):94–105. (A discussion of Inca stone-working techniques.)

1993. *Inca Architecture and Construction at Ollantaytambo.* Oxford: Oxford University Press. (A detailed study of the architecture of the Inca royal estate at Ollantaytambo.)

2004. "The Fortress of Saqsa Waman: Was It Ever Finished?" *Ñawpa Pacha* 25–27: 155–175. (Author presents evidence that Sacsayhuaman was still under construction at the time of the Spanish Conquest.)

Quilter, Jeffrey, and Gary Urton, eds.
2002. *Narrative Threads: Accounting and Recounting in Andean Khipu.* Austin: University of Texas Press. (A compilation of papers dealing with the current state of knowledge about the knotted cord record-keeping devices of the Incas that were called *quipu.*)

Ramírez, Susan E.
1990. "The Inca Conquest of the North Coast: A Historian's View." In *The Northern Dynasties: Kingship and Statecraft in Chimor,* edited by Michael E. Moseley and Alana Cordy-Collins, 507–537. Washington, DC: Dumbarton Oaks. (A discussion of the conquest of the Kingdom of Chimor by the Inca Empire.)

Reinhard, Johan.
1991. *Machu Picchu: The Sacred Center.* Lima: Nuevas Imagines S.A. (An argument that the location of the royal estate of Machu Picchu was determined by its relationship to the sacred mountain peaks that surround it.)

1992. "Sacred Peaks of the Andes." *National Geographic* 181(3): 84–111. (A popular article on Andean mountain worship.)

1992   "An Archaeological Investigation of Inca Ceremonial Platforms on the Volcano Copiapo, Central Chile." In *Ancient America: Contributions to New World Archaeology,* edited by Nicholas J. Saunders, 145–172. Oxford: Oxbow Monographs no. 24. (A report of original research of the high-altitude ritual platforms constructed by the Incas on Cerro Copiapo.)

1996. "Peru's Ice Maidens." *National Geographic* 189(6): 62–81. (Popular article on the frozen mummies of Inca human sacrifices discovered on snow-capped peaks in the Peruvian Andes.)

Rivera D., M.
1971. "Disenos decorativos en la ceramica Killke." *Revista del Museo Nacional* 37: 106–115. (Rivera discusses the decoration of pre-Inca ceramics in the Cuzco region.)

1971. "La ceramica Killke y la arqueologia de Cuzco." *Revista Española de Antropologia Americana* 6: 85–123. (An examination of the K'illke ceramic style found in the archaeology of Cuzco.)

Rostworowski De Diez Canseco, Maria.
1972. "Succession, Cooption to Kingship, and Royal Incest among the Incas." *Southwestern Journal of Anthropology* 16(4): 417–427. (An important article in which the author points out that civil war over the Inca imperial succession was the norm rather than the exception.)

1972. "Los Ayarmaca." *Revista del Museo Nacional* (Peru) XXXVI: 58–101. (A description of one of the most powerful indigenous groups in the Valley of Cuzco with whom the Incas struggled in the early part of their history.)

1988. *Historia del Tahuantinsuyu.* Lima: Instituto de Estudios Peruanos. (A general history of the Inca Empire by one of the foremost Peruvian ethnohistorians.)

1999. *History of the Inca Realm.* Translated by Harry B. Iceland. Cambridge: Cambridge University Press. (An English-language translation of the author's 1988 work.)

Rowe, John H.
1944. "An Introduction to the Archaeology of Cuzco." *Papers of the Peabody Museum of American Archaeology and Ethnology* 27, no. 2. Cambridge, MA: Harvard University Press. (Published version of the author's doctoral dissertation; a classic work on Cuzco and Inca archaeology.)

1946. "Inca Culture at the Time of the Spanish Conquest." In *Handbook of South American Indians,* edited by Julian Steward, bulletin 143, vol. 2, 183–330. Washington, DC: Bureau of American Ethnology. (A classic work describing Inca culture and the sources of information available about the Incas.)

1956. "Archaeological Explorations in Southern Peru, 1954–55." *American Antiquity* 22(2): 120–137. (A report of original research in Peru.)

1963. "Urban Settlements in Ancient Peru." *Ñawpa Pacha* 1: 1–27. (A discussion of urban settlements in the ancient Andes and how they differ from European cities.)

1965. "An Interpretation of Radiocarbon Measurements on Archaeological Samples from Peru." *Proceedings of the Sixth International Conference, Radiocarbon and Tritium Dating, Held at Washington State University,* 187–198. Pullman, Washington, June 7–11, 1965. (Another classic work that laid the foundation for the most commonly used chronological system in the Andes.)

1967. "What Kind of Settlement Was Inca Cuzco?" *Ñawpa Pacha* 5: 59–77. (A discussion of the Inca capital of Cuzco and how it differs significantly from European capital cities.)

1979. "An Account of the Shrines of Ancient Cuzco." *Ñawpa Pacha* 17: 2–80. (The author examines what is known about the religious shrines, or *huacas,* of Cuzco.)

1982. "Inca Policies and Institutions Relating to Cultural Unification." In *The Inca and Aztec States 1400–1800.* Edited by G. Collier, R. Rosaldo, and J. Wirth, 93–117. New York: Academic. (A discussion of Inca policies that were designed to prevent revolts by the Incas' conquered subjects. These included the implementation of *camayo, yanacona,* and *mitima,* statuses that served to disrupt previous provincial loyalties.)

1990. "Machu Picchu a la luz de documentos de siglo XVI." *Histórica* 14(1): 139–154. (Reports on original research showing that Machu Picchu was a royal estate belonging to the Inca Pachacuti and was abandoned later than previously assumed.)

2004. "How Did the Incas Say 'Sacsahuaman' in the Sixteenth Century?" *Ñawpa Pacha* 25–27: 151–153. (A discussion of the linguistic problem of proper pronunciation of sixteenth-century Inca words.)

Salazar, Lucy.
2004. "Machu Picchu: Mysterious Royal Estate in the Cloud Forest." In *Machu Picchu: Unveiling the Mystery of the Incas,* edited by Richard L. Burger and Lucy Salazar, 21–47. New Haven, CT: Yale University Press. (Author provides an overview of how the understanding of Machu Picchu has changed in the ninety years since its discovery. The article also contains a good selection of Hiram Bingham's original photographs of the site.)

Salomon, Frank.
1995. "'The Beautiful Grandparents': Andean Ancestor Shrines and Mortuary Ritual as Seen through Colonial Records." In *Tombs for the Living: Andean Mortuary Practices,* edited by T. D. Dillehay, 315–354. Washington, DC: Dumbarton Oaks Research Library and Collection. (A discussion of Andean attitudes and ideology toward death based on original research of colonial documents.)

Sancho de la Hoz, Pedro.
1917. *An Account of the Conquest of Peru.* Translated and edited by P. A. Means. New York: Cortés Society. (An English-language translation of an eyewitness account of the conquest of the Incas written by one of Pizarro's soldiers soon after the event. First published in 1543.)

Sarmiento de Gamboa, Pedro.
1960. *Historia de los Incas.* Biblioteca de Autores Españoles, vol. 135, 193–297.

Madrid: Ediciones Atlas. (A valuable early account of Inca history written for the king of Spain at the order of the Viceroy Toledo and based on reliable sources.)

1999. *History of the Incas.* Translated and edited by Sir Clements Markham. Mineola, NY: Dover. Originally published 1907. Cambridge: Hakluyt Society. (An English-language translation of the above work.)

Savoy, Gene.
1970. *Vilcabamba: Last City of the Incas.* London: Hale. (Author describes the discovery of the Vilcabamba site, the last refuge of the Incas during the Spanish Conquest.)

Schaedel, Richard P.
1978. "Early State of the Incas." In *The Early State,* edited by Henri Claessen and Peter Skalnik, 289–320. The Hague, The Netherlands: Mouton. (Schaedel discusses early state formation of the Incas.)

Schreiber, Katharina.
1993. "The Inca Occupation of the Province of Andamarca Lucanas, Peru." In *Provincial Inca,* edited by Michael Malpass, 77–116. Iowa City: University of Iowa Press. (Discussion of the evidence for and nature of the Inca occupation of the Lucanas.)

Sherbondy, Jeanette.
1982. *The Canal System of Hanan Cusco.* Cuzco: Biblioteca Bartolomé de las Casas. (A discussion of the water canals of the upper division of Inca Cuzco.)

1987. "Organización hidráulica y poder en el Cuzco de los Incas." *Revista Española de Antropologia Americana* XVII. (The author examines power and water control among the Incas.)

1992. "Water Ideology in Inca Ethnogenesis." In *Andean Cosmologies through Time,* edited by Robert H. Dover, Katharine E. Seibold, and John H. McDowell, 46–66. Bloomington: Indiana University Press. (An examination of water ideology of the Incas and how it related to their view of their own origins.)

Silverblatt, Irene.
1987. *Moon, Sun, Witches: Gender Ideologies and Class in Inca and Colonial Peru.* Princeton, NJ: Princeton University Press. (Silverblatt looks at the role of women in the Inca state.)

Squier, E. George.
1877. *Peru, Incidents of Travel and Exploration in the Land of the Incas.* New York: Harper and Brothers. (A classic nineteenth-century account of travel to Inca ruins and a description of their condition at that time.)

Sullivan, William.
1996. *The Secret of the Incas: Myth, Astronomy, and the War Against Time.* New York: Crown. (An important work on Inca astronomy suggesting that the behavior of the Incas was governed to some extent by what they observed in the heavens.)

Thompson, Donald E., and John V. Murra.
1966. "The Inca Bridges in the Huánuco Region." *American Antiquity* 31: 632–639. (A description of Inca bridges in the north-central highlands.)

Topic, John R., and Theresa Lange Topic.
1993. "A Summary of the Inca Occupation of Huamachuco." In *Provincial Inca,* edited by Michael Malpass, 17–43. Iowa City: University of Iowa Press. (A discussion of the Inca remains in the Huamachuco region of the north-central highands.)

Uhle, Max.
1903. *Pachacamac: Report of the William Pepper, M.D., LL.D., Peruvian Expedition of 1896.* Philadelphia: Department of Archaeology, University of Pennsylvania. (A classic work that represents some of the first scientific archaeology ever carried out in Peru. This study became the foundation for most of the Andean chronology schemes adopted by later archaeologists.)

Urton, Gary.
1981. *At the Crossroads of the Earth and the Sky: An Andean Cosmology.* Austin: University of Texas Press. (Urton discusses the Andean contemporary worldview and relates it to Inca cosmology.)

1990. *The History of a Myth: Pacariqtambo and the Origin of the Incas.* Austin: University of Texas Press. (The author examines the evidence for the existence of the mythical Inca origin place at the modern town of Pacariqtambo.)

1999. *Inca Myths.* London: British Museum. (A compilation of surviving Inca mythology.)

2003. *Signs of the Inka Khipu.* Austin: University of Texas Press. (Author argues that the knotted cord recording system called *quipu* is based on a binary recording system.)

Valcárcel, Luis E.
1946. "Cuzco Archaeology." In *Handbook of South American Indians,* Bureau of American Ethnology, bulletin 143, vol. 2, edited by Julian Steward, 177–182. Washington, DC: Smithsonian Institution. (A brief overview of Cuzco archaeology up until 1946.)

Valencia Zegarra, Alfredo.
1970. "Dos tumbas de Saqsaywaman." *Revista Saqsaywaman* 1: 173–177. (The author reports on the excavation of two tombs at the Inca monument of Sacsayhuaman.)

1982. "Complejo arqueológico de Yucay." In *Arqueología de Cuzco,* edited by I. Oberti, 65–80. Cuzco: Ediciones Instituto Nacional de Cultura. (A report of archaeological work at the town of Yucay.)

1984. "Arqueologia de Qolqampata." *Revista del Museo e Instituto de Arqueologia* 23: 47–62. (A report of the author's excavations in the Colcampata sector of the Inca city of Cuzco.)

2004. "Recent Archaeological Investigations at Machu Picchu." In *Machu Picchu: Unveiling the Mystery of the Incas,* edited by Richard L. Burger and Lucy Salazar, 71–82.

New Haven, CT: Yale University Press. (The author reports on recent archaeological work that he carried out at Machu Picchu together with Kenneth Wright between the years of 1995 and 1999. They discovered new canals, fountains, and roads at the site.)

Valencia Zegarra, Alfredo, and Arminda Gibaja O.
1990. *Excavaciones y puesta en valor de Tambomachay.* Cuzco: Instituto Nacional de Cultura. (A report of archaeological investigations at the royal Inca site of Tambo-machay in Cuzco.)

van de Guchte, Maarten.
1990. "'Carving the World': Inca Monumental Sculpture and Landscape." Ph.D. dissertation, University of Illinois at Champaign-Urbana. Ann Arbor, MI: University Microfilms. (The author reports on original research on the Inca monument at Sahuite, near Cuzco.)

Von Hagen, Adriana, and Craig Morris.
1998. *The Cities of the Ancient Andes.* London: Thames and Hudson. (Highly readable text that deals with the subject of Inca cities and those of earlier Peruvian cultures.)

Von Hagen, Victor.
1955. *Highway of the Sun.* Boston: Little, Brown. (A descriptive account of the royal Inca highway by the leader of an expedition to trace its route.)

Wachtel, Nathan.
1977. *The Vision of the Vanquished: The Spanish Conquest of Peru through Indian Eyes: 1530–1570.* Translated by B. Reynolds and S. Reynolds. Brighton, England: Harvester. (A highly regarded study of how the native South Americans viewed the European Conquest.)

1982. "The Mitimaes of the Cochabamba Valley: The Colonization Policy of Huayna Capac." In *The Inca and Aztec States 1400–1800,* edited by G. Collier, R. Rosaldo, and J. Wirth, 199–235. New York: Academic. (Author discuss late Inca colonial policy in the Cochabamaba Valley of Bolivia.)

Wright, Kenneth R., and Alfredo Valencia Z., eds.
2000. *Machu Picchu: A Civil Engineering Marvel.* Reston, VA: ASCE. (An excellent work presenting Machu Picchu from the point of view of a civil engineer.)

Xérez, Francisco de.
1872. *Reports on the discovery of Peru.* Translated and edited by C. R. Markham. London: Hakluyt Society. (An English-language translation of an eyewitness account of the Spanish Conquest written soon after the event by one of Pizarro's soldiers. First published in 1534.)

1985. *Verdadera Relación de la Conquista del Perú y Provincia del Cuzco llamada la Nueva Castilla.* Edited by Concepción Bravo. Madrid: Historia 16. (Modern Spanish-language edition of Xérez's 1534 account.)

Zuidema, R. Tom.
1964. *The Ceque System of Cuzco.* Translated by Eva M. Hooykaas. International

Archives of Ethnography, supplement to vol. 50. Leiden, The Netherlands: E. J. Brill. (A classic work from a structuralist perspective concerning the organization of shrines and the *ceque* system of Cuzco.)

1973. "The Origin of the Inca Empire." In *Les Grands Empires. Recueils de la Societe Jean Bodin Pour L'Histoire Comparative Des Institutions.* Brussels: Editions de la Librairie Encyclopedique. (Zuidema discusses the origin of the Inca Empire in terms of the influence of the earlier Wari Empire. Author argues that the legend of the Chanca Wari and the accession of Inca Pachacuti may reflect a cultural memory of the expulsion of the Wari invaders.)

1990. *Inca Civilization in Cuzco.* Austin: University of Texas Press. (A structuralist approach to explaining the organization of Inca society.)

1995. *El sistema de los ceques.* Lima: Pontificia Universidad Católica del Perú, Fondo Editorial. (Spanish-language version of the author's studies of the Inca shrines and *ceque* system.)

# Index